REALITY AND ILLUSION IN NEW TESTAMENT SCHOLARSHIP

A Primer in Critical Realist Hermeneutics

Ben F. Meyer

A Michael Glazier Book
THE LITURGICAL PRESS
Collegeville, Minnesota

A Michael Glazier Book published by The Liturgical Press.

Cover design by David Manahan, O.S.B.

Photo by Robin Pierzina, O.S.B.

Index compiled by Aldemar Hagen.

1	2	3	4	5	6	7	8

Library of Congress Cataloging-in-Publication Data

Meyer, Ben F., 1927–
    Reality and illusion in New Testament scholarship : a primer in critical realist hermeneutics / Ben F. Meyer.
        p.   cm.
    "A Michael Glazier book."
    Includes bibliographical references and indexes.
    ISBN 0-8146-5771-0
    1. Bible. N.T.—Hermeneutics 2. Lonergan, Bernard J. F.
Method in theology. 3. Bible. N.T.—Criticism, interpretation, etc.
4. Critical realism. I. Title.
BS476.M36 1995
225.6'01—dc20   94-23991
                                                                CIP

To "the Not Too Numerous Centre"
    and, among its partisans,

to: Frederick E. Crowe and Robert M. Doran
    Sean E. McEvenue and Quentin Quesnell
    Fred Lawrence, Matthew Lamb, and Sebastian Moore
    Charles C. Hefling, Michael Vertin, and Hugo Meynell
    Elizabeth A. Morelli and Mark D. Morelli
    Bernard J. Tyrrell, Timothy P. Fallon, and Philip Boo Riley
    Philip McShane, Kenneth R. Melchin, and Cathleen Going
        (Sor Maria del Salvador, O.P.)

Contents

Preface

The present work accords with my *Critical Realism and the New Testament* (Allison Park: Pickwick, 1989), but it is an integral, independent text, more fundamental than the essays in the latter volume. It is a primer in hermeneutics, intended to make solid philosophic resources more easily available to New Testament readers, students, and scholars. Those engaged in studies that include interpretation and history eventually discover that these activities are not self-explanatory. For an explanatory account of them, one must look to hermeneutics, which is a subquestion in the philosophy of knowledge.

The explanatory account offered here is that of the late Bernard Lonergan (d. 1984). Over a period of thirty-five years (from the 1940s to 1982), Lonergan published a large body of systematic work on issues of knowledge relevant to method in theology. Inquiry into fully human functioning (intentionality analysis) laid the foundations. This was followed by why this functioning generated knowledge of truth and love of the good (epistemology and theory of the good). There followed an account of the reality that we come to know and love (metaphysics). In his 1972 masterwork, *Method in Theology*, Lonergan made hermeneutics a richly inclusive resource: supposing all the above, it focused on interpretation, history, radical debate on such topics (dialectic), and the way to resolving such debate (foundations).

A striking trait of Lonergan's intentionality analysis (see below, chapters one, two, and three) is its reliability. In fact, there are excellent reasons, as we shall see, for taking it to be impervious to fundamental reversal. Verifiable analysis of human performance lays firm foundations for what follows.

A critical-realist epistemology (especially chapter four) has as its most striking trait a clean break with the naïve philosophic habit of relying on sense perception to guarantee the objectivity of knowledge. This "perceptualism" finds a cure in attention to consciousness and its explanation, to the experiences of wonder, of questioning, and of question-answering. What emerges from this is the discovery of two kinds of knowing, two kinds of object, and two kinds of objectivity. In fully human knowing, it turns out, we arrive at objectivity not by quelling subjectivity (with variations among empiricists, positivists, and behaviorists), but through intense exercises in subjectivity made authentic by its accord with the human drive to reality. This drive ("the intention of being") is the key to normative human functioning.

In the theory of interpretation and theory of history (chapter five) intentionality analysis and epistemology are applied to the tasks of interpretation and history. This allows us to distinguish between effective procedure and ideological procedure (on ideology in literary and historical studies, see chapter six).

The six chapters referred to make up the bulk of this primer. Consequently, the book primarily belongs to the field of philosophical hermeneutics. This might be overlooked in view of our applications and examples, almost all of them drawn from the New Testament. The examples are mine. The philosophic stance is entirely that of Lonergan. He is often cited; intended originality vis-à-vis his work is negligible. My purpose is thus in one sense modest (no attempt to improve on the master), in another ambitious, for the work is meant to afford students and scholars access to an extraordinarily deep and deft philosophic achievement.

The accent on philosophical hermeneutics has an ecumenical function: to be of service to whoever finds it possible to share the philosophical enterprise of critical realism. This realism is by no means limited to those sharing Lonergan's (and the writer's) religious allegiances (specifically Catholic) or theological preferences. It is essentially open.

The purposes spelled out above are open to believers and non-believers, but the view of the New Testament and its importance is that of a believer. As Heinrich Schlier put it, every "event" in the full sense of the term has its text; for *its* text the event of Christ's resurrection has the whole New Testament. These writings reflect a brief but climactic moment in history: the mission of John the Baptist and the mission of Jesus, climaxed by the resurrection of the crucified Messiah and followed by the launching of a world mission.

Part Three of the present book is theological hermeneutics. I use the term despite not offering a full treatment of such classic themes as divine inspiration, the canon, the senses of scripture. The theological concerns of Part Three relate, first, to finding an entrée to New Testament horizons. Access to the New Testament is not automatic, not easy; it is a steep challenge. Theological achievement among exegetes is uncommon because to meet its conditions is to have successfully surmounted great challenges. Further concerns of Part Three include recognition of the unity-amid-plurality in the New Testament and full acknowledgement of the role of faith in measuring up to the text as "word of God."

In the perspective of the present work the importance of the New Testament lies in its status as God's climactic and definitive revelation. The texts are unique less for their literary excellence than for their unparalleled content and consequences. "Content" is summed up in "the gospel," the news of the life, death, and resurrection of Jesus, divinely vindicated as Savior of the world and normative paradigm of human life, the one who (in Ignace de la Potterie's reading of the Prologue of John's gospel) "has opened the way." Because the gospel reveals the peculiar relation of Jesus Christ to the world, human destiny in history and eternity turns on the human response to the gospel. This uniqueness of role and status is among the primary reasons for searching out and seeking to articulate a thoroughly grounded hermeneutics.

Human destiny hinging on response to the gospel implies an age-old view which has undergone development and refinement in the past hundred-and-fifty years: the indispensability of Christ as Savior of the world, a normative relation that holds for every individual, community, and nation, every generation and era, every culture and civilization. Hence, nothing in human history is more crucially a ground of celebration or lament than the human response to the gospel. This should not be read as limiting or diminishing God's all-inclusive saving will. We affirm this all-inclusive will without therely cancelling the definitive and normative economy of salvation in Christ.

The gospel in a secondary sense is the story told by the evangelists. In neither sense can the gospel be reduced to one among many stories or "paradigms of transcendence." Why not? Because of the story's protagonist, plot, climax, and unfinished ending. The gospel cannot be reduced to one among many paradigms unless it can be shown that the story is essentially illusory: that the protagonist is not who the story says he is, that he does not do what the story says he does, that he has not been "raised from the dead," as the story says he has, and that he will not bring the story to the end that, in the story itself, he says he will.

This view might be thought to violate the pluralism in which we of the West currently take great pride. Indeed, it does violate the bumptious pluralism of "postmodernism," which surveys all philosophies and religions from a superior vantage point and reduces them all to interchangeable status on a single level, or to building blocks for some Toynbeesque synthesis in the suitably indefinite future. It does not, however, violate the pluralism that ascribes positive value to many philosophies and to all major religions. It does not violate the pluralism that simultaneously affirms the universal saving will of God and the economy of salvation in Christ. God dispenses the grace of Christ in accord with his infinite resourcefulness in making all the world's religions and philosophies, and other social and cultural values, serve his saving will.

The reductionist pluralism alluded to above, incompatible with the truth of the kerygma/gospel of the New Testament but adopted, it seems, in view of its good intentions, is a key to why numerous moderns and postmoderns, including some New Testament scholars, are intent—while smiling and applauding—on cutting Christianity, its meaning and truth, down to a size they think more suitable. Among the tasks and roles of hermeneutics there is that of deciding between the gospel and its reductionist interpreters.

Access to the gospel is not to be taken for granted. Nothing guarantees it. It is helped or hindered in accord with humanly generated conditions. Millions live without the slightest contact with Church or gospel. Again, many have made a failed contact, owing to misunderstanding, deliberate or indeliberate, or to superficiality, vacillation, immersion in anxiety or pleasure (Mark 4:14-19; Matt 13:19-22; cf. Luke 8:12-14). To the tendency to drift, which infects all generations, we might add what is special to our own time: the noxious-to-lethal impact of *ideology* on the history of our century.

"Ideology" in this context has a negative, not neutral, sense. It is the rationalizing talk and doubletalk that in the first half of our century camouflaged the nature and purposes of Communists, Fascists, Nazis, and many others, and in the second half of the century never ceased to connive with ideological mendacity, which, however, remained as vicious and murderous as ever. As history in our time has made crystal-clear, neither natural gifts nor acquired culture supply enough antibodies against it. Counter-instances are all too many. Martin Heidegger, that great unmasker of the "incomprehensible triviality" of the age of the masses, its empty chitchat and anonymous "they," himself fell victim to his own affinities with the *Volk* and *Boden* ideology of the Third Reich.

In a century of technological brilliance and of mendacious and murderous ideology, the gospel for millions has been like a letter undelivered, lost in the shuffle. Hermeneutics, of course, is no more than a philosophic discipline. The task of New Testament hermeneutics, however, is sublated by the Christian missionary task: to open, to keep open, or to reopen access to the gospel; to remove the blocks that stop the flow of meaning and extinguish the light of truth. New Testament hermeneutics is not an emergency task, but it does become most meaningful when, in one way or another, things have gone awry with New Testament interpretation.

In keeping with its character as a primer, this book includes a glossary of terms relevant to hermeneutics.

Friends and colleagues have helped me to organize and produce this book, especially Frederick E. Crowe, E. Earle Ellis, Sean McEvenue, Alan Mendelson, C.F.D. Moule, Quentin Quesnell, John C. Robertson, and Peter Stuhlmacher.

Ben F. Meyer
Les Verrières, Switzerland

Part I

Insight, Judgment, Reversal

In Part I we shall deal in introductory fashion with the two main intellectual acts that constitute fully human knowing: insight (construal, understanding) and judgment (cognitive self-committal, namely, to a verdict of true or false).

We begin immediately with "reading as paradigm of knowing," in other words, of understanding and judging. We shall return to this paradigm to specify, ponder, and highlight its implications.

In chapter one, after an effort to "place" or "locate" the act of insight in the contextual sequence of human knowing, we shall review *several kinds of insight* that illustrate, quicken, and advance New Testament scholarship.

In chapter two we shall do the same with the theme of judgment: first "place" it in the sequence of human knowing, then, by way of exhibit, present a solidly probable judgment that offers foundational support to countless other judgments and limits a priori some of the more unlikely, not to say marginally irrational, proposals touching the field of studies as a whole.

Finally, having dealt with progress-generating insights and judgments, we shall review (in chapter three) the phenomenon of "self-reversal"; we shall then build on it by making thematic first "horizons," then the correlation of horizons in "dialectic" with a view to confirming or reversing them.

Reading as Paradigm of Knowing

In the late twentieth century the most basic hermeneutical is-sue has become explicitly central: do *texts* mediate meaning *to us,* or do *we* lend meaning to *texts?*

Early in his career the late Northrop Frye recalled a comment on Jacob Boehme: "His books are like a picnic to which the au-thor brings the words and the reader the meaning." This, said Frye, may have been intended as a sneer at Boehme, "but it is an exact description of all literary works without exception." And Frye lived to see this conception of reading adopted almost univer-sally among North American theorists (though not among ordi-nary readers anywhere).

That a view so removed from common experience and com-mon sense should have come to have so wide a success in the sphere of theory is hardly explicable apart from reaction against the simplistic notion of reading that it replaced. This was the "naïve realism" that took the meaning of the text to be already fully constituted just as it stood on the page. But what exactly is it that stands on any page? Inkspots, or what R. G. Colling-wood called "curious marks on paper."

These inkspots are, of course, signs; the reader's deciphering of the signs yields a word-sequence which the reader construes to mean such-and-such. Frye had the wit to notice, first, that the page yielded not meaning, but inkspots; second, that the inkspots were signs; third, that anything over and above a reissue of the same signs in the same order was bound to be the product of the reader. In this sense every text is a picnic to which the writer brings the words and the reader the meaning.

Frye's view, however, suffers from a fundamental oversight. Not only are the inkspots signs, which, deciphered, yield word-sequences; further, *the reader takes his marching orders from them.* The signs yield *this* word-sequence and no other; and, nor-mally, the meaning that the reader brings to the picnic is the mean-ing that the writer had managed to express—to objectify verbally and textually. It is perfectly true that the reader's hold on the meaning of the text is mediated by the reader's own experience, intelligence, and judgment; but, when the reader is competent and his reading accurate, the meaning so mediated is precisely the meaning that the writer intended and more or less skillfully expressed in words signified by letters (= inkspots).

It follows that in every successful act of reading we have a perfect illustration of critical realism. Whenever the reader catches the meaning of the writer, the picnic is a success—a phenomenon attributable to two distinct factors, the skill of the writer as writer and the skill of the reader as reader.

The two go together. No matter how bright the reader, the picnic is a dud if the writer has nothing of interest to say or lacks the skill to say it well. And nothing and nobody can save the day, not even a Homer or a Shakespeare, if the reader is unable somehow to measure up to the text.

In any case, reading is neither the mere passive registering of a meaning already fully constituted on the page, as naïve realists assumed, nor is it the entirely creative response of the reader, as Northrop Frye and countless allies and followers with nearly equal infelicity have supposed. Every act of successful reading illustrates the middle position, corresponding (as we shall see) to the critical-realist view of insight.

Furthermore, at the heart of critical realism is the theorem that the way to objectivity is through *the subject, operating well.* The objective element in successful acts of reading is—what? It is not the writer's meaning (which might be inept, mendacious, dead wrong), but the *accurate recovery* of whatever meaning the writer has managed to objectify in words. That meaning is mediated, communicated, recovered, only if the reader reads *well,* only if he or she attends to an exact decoding of signs, to the particularities of the word-sequence that emerges, to how every element in it works with every other.

Above we used the expression "measuring up to the text." Everyone can read the funnies, but not everyone can read Tolstoy, much less Virgil and Dante. A basic aspect of successful reading is a state of potential adequacy to the text. The reader must have some *entrée* to the world of the writer. Over and above that, he must attend to the sense of the words he is reading, and not only to their sense, but to their sound—timbre, color, rhythm— and to all the other clues to feeling and tone, for these qualify the sense. The more at home the reader is with the writer's field of vision, the more alert, sensitive, and discerning his attention to singularities of the text, the more successful the retrieval of intended and realized textual meaning. The more authentic the acts of the subject, or reader, the more objective his reading. Or, to put it in the general terms in use among critical realists, the way to objectivity is through authentic subjectivity.

Another title for the present work might be: *New Testament Scholarship: The Cultivation of Authentic Subjectivity,* for the cultivation of authentic subjectivity is the purpose, the heart, the central theme of the book. This is a primer on subjectivity. When is subjectivity authentic? When the subject does things the right way. So far as interpretation is concerned, two questions arise. What must an interpreter do? And, how does he discover the right way of doing it?

Ultimately, the point of interpretation is the truth and value of the text. If there were not texts worthy of eliciting a maximum effort to understand them, what point would there be in interpretation and interpretation theory? We are supposing that such worthy texts exist. Given this, the *immediate,* not ultimate, point of interpretation (and of hermeneutics as theory of interpretation) is to arrive at the intended sense of the text and to articulate it well. To do this well is to attain the truth of interpretation.

All truth, whether it be the sense and truth of the text or the truth of interpretation (the successful recovery and mediation of the sense and truth of the text), hinges on objectivity. Objectivity, in turn, hinges on the subject's effort to perform his task well. Contrary to a stubborn illusion born of naïve realism, *objectivity is not achieved by the flight from subjectivity nor by any and every cultivation of subjectivity, but by an intense and persevering effort to exercise subjectivity attentively, intelligently, reasonably, and responsibly.*

Coups and Breakthroughs:
Insights That Make a Difference

Locating "Insight"

Our first concern is understanding (construal, insight). To get hold of this act is, first of all, to set it in experiential context. Where does it come in the sequence of acts that collectively and cumulatively constitute knowledge?

We may begin by noting that it must come after sense-knowledge and after the wonder that, in human beings, supervenes on sense-knowledge.

One wonders about something, perhaps about the data present to the wonderer by eye or ear or imagination. There follow several quite distinct moments: formulating the wonder in a question, cudgelling one's wits until—sometimes suddenly, sometimes laboriously—an answer occurs. Finally, one weighs how good the answer is.

The first moment is the act of shaping and sharpening wonder by formulating it as a question. This is spontaneous; questions naturally "arise." Still, anything like a precise formulation of the question is not so spontaneous. By experiment, by sticking with the as yet unfocused issue through a process of trial and error, the question begins to take shape, to fit into an order of questions, and—little by little, through subtractions as well as additions—to become more exact.

The second follow-up moment is the search for an answer. The search culminates in a flash of construal, understanding, insight. In response to whatever one had wondered about, one not only attends to what look like promising data, but *so construes these data as to provide an answer to the question.*

This active forward step of construal is something new. It is an addition that responds to or answers the question. It is new vis-à-vis the data about which one wondered, and it is new vis-à-vis the question that focused one's wondering about the data. It would be a mistake, then, to suppose that an act of construal or insight is somehow already present, actual, pre-constituted in the data, itself a given, immanent in the data and imposed by the data. No. An act of construal or understanding or insight is an active movement of intelligence. It is true that we could never come to a geometrical understanding of a circle without some image, like a wheel; still, the definition of a circle is not somehow already actual and present in the image. And since it is not actually present, it cannot imprint itself on the mind.

Insight, accordingly, is not like sight. Sight is called into being when an image has been registered on the eye. It may image only a part or aspect of the object, but, as image, it is fully constituted, it stands in integral relationship to a colored, lighted object. Once the eye is acted upon by the object, sight follows as the night the day. Seeing is immediately present to what is seen, and (supposing that the eye is in good condition and the object is colored and lighted) seeing has a kind of infallibility.

With insight, on the other hand, the presence of the to-be-understood does not automatically trigger understanding, much less accurate understanding. If it did, then the classroom phenomenon of some children understanding and others remaining puzzled could not happen. All would simultaneously find themselves in possession of the same sought-after insight, just as all (if all are looking) see the drawing that the teacher holds before them in his or her hand.

We have begun to locate construal, insight, understanding, answer: it follows on sense-knowledge, wonder, the forming of a question, the search that finds release in an answer. But insight or construal is not terminal. It sparks a new question: is the construal exact? Does the insight hold? Or, is this way of understanding any good? Having come up with what might seem like a hot idea, we find ourselves wondering whether idea/construal/insight/understanding/answer is good and, if so, how good. Coming up with an answer has merely raised a further question, a question for reflection, which calls for an answer or verdict or judgment saying "true" or "false," and "certainly" or "probably." Insight, in short, is an event located *after* wondering and *before* judging.

Illustration: let the data be a text, such as: "Look, I tell you a secret: we shall not all sleep but we shall all be changed" (1 Cor 15:51). I wonder just what that means. Let the wondering be sharpened into a question, and let the precise question be: what does "the secret" consist in? Finally, let the act of construal/insight/understanding be exemplified in and by each of three tries at an answer.

First try: "the secret" is that we shall not all sleep, that is, that *not all of us will die.* Maybe; but a distinction between the living and the dead at the parousia had been a commonplace from the earliest Christian scenarios we know of; moreover, it looks as if the secret in any case takes that into account but somehow includes more. Second try: "the secret" is the transformation of the two classes, or better yet, *the timing of the transformation,* namely, at the parousia (not, as in 2 Baruch, only after the judgment). Maybe; but is there any reason in the text to lead us to think that Paul is dealing with the same problem that 2 Baruch was dealing with? No such clue is evident. Third try: "the secret" focuses on the living. It consists in this, that (though not all will die) *all—not only the dead (1 Cor 15:42-44), but the living as well—will be changed (at the parousia).*

Arguments have been adduced in favor of all these (and several other) efforts of construal or insight; clearly some argument is needed. None of these insights/construals/understandings is self-authenticating. Insight is integral of itself, without its including any guarantee of adequacy to the object of inquiry (objectivity). To push further toward a real knowledge of truth, a further increment, a new cognitive moment, is called for.

This new moment we shall hold off until chapter two. Right now we shall say only that it is inevitable. For, once one has placed the act construal/insight/understanding, it is inevitable that one ask whether it is supported by relevant evidence, whether the evidence is sufficient to establish it as at least probably true. Meantime, we shall concentrate our efforts on the moment of insight/construal/understanding.

We intend to stay close to experience, adopting a strategy that ought to cheer the heart of any practicing New Testament scholar or student, namely, with a series of bright and probably successful insights. Though our main topic in this chapter is not the rational level of evidence and judgment, we shall anticipate to the extent of indicating why these insights were not only striking but solid. Finally, we shall find ourselves led to the question: how can we cultivate the sources of insight and the habits that foster the incidence of insight? But we are not beginning, so to speak, at the deep end of the pool. We begin with examples meant to show that the natural appetite for and drive to the true and the good has an intrinsically normative character. Critical realism is grounded in spontaneous human functioning, which is itself the key to how to do the job.

Perhaps the most fascinating and persuasive aspect of this normativeness—"the key to how to do the job"—is the negative phenomenon of "self-reversal." When I spontaneously operate in one way, but laboriously theorize in another, some inner contradiction or doublethink is bound to turn up, as we shall see in chapter three.

Linguistic Insights

Until the appearance nearly a hundred years ago of Gustaf Dalman's *Die Worte Jesu,* the concentrated study of gospel texts in Greek (which in the Western world dated only from the Renaissance) proceeded perforce without a satisfactory grasp of the linguistic singularity of Synoptic texts. Dalman's effort to define this linguistic singularity has stood the test of time exceedingly well. These gospel narratives were not free compositions but in significant part literary fixations of oral tradition; the traditions were not first formulated in Greek but in Aramaic; finally, as they stand, the gospels are neither translations from Aramaic nor fully, precisely intelligible apart from attention to their Aramaic substratum.

Dalman did not put the accent on the traits of oral transmission, though he was well aware of the oral character of Jesus' words and of the oral factor, for example, in early liturgy. His focus on languages, however, has helped define the conditions of insight into the meaning of words in the Synoptic gospels. Here we shall offer some insights into the sense of words, of which the first few relate to the sense of words and idioms in the light of the Aramaic substratum.

The last petition of the Our Father (Matt 6:9-13, Luke 11:2-4) is a distich in Matthew, a monostich in Luke. The line, *kai mē eisenegkēs hēmas eis peirasmon* (Matt 6:13a; Luke 11:4c) appears in Jerome's rendering as *et ne nos inducas in tentationem:* "and lead us not into temptation."

What can this possibly mean? That, unless dissuaded, the Father might well entice us to evil? This sort of question may stand behind the text in James:

> Let no one say when he is tempted, "I am tempted by God"; for God cannot be tempted with evil and he himself tempts no one; but each person is tempted when he is lured and enticed by his own desire (1:13-14). (Revised Standard Version)

Such considerations have prompted some to interpret *peirasmos* differently, and to translate it by a word other than "temptation," so accenting the distinction that James evidently made between *peirasmos* as "trial, ordeal" and *peirasmos* as "enticement to evil." "Trial" or "ordeal" probably does accord better than "temptation" with the original sense of the petition.

It is true, of course, that the two senses ("temptation" and "test/trial/ordeal") tend to converge inasmuch as a trial or ordeal entails the danger of moral or religious collapse under pressure. Still, James is surely right both in his implicit acknowledgment that God may indeed "put to the test" and in his explicit denial that God entices to sin. Though the one tested might fail, God's intention in testing is to produce "steadfastness" (Jas 1:2-3).

This line of thought or one like it must have lain behind the widespread abandonment of the RSV's "Lead us not into temptation" and the adoption of the following translations:

> And do not bring us to the test (New English Bible);
> And do not put us to the test (Jerusalem Bible; New Jerusalem Bible; Revised English Bible);
> Subject us not to the trial (New American Bible);
> Do not bring us to hard testing (Good News Bible).

There are several reasons, however, for doubting whether any of these yields the true sense of the petition. First, though there are Jewish and Christian prayers, including New Testament prayers, that reflect this kind of petition, there is also a countercurrent to the effect that trials and ordeals are inescapably part of our lot as human beings. As for the supreme eschatological affliction or ordeal, we find (in John 12:27) Jesus' cry, "And what shall I say? 'Father, save me from this hour?' No, for this purpose I have come to this hour." A text in Tertullian may reflect an authentic agraphon of Jesus: *neminem intemptatum regna caelestia consecuturum* ("no one will attain to the reign of heaven without passing through trials"). It would probably be too much to say that this in and of itself rules out the above translations (according to which the petitioner prays to be saved from trials, or from the trial); it nevertheless does offer grounds for doubt.

Moreover, the above translations *are* ruled out by a different consideration: we have a splendid parallel to this petition among ancient Jewish prayers (bBer 60b), which points in a different direction. In morning and evening prayers that may well go back to the time of Jesus, we find:

> Lead me/my foot not into the hands (= power) of sin,
> and bring me not into the hands (= power) of guilt,
> and not into the hands (= power) of temptation/trial(s),
> and not into the hands (= power) of anything shameful.

Here we should notice four elements that run parallel to the Our Father petition under consideration: (1) the negative formulation, "Lead . . . not"; (2) the word "lead" (in the Jewish prayer, this is the causative *(hiphil)* of "to go"; (3) the expression "into"; (4) the series "sin, guilt, temptation, and anything shameful." Whereas the phrases *mē eisenegkēs hēmas* ("lead us not") and *eis peirasmon* ("into temptation") in the Greek text of the Our Father are both problematic, the phrasing of the Jewish prayer is clear. The negative with the causative of "to go" may be rendered "lead . . . not," but may be as well or better rendered, "do not allow": do not allow my foot/me to go. . . . Again, *eis peirasmon* and "into temptation" both represent a thoroughly baffling idiom, on which excellent scholars have spent enormous ingenuity, more or less in vain, whereas the sense of the petition in the Jewish morning and evening prayers is plain as a pikestaff.

The petitioner calls on God to keep him clear of the power of sin, guilt, etc., that is, *to keep him from sinning.*

Inasmuch as we have here a parallel that illuminates the whole line *(mē eisenegkēs hēmas eis peirasmon),* we are positioned (1) to construe mē *eisenegkēs* as reflecting the Aramaic causative ('afel) of "to go." This might be hamhandedly rendered, "lead . . . not," but the intended sense, no doubt, included the permissive nuance: "do not allow . . . to go"; (2) to construe *eis peirasmon* as equivalent to a fuller Aramaic expression: *lîdê nisyôn = eis cheiras peirasmou,* "into the hands [= power] of temptation/the test." In the light of the parallel, it is evident that "into temptation/the test" and "into *the power of* temptation/the test" are perfectly synonymous. (The Aramaic substratum of *eis peirasmon* was probably *lĕnisyôn,* understood as the equivalent of *lîdê nisyôn;* it is noteworthy that in the late-nineteenth-century Delitzsch/Dalman Hebrew translation of the New Testament we have *lîdê nissāyôn,* "into the hands [= power] of temptation/[the] trial.")

The sense of the last petition of the Our Father, therefore, is not "save us from being put to the test!" but "save us from cracking under pressure of the test!" It is a petition that God save us not from being tested, but from ourselves, from our own weakness, our liability to fall into sin under pressure. If, as is probable, the *peirasmos* (at least originally) referred to the eschatological ordeal, the petition is that God keep us from falling away, from committing apostasy under pressure of persecution.

Suggestions for revising the English translation of the Our Father might include:

> "and keep us from failing when tested";
> "and make us stand firm in (our) trial(s)";

or, if one wishes to keep the original negative formulation and eschatological reference:

> "and do not let us fall victim to the ordeal";

or, keeping the negative formulation but generalizing the eschatological reference:

> "and do not let us crack under pressure."

We said above that Dalman gave the first thoroughly informed
and thought-through account of the linguistic situation of the
gospels, especially the Synoptic gospels. In the light of this account, we must make room for the possibility that the Greek text
itself is here and there semantically problematic. The "insight"
that opens up the last petition of the Our Father turns less on
a resourceful exploitation of Greek philology than on a striking
and persuasive parallel between this petition and a series of four
synonymous lines in two ancient Jewish prayers.

A similar situation obtains elsewhere in the Our Father,
namely, in the bread petition: *ton arton hēmōn ton epiousion dos
hēmin sēmeron* (Matt 6:11), which Jerome rendered, *panem nostrum cotidianum da nobis hodie,* "our daily bread give us this
day" or, inverting the order, "give us this day our daily bread."
But Jerome himself has provided us with an item of information
that tips the scales on how best to analyze the problematic adjective *epiousios.* He recounts that the Aramaic gospel of the
Nazoraeans had, for *epiousios,* the word *maḥar,* "tomorrow."
That orients us toward *epeimi/epienai* from the root "come"
rather than toward *epeimi/epieinai* from the root "be." Thus,
epiousios was in all probability formed from the present participle used in phrases such as *tę epiousę hēmera/nukti* ("on the
following day/night"), just as the adjective *tetartaios* ("pertaining to the fourth day") was formed from *hē tetartē hēmera* ("the
fourth day"). On this basis *epiousios* means "pertaining to tomor-
row/the future"; and the text should have been rendered *panem
nostrum crastinum da nobis hodie,* "our bread of tomorrow give
us today." The petitioner begs for a share already, now, in the
coming banquet of salvation, an image that often occurs in the
words of Jesus, for example,

> Many will come from east and west
> and recline at table with Abraham, Isaac, and Jacob
> at the coming of the reign of heaven . . . (Matt 8:11; cf. Luke
> 13:28b-29).

The scene evoked is the messianic banquet on the world mountain. In the parables, too, Jesus more than once presented the
reign of God as a great banquet. His words draw on the closely
related imagery of "new wine" both in his public ministry (Matt

9:17 = Mark 2:22 = Luke 5:37-38) and at the Last Supper (Mark 14:25 = Matt 26:29).

All this might have emerged (indeed, probably did emerge) as a likely possibility even without the testimony of Jerome on the gospel of the Nazoraeans. But that testimony, a factor extrinsic to the Greek text of the Our Father, is what lends the reading "bread of tomorrow" its clear edge of probability. Once again, insight into the text has depended on data from outside the text.

Massive indirect verification has accrued to Dalman's hold on the linguistic state of affairs in the Synoptic gospels, especially owing to his contemporary Charles Fox Burney and to the following generation of Paul Joüon. We shall offer here a rapid survey of quite ordinary semantic insights proposed by Joüon and others. Collectively, they verify Dalman's theses.

The last and climactic antithesis in the Sermon on the Mount reads, "You have heard that it was said, 'You shall love your neighbor and hate your enemy.' " In Joüon's reading, however, the second stich, no doubt a current halakic refinement on Leviticus, may be read taking "hate" as a simplifying expression for "not to love" (Gen 29:31; Mal 1:2-3), and taking the underlying Aramaic imperfect/future as intending a permissive nuance, "You shall love your neighbor [= fellow countryman] though you need not love your [personal] adversary."

Again, in the Sermon on the Mount: did Jesus urge his hearers to "enter by the narrow gate" or to "travel by the narrow pass"? The word *pulē* in the New Testament is usually a monumental gate, such as a portal of entry into a city. But "narrow" suggests that here Aramaic *tar'ā'*, which may equally refer to a gate or a pass/defile (cf. "the Gates [mountain passes] of Cilicia"), ought to have been rendered "pass." (If this is on the right track, the Aramaic substratum exhibited *'atā'* with *b*, not *l*. The original text has been modified as part of the translation process.)

Joüon, a remarkable grammarian and semanticist, published (in 1930) one of the most useful vernacular translations of the gospels in existence. Its notes point out hundreds of semantic refinements and improvements. Any number of quasi-cranks have attempted the same sort of clarifications; here, by contrast, we have a sober scholar as well as a thoroughly qualified linguist. The oral-tradition translators into Greek were far less often flatly mistaken than merely somewhat hurried or approximate or inept. In a number of instances a slight woodenness can turn out to be utterly misleading. Dalman resolved the baffling language of the so-called "thunderbolt from the Johannine sky" (Karl Hase on the text of Matt 11:27 = Luke 10:21, which treats of reciprocal knowledge of Father and Son) simply by reference to Aramaic idiom (use of article for generic sense, lack of reciprocal pronoun "one another, each other," etc.). So, instead of referring to a mystical union of Father and Son, the text said, more simply, "As only a father knows his son, so only a son knows his father. . . ."

The following is an example of semantic insight within the sphere of Greek alone. Mark 14:2 and Matthew 26:5 tell us that the conspirators against Jesus ("chief priests and scribes") were intent on seizing him "by stealth . . . for they said, 'not *en tē heortē* lest there be a riot among the people.'"

This text occasions both interpretative and historical problems. If "not *en tē heortē*" means "not during the feast," what time-period, as Passover approached, did the conspirators have in mind? Earlier, before the feast? If their problem was to avoid inciting a riot among the people, that would hardly serve, for in the short period left before Passover, masses of pilgrims were already arriving; hence, the prospect of a riot could hardly be obviated. Or did the conspirators think rather of waiting until after Passover? That, too, is problematic: what guarantee would they have had that Jesus would stay in Jerusalem rather than leave with the mass of pilgrims? The more concretely one tries to make sense of the notice, the more enigmatic it becomes. The arrest was to take place "by stealth"; but that makes sense only if it was to take place *during the feast*.

In 1922 Georg Bertram resolved these and related problems (for example, how the betrayal by Judas fitted into the conspirators' plans) by proposing a different meaning for *hē heortē*: not "feast," but "festival crowd," a sense well attested in secular Greek. First of all, the implied antithesis between "by stealth" and *"en tē heortē"* was enigmatic if "stealth," which expresses manner or means, were being played off against "during the feast," a time-notice. In Bertram's proposal there is no time-notice and no problem: "stealth" correlates perfectly with "not in public" ("by stealth . . . for they said, 'not in the festival crowd . . .'"). Second, with the dropping of the time-notice Markan chronology no longer entails implicit contradictions. Third, the service that Judas rendered now makes sense: what was needed was to know where Jesus would be and to have access to him when he was out of the public forum and public eye. (Previous to the brilliant simplicity of Bertram's proposal there had been some fancy footwork and guesswork on what Judas' service to the conspirators was to consist in. In Albert Schweitzer's view, Judas told the conspirators of how Jesus and the disciples harbored the idea of Jesus' being the Messiah.)

Literary Insights

Ernst Lohmeyer must be credited with the discovery (published in the late 1920s) that the text of Philippians 2:6-11 was a pre-Pauline Christian hymn. Lohmeyer launched what became over the following years a fascinating sequence of efforts to specify its literary structure. He himself proposed two parts, each part comprising three three-line strophes. *La Bible de Jérusalem* adopted a form not far removed from Lohmeyer's:

Lui, de condition divine,
ne retient pas jalousement
le rang qui l'égalait à Dieu.

His state was divine,
yet he did not cling
to his equality with God

Mais il s'anéantit lui-même,
prenant condition d'esclave,
et devenant semblable aux hommes.

but emptied himself
to assume the condition of a slave
and became as men are;

S'étant comporté comme un
    homme,
il s'humilia plus encore,
obéissant jusqu'à la mort,
    et à la mort sur une croix!

and being as all men are,

he was humbler yet,
even to accepting death,
    death on a cross.

Aussi Dieu l'a-t-il exalté
et lui a-t-il donné le Nom
qui est au-dessus de tout nom,

But God raised him high
and gave him the name
which is above all other names

pour que *tout,* au nom de Jésus,
s'agenouille, au plus haut des
    cieux,
sur la terre et dans les enfers,

so that *all beings*
in the heavens, on earth and
    in the underworld,
should bend the knee at the
    name of Jesus

et que *toute langue proclame,*

and that *every tongue should
    acclaim*

de Jésus Christ, qu'il est Seigneur,
à la gloire de Dieu le Père.

Jesus Christ as Lord
to the glory of God the Father.

There was an insuperable difficulty with this structure, namely, that it violated the *parallelismus membrorum* (a stylistic trait noticed by Johannes Weiss and, half a century later, by Rudolf Bultmann) exemplified by the lines

> *en homoiōmati anthrōpōn genomenos*
> *kai schēmati heuretheis hōs anthrōpos.*

In 1947 and 1953 there appeared two new efforts, by Lucien Cerfaux and Joachim Jeremias respectively, which, though independent, were closely parallel to one another. Both did full justice to this and other parallelisms in the hymn. The text was in two parts, but three strophes. The following is Jeremias' effort:

(v. 6) *hos en morphę̄ theou huparchōn*
      ouch harpagmon hēgēsato to einai isa theǭ
(v. 7) *alla heauton ekenōsen*
      morphēn doulou labōn.

      en homoiōmati anthrōpōn genomenos
      kai schēmati heuretheis hōs anthrōpos
(v. 8) *etapeinōsen heauton*
      genomenos hupēkoos mechri thanatou
      [*thanatou de staurou*].

(v. 9) *dio kai ho theos auton huperupsōsen*
      kai echarisato autǭ to onoma to huper pan onoma
(v. 10) *hina en tǭ onomati Iēsou pan gonu kampsę̄*
      [*epouraniōn kai epigeiōn kai katachthoniōn*]
(v. 11) *kai pasa glōssa exomologēsētai hoti KURIOS IĒSOUS*
      CHRISTOS [*eis doxan theou patros*].

This proposal (with putative Pauline additions enclosed in square brackets) respected the following data relevant to structure: (1) the caesura between *dio* in verse 9 and what precedes; (2) three examples of *parallelismus membrorum:* the first in verse 9 *(huperupsōsen/echarisato);* the second, in verses 10-11 *(pan gonu kampsę̄/pasa glōssa exomologēsētai);* the third, in verse 7c and d *(en homoiōmati anthrōpōn genomenos/kai schēmati heuretheis hōs anthrōpos).*

Moreover, once Jeremias' proposal is taken as settled, it reveals some further quite remarkable structural and stylistic parallelisms between the first strophe and the second. Both begin with a prepositional phrase *(en morphę̄/en homoiōmati),* each immediately followed by a participle at the end of the line *(huparchōn/genomenos)*, both exhibiting a reprise *(Wiederaufnahme)* by a comparative particle in the second line *(isa/hōs)*. Further, in both strophes the emphatic main verb occurs in line three *(ekenōsen/etapeinōsen);* in both strophes the object of the main verb is the reflexive, but in chiastic order *(heauton ekenōsen/etapeinōsen heauton)*. The fourth line of both strophes explains the sense of the main verb with the help of an aorist participle *(labōn/genomenos)*, the placement of which (once again) varies chiastically. Finally, both strophes end (fourth line) with a reprise from line one. In strophe 1, this is *morphē;* in strophe 2, it is *genomenos*. In each case this reprise is the first word of line four. This kind of minute parallelism would appear to confirm definitively the proposed strophe division.

With respect to the thematic progression of the hymn, it is widely agreed that the major caesura is between *dio* and what precedes; that is, the main thematic sequence is "humiliation" followed by "exaltation." It is also agreed, though less widely, that the motifs of pre-existence and incarnation are present in the part dominated by the humiliation theme. How do these motifs tie in with the hymn's structure?

The answer turns in large part on how one interprets *heauton ekenōsen*. Here two observations are appropriate. First, *mōrphēn* in line four is not only a reprise of *morphē* in line one, it also serves to point up an antithesis: *morphē doulou* vs. *morphē theou*. The deliberate contrast commends the view that in both lines *morphē* has a generically ontological sense. Second, in both strophes the participial clause of line four helps specify the sense of the main verb in line three. We cannot, then, take *heauton ekenōsen* to mean, "he poured out his (mortal) life." Rather, he who was *en morphē theou,* and who thus enjoyed equality with God, "emptied himself" and took on the *morphē* of servant: a creaturely status, and so a status of submission to God.

On the other hand, as Jeremias rightly argued, there is no solid linguistic objection to the phrase *heauton ekenōsen* as a rendering of *he'ĕrāh lammāwet napšô*, he poured out/surrendered his life to death (Isa 53:12b). Inasmuch as (1) *'rh* in the sense of "to empty" is generally rendered by *ekkenoun;* (2) the reflexive form is a *hapax* in both Greek (Phil 2:7) and Hebrew (Isa 53:12); and (3) there are other ties between the Philippians' hymn and the great

Servant text (Isa 52:13–53:12), it seems inescapable that the phrases "he emptied himself" and "he poured out his life to death" are related. But how are they related? The uniquely plausible solution would seem to be that the author of the hymn has deliberately transposed a text on the suffering Servant to the realm of pre-existence and made it interpret incarnation as ineffably heroic humiliation.

As a Greek version of *he'erāh lammāwet napšô, heauton ekenōsen* is linguistically impeccable, but the drawing of it into the ambit of the humiliation theme has radically altered its sense. As developed in the hymn, the humiliation theme has two coherent phases: incarnation (strophe 1) and obedience unto death (strophe 2). If there is here an allusion to the Adam/Christ typology, it too is transposed to the pre-existing One, who, unlike Adam, in already being in the *morphē* of God, relinquished his status and emptied himself—the exact contrary of what Adam attempted to do.

If this transposition from the earthly and historical sphere to that of the heavenly pre-existence of the savior seems a priori implausible, it might be recalled that in the hymn's third strophe the *Kurios* motif is similarly transposed from the earthly and historical sphere to that of Christ's glorification after death. Although the two-part division of the hymn still holds, the two transpositions signaled here establish the sequence: pre-earthly event (strophe 1), earthly event (strophe 2), post-earthly event (strophe 3). For the first time Christians (Antiochene *hellēnistai*) have produced a universalist christology (no reference to Israel). The world of the hymn is unrestricted. The scene is already set now for an event which will take place at the consummation of time, when every knee shall bend and every tongue confess Jesus as Lord. The salvation of the nations is already an implied imperative. Salvation history had previously (in the view of the *hebraioi*) climaxed in the image of the nations reclining to banquet with the patriarchs on Zion. In virtue of a new way of viewing the Easter event, it now climaxes in cosmic worship "to the glory of God the Father."

Here structure, theme, and logopoeia (Ezra Pound's name for charging language through implied allusion to texts familiar to the readership) come together smoothly, organically, and with brilliant originality. The recovery of this superb lyric has been effected by Ernst Lohmeyer's alertness to non-Pauline conceptuality and vocabulary (1927/28), construal of certain lines as parallel by Weiss, Bultmann, and others, the Lucien Cerfaux/Joachim Jeremias literary analysis of style and structure, Cerfaux publishing earlier (1946), Jeremias later but independently (1953). Since then we have had instances of insight into the conceptual resources of the hymn (Dieter Georgi, 1964) and helpful currents and countercurrents contesting, revising, completing the reading of the hymn (Otfried Hofius 1976, Joseph A. Fitzmyer 1988, and many others).

Historical Insights

An insight that has long seemed to the present writer one of the genuine breakthroughs in historical-Jesus research was that of Charles Harold Dodd on Jesus' prophetic view of the future. In chapters two and three of Dodd's 1935 work, *The Parables of the Kingdom,* he put on a solid basis a hypothesis (first floated in 1873 by Wilhelm Weiffenbach) to the effect that Jesus envisaged a near future of (1) tribulation and (2) parousia. That is, the common Christian scenario that posited a distinct resurrection-event to be followed by the Church-and-mission era *and then* the parousia did not go back to Jesus himself, whose view was simpler and more schematic.

Weiffenbach, however, was distracted by an a priori concern to free Jesus of the trappings of Judaic eschatology. Dodd was simply intent on making sense of the mass of Jesus-sayings about the future in the tradition. He presented his reconstruction most tentatively and, when he was finished, he yielded to the temptation to complicate it with a further hermeneutic effort to interpret the whole in accord with "(totally) realized eschatology." This was in a sense to take it all back, an attitude that shows how little Dodd was being tempted to reconstruct Jesus' future scenario in a way meant to please Dodd himself.

As for the two-act scenario of "ordeal" and "resolution" or, as he put it, of an "eschatology of woe" (to be opened by Jesus' suffering) followed by an "eschatology of bliss" (to be opened by a globally conceived resurrection/exaltation/parousia of Jesus), Dodd accordingly had no theological axe to grind. He was perfectly ready to abandon his reconstruction if another met the data more effectively. He made no secret of his own favorite stance, "realized eschatology," which he indeed proposed as a hermeneutical way of aborting his extraordinarily perceptive reconstruction.

Dodd's reconstruction moved through the following sequence: (1) the sense of kingdom *(basileia/malkût)* of God; (2) use of the expression in Jewish literature of the era; (3) texts organized in accord with Synoptic source criticism (two-source hypothesis); (4) first distinctive trait of Jesus' usage: *Schonanbruch*/advance arrival of reign of God; (5) specific future coming of reign of God; (6) two times and modes of eschatology: "woe" in history, "bliss" in the post-historical future opened by "the Day of the Son of Man."

This reconstruction has recently come under detailed critique under two main heads: first, as relying too much on the two-source theory of Synoptic source criticism; second, as failing to take account of all the data. Neither point, however, is effective. It is true that Dodd did not discuss all reign-of-God texts; but with specific reference to the question at hand he left out of account no significant items in the eschatological calendar of the gospel tradition. The critique accordingly fails to detract significantly from Dodd's reconstruction. There is no doubt about its having many minor blemishes. They relate mostly to schematizing (e.g., Dodd tended to correlate the eschatology of woe with prophetic tradition and the eschatology of bliss with apocalyptic tradition, whereas all of Jesus' sayings about the future reflected both traditions). The only real failure lay in Dodd's all-too-keen readiness to take the whole reconstruction back in favor of a Johannine "realized eschatology." All the blemishes, however, were corrected as early as 1941.

All in all, Dodd's effort was a brilliant breakthrough. It both recovered the substance of the historical Jesus' scenario of future events and showed how the early Church, in reaffirming Jesus' scenario, had no choice but to insert, *ex eventu,* Jesus' resurrection from the dead and the mission (originally conceived as limited to Israel) launched under the kerygmatic banner of the death and resurrection of Jesus, made Christ and Lord.

In this way the many data of Jesus' "imminent expectation" of the end—like the data on John the Baptist's imminent expectations —make sense; the Church's own imminent expectation, which appears to have reigned supreme until the fall of Jerusalem and which disappeared only in the course of the following generation (toward the end of the first Christian century), makes sense; the frequently transparent accommodating of words of Jesus to the new scenario (resurrection/mission/parousia) makes sense. Finally, we have now had a hundred years of efforts on this issue with (so far as the present writer can see) no truly satisfactory competitor to Dodd's version of the Weiffenbach hypothesis: historic events broke the globally conceived triumph of resurrection/exaltation/parousia into its component parts.

Conclusion

Insights are legion. The insights that open to us the New Testament are of all kinds. We have had a festival of insight in the twentieth century. Never have the tool books (concordances, dictionaries, grammars, collections of background literature, fauna, flora, social history, and the rest) been more expert and plentiful. Never before have so many worked so long and hard from so many angles of vision on understanding these texts. Yet, and yet . . .

Well, what has been missing—more than a hermeneutic to give guidance to this immense, extraordinary effort? What is needed more than a powerful, critically grounded hermeneutic resource designed to allow this effort to move in the right directions, to catch sight of *die Sache* (the object of these texts), to reach up to, measure up to these incomparable texts with their unique burden and power?

2

Marshalling and Weighing Evidence: A Judgment That Has Counted

"Placing" Judgment

Of themselves, so said Bernard Lonergan, insights are a dime a dozen; the hard work of finding out which ones are true is what separates the men from the boys.

The whole sequence of acts that constitute human knowing has its ground or secret in the drive to know. Reflection accordingly centers first of all on this drive, appetite, desire. It is soon borne in on us that the desire to know is distinctive and puzzling.

Distinctive: it is an appetite; it is a conscious appetite; but, above all (and this is why we call it a "notion"), it is an intelligent and rational appetite open to our recognizing it as the condition of our intelligent and rational operations. It is an appetite that we not only feel, but know as the root of all our knowing. It does not stop at its intermediate goals—for example, at wonder and questioning, or at insight, or at reflection on the sufficiency of evidence. It does come to term, so to speak, with judgment, but even then, so far from bringing a halt to the process, judgment itself only serves to launch the sequence anew, starting with wonder and pushing further ahead in a way that seems simply open-ended.

Puzzling: for the notion of being differs from all other concepts. It does not derive from the formulation of an insight. It cannot be defined, except functionally. Moreover, even as desire, it is puzzling, for other desires show themselves to be severely limited in their objects and clearly self-centered. This desire, on the contrary, orients us toward a goal far greater than us, a goal that far surpasses the bearers and subjects of the desire. Nor is this desire narrowly self-interested, turned in on the subject. Rather, it is self-forgetfully turned outward onto the world.

We find that we cannot dispense with the acknowledgement of this appetite/orientation/desire and still come to anything like a satisfactory account of the acts that constitute knowledge. We cannot, for example, suppose that the drive to know is illusory, a figment of fancy. Nor can we suppose that our orientation to cognitional acts is a dumb, blind appetite, nor that its goal might in any way at all be restricted. It transcends every limited category of objects. Above we have touched on only a few traits that set this desire apart. It is unlike others in being not in need of regulation, but a source of regulation. We may call this desire a "notion," insofar as understanding discerns itself, its own inner root and cause and character, in this appetite or orientation.

Apropos of wonder, we shall return to the topic. We can hardly return too often to this great resource built into the human subject as the root of self-transcendence and fulfillment. Here let it suffice merely to notice two things: first, that this drive reveals itself in a fashion constantly fresh. At the phase or level of wonder, it is curious; at that of insight, quick and bright; at that of reflection, sober. It is an appetite/desire/orientation that is conscious, purposeful, intelligent, rational. Second, because in virtue of it we come to know, and because to know is to know what is, we conceive of "reality" or "being" in functional terms as "what it is that we desire to know." If the desire to know stands apart, unique and puzzling in virtue of its being conscious, inclusive, and unrestricted, it is nevertheless transparently recognizable by everyone, for it makes itself known as "wonder." We are constantly wondering about this, that, or the other thing. Our wondering, in fact, is as open as can be, utterly without limit, able to focus on anything.

In the last chapter we took note of the spontaneous experience of wonder and its spontaneous translation into questioning. We observed that questions make wonder effective and that answers—construals or insights—are concrete attempts to satisfy it. Let these questions be called "questions-for-intelligence": Who? What? When? Where? Why?

Now, we go further to observe that the satisfaction of wonder has a further dimension. It involves one in the reflective search for evidence apt to settle how good some given answer might be and actually is. The "question-for-intelligence" has been met with an act of construal/understanding/insight. This act now raises a "question-for-reflection," which calls for relevant and sufficient evidence. It asks, "Is the answer true?" and is answered by "Yes" or "No."

One of the ascertainments of the previous chapter was that construal or insight comes without guarantee. It is a creative act. Intelligence is unlike sense knowledge; the senses are indeed active and operate, but merely by registering their objects. In that limited sense the senses are passive. Accordingly, sense knowledge has a kind of *per se* infallibility; insight, on the other hand, is entirely hypothetical. Sense knowledge, though oriented toward higher acts initiated and generated by wonder, nonetheless has a kind of intrinsic integrity and completeness. Insight is incomplete and calls for completion in judgment. This is how we "place" or "locate" the act of judgment: it pronounces on how good any given act of understanding is. The verdict is "true" or "false," "certain" or "probable."

From the beginnings of philosophy in ancient Greece, there have been wits to call into question the possibility of making true judgments. We need not find fault with this calling into question. It nevertheless betrays a certain intrinsic futility. The wit announces: we cannot know what is really and truly so. This latently self-reversing statement becomes patently self-reversing when we make thematic *the performance of stating:* "I am stating what is really and truly so, when I say that we cannot know what is really and truly so." Such is an act of self-reversal. It is caught in the image of sawing off the branch one is sitting on.

If, then, what the wit said is false, its contradictory is true: we *can* know what is really and truly so. Suppose, on the other hand, that what the wit said is true. Then at least in this one instance we—with the help of the wit—would have penetrated to a real state of affairs, and so have known something that was really and truly so. In short, the wit's self-contradictory stand demonstrates *the utter futility* of denying the common experience of making true judgments.

True judgments have conditions and traits. The conditions change with every change in the content of the conditioned, i.e., of the understanding or insight we propose to ourselves; the traits remain constant and appear to be somewhat paradoxical. It seems, on the one hand, that judgment is a highly personal act; on the other that, if true, a judgment is objective, and if objective, impersonal. Here too we must distinguish. There is a sense in which every judgment depends on the subject who passes judgment. The subject is the ontological home of truth: if there were no judging mind there would be no true judgment. But there is also a sense in which true judgments do not hinge on me, the subject. In terms not of ontology (or conditions of existence), but of intentionality (or reference to the real), the true judgment would be true whether I am there to pass it or not.

The paradox is real. Just as, at the level of wonder, the drive to know is curious, and at that of insight, quick and bright, so at the rational level, the drive to know has a certain moment of impersonality. What does this impersonality derive from? From, evidently, the hold on evidence, from a grasp (1) of the conditions that condition the insight, and (2) of their fulfillment. This is called "grasp of the virtually unconditioned."

It may be well to think about this concretely. In the last chapter we posed an interpretative question: in the text of 1 Corinthians 15:51 ("Look, I tell you a secret: we shall not all sleep, but we shall all be changed"), what (in Paul's intended sense) did "the secret" consist in? We entertained three possible answers: "the secret" was that we would not all die; "the secret" was that the living and the dead would be changed not after the judgment which would follow the parousia, but already at the parousia; or, "the secret" was that, though we would not all die, those who lived to the parousia (when the dead would be raised) would themselves at that same moment be transformed.

Now, we know from elsewhere in Pauline texts that Paul and the communities he founded envisaged a parousia at which "the living" (who Paul originally expected would include most of his converts) would welcome the return of Christ, and "the dead," prominently including those who had been baptized but had died prior to the parousia, would be raised. Hence, it is difficult to suppose that "the secret" in 1 Corinthians 15:51 was the well-known and long-expected parousiac state of affairs: some of the faithful would have died, others would still be alive. The distinction of living and dead at the parousia was hardly a secret.

The second view (that the secret was the timing, the exact moment at which the transformation of those newly raised from the dead would take place) is also improbable. For Paul "resurrection" was transformative (1 Cor 15:42-49) and in 1 Corinthians 15:23 he had already specified that it would take place at the parousia. How, by the end of the chapter, could this still be a secret?

The failure of the first two theories does not guarantee the success of the third, but in fact the third theory is correct. The "secret" bore on the destiny of those who would still be living at the parousia. The distich of 1 Corinthians 15:50 said,

> Flesh and blood cannot inherit the reign of God / nor does decay inherit immunity to decay.

The first line bore on the living, the second on the dead. Neither could enter into the life to come *as they were.* Both called for transformation. Now, Paul had already made clear how that problem would be solved for the dead: namely, by resurrection, which was intrinsically transformative (1 Cor 15:42-49). But now Paul revealed how the problem would be solved for the living: at the parousia, they would be transformed without having to die.

To grasp that theory three is correct, the inquirer must have gotten hold of just what conditions would have to be fulfilled if the theory was to hold. One such condition, regularly recurrent in interpretation, is that the interpretation in question allow the whole text in all its relevant details to make good sense. Here the relevant whole is, roughly, chapter 15, and among the most relevant details we should include: verse 23, where it is clear that the coming resurrection of the dead is to take place at the parousia; verses 42-49, where the transformative character of resurrection is made clear; verse 50, which differentiates between the living ("flesh and blood") and the dead ("decay," an instance of the abstract standing for the concrete, *abstractum pro concreto*); we should doubtless add a further condition, that is, that "interpretation three" be plausibly named a "secret"—so, for example, we should not find Paul dealing earlier with the special problem posed by verse 50, the distich or couplet that says that the living and dead *both* needed to be transformed in order to enter the life to come ("the reign of God" or "immunity to decay"). Once one has concretely faced the problem of defining the "secret" of 1 Corinthians 15:51, these items are all graspable as meeting conditions that must be met if the third interpretation is to be pronounced "probably adequate." (We should acknowledge that usually textual interpretations will be, at best, not "true without any possibility of error," but "probably true.")

Before coming to the point of placing that free and highly personal act of judging (namely, judging that interpretation three is probably true), one must have grasped the concrete data and considerations adduced above as "fulfilled conditions of adequacy" for the probable truth of interpretation three. This "grasp" is the crucial antecedent of judgment. It solicits judgment itself, the act of committing oneself to the proposition: "By 'secret,' Paul intended option three, transformation of the living at the parousia."

Here we find the resolution of the paradox we began with: true judgment is paradoxical in being simultaneously impersonal and personal. The paradox is not resolved by relativizing one or the other of these seemingly contradictory traits. It is resolved by locating the acts that account for both traits. The grasp of the virtually unconditioned—that is, of sufficient evidence or of the conditions that must be met if the proposition is to stand, along with the ascertainment that these conditions are in fact met—is a cool, sober, measured, and measuring act, which not only makes the truth of a true judgment possible, but lends it its quality of impersonal objectivity. It says: here the demands of rationality are fulfilled. The inquirer who has arrived at this point is under the inducement of rationality (or the drive to know) to commit himself to the proposition now presenting itself as objectively grounded. But he has still not placed the act of judgment; hence, the increment of knowledge that occurs in and through conscious conformity to the real has not yet taken place. The inquirer has not committed himself until he places the personally self-involving act of judgment itself.

To complete the account of judgment, I would like to review three points in the theory, and then pose a crucial question for the reader. The three points are: first, the grasp of sufficient evidence; second, the fact of individual and collective fallibility;

third, judgment as expression of the desire to know. (We shall hold off, for the moment, the "crucial question for the reader.")

The "virtually unconditioned" is so named, first, to make the point that any insight/construal/understanding is hypothetical, in other words, conditioned; unless its conditions can be specified and ascertained to be fulfilled, it remains what it is, a hypothesis pure and simple. But if it turns out that the inquirer *can and does* list the relevant conditions, and *can and does* ascertain that they are fulfilled, the same insight is no longer mere hypothesis. We use the term "virtually" unconditioned to differentiate between an insight/construal thus grounded (and so relieved of its merely conditional status) from an unconditioned that is without conditions at all. (God is unconditioned in this way.) A "virtually unconditioned," in short, has conditions, but (in the case that we are evoking) they are known and known to be fulfilled.

Second point: as individual interpreters we do our best to marshall all the conditions that must be met. But we may (and in fact often do) overlook some condition or conditions; or we may erroneously estimate the fulfillment of some condition or other. The mistaken judgment that follows may be corrected by other interpreters. So, our view of judgment by no means overlooks fallibility. It simply operates on the basis that, in fact, we sometimes do make true judgments, and seeks to explain how this happens. We should add that the fallibility in question may be collective. In 1932 Olof Linton described "the 1880 consensus" among (some British but mostly German) New Testament scholars to the effect that there were no discernible historical ties between "Jesus" and "Church." Here is a beautiful example of collective fallibility. The year 1880 may be remembered for several things; among them we should include the fact that the whole community of historical-critical exegetes, on a significant issue, was way off the track.

Third, it is *the desire to know* that, at the level of judgment, calls for the effort to measure insight in terms of evidence. But once this is done (by grasp of the virtually unconditioned) this same desire calls for affirmative judgment to follow. Now, we are by nature rational beings in the sense of registering in some measure the demands of rationality, not necessarily in the sense of easily, habitually, gladly, regularly, and in timely fashion acceding to the exigences of our own rationality. Just as we may act against the immanent norms of our own rationality by habitually skipping the laborious and bothersome business of looking for relevant evidence and weighing its adequacy, so we may act against those same immanent norms by obscuring the evidence because it is not what we expected or wanted or find advantageous, or by fixing our attention on objections and problems and looking for excuses to disqualify the prospective judgment, or indeed, to make a judgment contrary to what the grasp of the virtually unconditioned commends. Habitually overcautious men or women may be guilty of irrationality just by their hemming and hawing, their postponing of judgment and looking for possible exits from it. The *personal* character of judgment thus comes to the fore, just as it does when one simply follows the dictates of rationality and judges in accord with the disinterested desire to know.

Finally, we arrive at our "crucial question to the reader": whether the above account of judgment squares with his/her own experience of judging. Does it, or does it not? Reread and reconsider. Much follows from the answer. If the answer is "yes," then for the reader it is settled that judgment mediates a real increment of knowledge.

A debate from the early 1950s will illuminate the point in question. Consider the statement: "The 'secret' of 1 Corinthians 15:51 refers to the transformation of the living at the parousia." Notice that this statement states indifferently (1) theory number three, and (2) the judgment that theory number three is correct. That is, the same words specify theory number three (while taking it to be a mere hypothesis) and the judgment that restates the theory (while taking it to be not a mere hypothesis but a verified hypothesis, i.e., a true statement). Peter Strawson in an article that appeared in 1949 called attention to this singularity. If the same words serve for insight and judgment, what has judgment added to insight?

In a sense it suffices to say, with Strawson, "agreement" with the hypothetical proposition. But any reader who finds that the description of judgment offered above squares with and expresses his or her own experience of judging, must observe further that judgment and *true* judgment are not on a par. Any affirmative or positive or "yes"-judgment signifies agreement with the hypothesis; but there is a significant difference between those judgments which were preceded and made ready by the act of grasping the virtually unconditioned and those judgments in which no such grasp has taken place. In the former case judgment adds *knowing the hypothesis to be true.*

The debate that followed Strawson's article turned on the correspondence theory of truth. Strawson could not acknowledge the truth of the correspondence view of truth precisely because he took the description of cognitive acts to bear on language, in other words, on something outside, distinct from, the very experience of those mental acts called construing and judging. This oversight amounted to an advance failure to take hold of "conscious correspondence." Inasmuch as Strawson attended to a proposition expressed in words, but failed to attend to judgment as a psychological event, he could hardly avoid overlooking factors crucial to correspondence. *True* judgment does something more than register "agreement"; it *effects the correspondence of intelligence with its object.*

Strawson thereby overlooked the mediation of reality that takes place with the event of true judgment. The Augustinianism of the high Middle Ages put it this way: *ens per verum innotescit,* "being becomes known through the true." Judgment reduces cognitive self-transcendence to act, so generating an increment in knowledge.

So much for placing the act of judgment. Its glory lies in that true judgment actuates what the pagans of antiquity called the divine element within us, the element that attunes us to truth, and in and through truth, to the real order of things.

A Judgment That Has Counted

We could pick all the examples of "insight" proposed in the last chapter and, by considering them in terms of evidence, use them as examples of judgment. It will be more profitable, however, to consider at moderate length an instance of judgment to which we are confident of winning the reader's assent as true, and which we shall draw on later in connection with the hermeneutical critique of ideology. (By contrast, it is hard to know how probably the mass of readers could be induced to agree with the view of Cerfaux and Jeremias on the structure of the Philippians hymn. It might be even dicier to count on winning over the mass of readers to Dodd's reconstruction of the historical Jesus' scenario of the future. To affirm such insights, merely to peruse a line-up of appropriate evidence is not enough; sustained personal contact with the evidence is indispensable.)

I do think it possible to win over the generality of readers to a judgment that has come gradually but firmly into existence since early in our century, that is of still greater significance to New Testament scholarship than the above issues, and that has been confirmed by scholars of all tendencies. I refer to the answer that Bultmann and the kerygma theologians gave to the question, "What did the first Christians take to be 'the center' of their faith?"

In the nineteenth century there were many answers to this question. Many, of course, were much less interested in what the early Christians thought than in what they, the progress-producing moderns of the nineteenth century, were disposed or inclined to think. Hence, the great variety of inquiries connected with "the essence of Christianity."

David Friedrich Strauss in the mid-1830s sank that flagship of the Enlightenment, the Rationalist school of biblical interpreters; attention thereafter turned toward the issues of ethics and moral theology or moral goodness. Among those who distinguished sharply between the way the early Christians thought and the way things really were, was Ludwig Feuerbach, who called himself "a natural philosopher in the domain of the mind." To Feuerbach the essence of Christianity, as of any religion, was the essence of man idealized, objectified, and projected in accord with the natural human drive to self-transcendence. For example, the specifically Christian doctrine of Incarnation objectified the supremely self-transcending dream of man to become God.

John Henry Newman, writing at about the same time, considered it presumptuous to think that it fell within the ambit of the human mind to define the essence of Christianity. But, he said, if one were merely in search of how most satisfactorily to correlate Christian ideas or doctrines among themselves, he saw point in the inquiry, and was personally inclined to organize the whole around the idea, "Incarnation."

At the end of the century there were those (Sigmund Freud, for example, or his contemporary, Adolf Harnack) who still retained the robust confidence of a Strauss or a Feuerbach in the access of the inquirer to the religious thinking of the ancients. That is, they thought that the ancients thought pretty much as we do, though with discernible variations. To Harnack, the essence of Christianity lay in the sphere of Jesus' ethical preaching: the Fatherhood of God, the infinite worth of the human soul, and the ethical idea of the kingdom of God (especially the commandment of love).

By contrast, to the new History-of-Religions School, born in Göttingen in the early 1890s (Eichhorn, Johannes Weiss, Gunkel, Heitmüller, Wrede, Bousset, Troeltsch), the early Christians were denizens of another world, their thought-processes far removed from those of nineteenth-century moderns. The more inaccessible the thinking of those strange syncretists, the early Christians, the more engaging it became to figure out how their minds worked. Theirs was not the thinking—the rational and moral concerns— of moderns. No, the first Christians were immersed in eschatological hopes such as the hope of resurrection, in redemption myths, cultic and sacramental practices, and other phenomena adopted from widely diverse sources (Judaism, gnosticism, mystery cults, philosophic schools).

The effort to find evidence of the earliest Christian beliefs soon fastened, in the first decade of the twentieth century, on short formulaic texts to be found in the letters of Paul and other New Testament letters and initially interpreted as fragments of a single credo. Thus began a now nearly century-long effort to place and analyze the earliest Christian faith-formulas (including hymnic texts such as Phil 2:6-11). Rudolf Bultmann (1884-1976) more than any other single figure highlighted *the kerygma as the center of earliest Christian faith,* and found early kerygmatic texts preserved in Paul's great letters.

Later, we shall return to consider this series of efforts, from the 1830s on, to grasp the identity or essence or leading idea of Christianity, to bring "faith" and "knowledge" into relation to one another, and see what light this long effort can be made to throw on contemporary efforts to construe the New Testament. For the present we shall content ourselves with a review of at least some of the evidence in support of the judgment that the gospel or kerygma gives expression to the center of early Christian faith.

Evidence of the Kerygma

Our purpose will not be to repeat what is already well and widely known, in other words, that the kerygmatic, confessional, liturgical, and other faith formulations of the New Testament are properly set apart (on the basis of language, conceptuality, and form or genre) from the literary contexts in which they are now embedded (e.g., the authentic Pauline letters, Colossians and Ephesians; 1 Timothy, 2 Timothy, Titus; Hebrews, James, 1 Peter). Nor shall we survey all early faith-formulations. Let it suffice to survey a few major representative texts on which to ground our anticipations with respect to the character of the earliest post-Easter Christian movement.

> Christ died for our sins in accord with the scriptures,
> he was buried;
> he was raised on the third day in accord with the scriptures,
> he appeared to Cephas, then to the twelve (1 Cor 15:3-5).

Some years ago I drew on the standard analytic literature to define the language, age, meaning, and function of this text:

> This handsomely sculpted kerygmatic formula, probably first composed in Aramaic, dating at least from the forties of the first century, attesting the common faith of the churches of the Levant and of the Mediterranean basin, doubtless served catechetical purposes as a summary in its own right and perhaps as a recapitulation of points to be developed.

Comparable early faith-formulas, less elaborate and probably still more primitive:

> who was delivered up for our transgressions
> and raised for our acquittal (Rom 4:25).

or again:

> who died,
> or rather was raised,
> who is at the right hand of God,
> who makes intercession for us (Rom 8:34).

All three texts juxtapose death and resurrection, accent the resurrection as climactic, appeal (implicitly or explicitly) to the

Old Testament scriptures (Isa 53 in Hebrew or Aramaic). In the
1 Corinthians 15 text the main carrier of meaning are lines one
and three (death for our sins in accord with scriptural promise,
resurrection "on the third day" in accord with scriptural promise); lines two and four provide, each of them, warrants for real
death (namely, burial) and real resurrection (namely, appearances
to Cephas and the Twelve). Scriptural witness is a qualifier. The
heart of the confession is: he died for our sins, he was raised on
the third day.

All three texts strike the expiatory note in accord with Isaiah
53; the first two apply it to the death, 1 Corinthians 15:3 allud-
ing to Isaiah 53:5 in Hebrew text or Targum, and Romans 4:25a
corresponding exactly to Isaiah 53:5 in the Targum. The third text
interprets an originally intended reference to the expiatory character of suffering and death (Isa 53:12 in Hebrew, or the Targum
for 53:11, 12) as the gracious intercession of the risen Christ seated
at God's right hand.

Why the heavy accent on Isaiah 53? There are several reasons.
It is the perfect hermeneutical resource for the earliest Church.
It meets the scandal of Jesus' repudiation by finding it prefigured
in the scriptures; it converts the shame of the death into the expiatory language, owing to the *'ašām*/expiatory offering theme
in this great Servant passage; finally, it extends the practice of
Jesus, who himself had drawn on the Isaian passage, especially
at the Last Supper, as the "for-you" formula in 1 Corinthians
11:24 indicates and its more primitive parallel in Mark 14:24 es-
tablishes. Indeed, of the thirty-odd uses of the *huper* + genitive
(signifying beneficiaries of Jesus' death) a solid fifteen (Mark
14:24; Luke 22:20; John 6:51; 1 Cor 15:3; Gal 2:20; Eph 5:2, 25;
Gal 1:4; 1 Tim 2:6; Titus 2:14; Rom 5:6-8; 2 Cor 5:14-15; 1 Pet
2:21; 3:18; 2 Cor 5:21) not only refer to expiatory death, but (in
impressively various ways) precisely to Isaiah 53.

Two further observations on the earliest ascertainable indices
to Christian understanding and self-understanding: first, there was
the clear dominance of the message of the resurrection of Jesus;
second, there was the summarizing of the life-history of Jesus in
a single decision, namely, to go to his death faithful to his saving
mission.

The primacy of the resurrection theme (if we may so name
it, taking it to comprehend the exaltation-phase of the humilia-

tion/exaltation thematic) is intrinsic to the death/resurrection texts despite the quasi-independent meaning accruing to the death by its expiatory value. Two factors establish this: its climactic status and its final-cause status. Thus, in the 1 Corinthians 15 text, the first distich (death for our sins was real death, as burial attests) is for the sake of the second distich (resurrection on the third day was real resurrection, as appearances attest). The point of thematizing the reality of the death could not be other than to thematize the reality of the resurrection. As Adolf Schlatter put it, "Jesus was buried *because* he was to be restored to life."

In the formula of Romans 8:34 the primacy and climactic status of resurrection is explicit: "Who died, or rather was raised."

A convergent phenomenon: in the early chapters of Acts all six of the explicit scriptural citations (Psalms and Deuteronomy) that are applied to Jesus in the schematic missionary speeches concern his resurrection/glorification: Psalm 16:10 (Acts 2:25-28; cf. 13:35); Psalm 132:11 (Acts 2:30); Psalm 110:1 (Acts 2:34-35; 5:31); Deuteronomy 18:15-16 (Acts 3:22); Psalm 118:22 (Acts 4:11); Psalm 2:7 (Acts 13:33).

The epitomizing of his life in a single decision (to go to his death, true to his saving mission) is most clearly thematic in the Philippians hymn: strophe 1 (kenotic Incarnation) is for the sake of strophe 2 ("he humbled himself / becoming obedient unto death"); at the same time strophe 2 brings incarnation to a completion or fulfillment in history. (The glorification/exaltation theme is, of course, climactic here too.) This concentrated focus on the will of Jesus to go to his death is equally evident in the cultic (eucharistic) text of 1 Corinthians 11:23-25 as well as in 1 Corinthians 15:3-5 and other formulaic texts, where Jesus' death is understood as *willed* (e.g., Rom 3:25-26; 4:25; Gal 1:4; cf. 2:20).

No matter what the nineteenth-century thinkers thought, for the early Christians themselves the heart of the meaning that bound Christians together was summed up in the formula of Romans 4:25: Jesus died for our sins, and his death found completion and realization in his resurrection from the dead for our acquittal. The kerygma theologians, despite the difficulties it made for them (in forcing them to deal somehow with motifs theologically alien to them, such as *expiatory* death and *physical* resurrection), put an end to the liberal chitchat on the merely moral center of earliest Christian faith and definitively vindicated the

claim of the kerygma and confession of Christ's death and resurrection to central status.

The kerygma, once again, was central not to some one group
or another, not to the group that finally won out over alternative
views, but to all Christianity, Aramaic-speaking or Greek-
speaking, in the Levant or the Mediterranean basin, pre-Pauline,
Pauline, para-Pauline, and post-Pauline. If this is occasionally
contested, as it has been recently once again, it is not on the basis
of data from any concrete, known Christian community, but exclusively on the basis of hypothetical communities of which we
lack concrete historical evidence.

Consequences of the Centrality of the Kerygma

The History-of-Religions School trained a generation of New
Testament scholars in Germany to familiarize themselves with the
Jewish and pagan literature of the intertestamental period, to
rediscover the impact of cult on religion, and to discover and acknowledge the existence of phenomena uncongenial to modernity:
apocalyptic eschatology (Johannes Weiss, 1892), syncretism (Hermann Gunkel, 1903), cult (Eichhorn, Bousset, Gunkel), miracles
and exorcisms, themes of triumph over Satan and the demons,
hope for a literal parousia (Christ coming on the clouds). This
shook up liberal theology, and the devastating impact of World
War I killed all such optimistic, moralizing movements. Theologians and biblical scholars were finally ready to consider the
evidence of the kerygma, or gospel, as the center of Christian
faith.

In *The Apostolic Preaching and its Developments,* C. H. Dodd
studied the use of such terms as *kērugma* and *didachē,* the forms
of the kerygma and its structure, the possible relation of the form
of the kerygma that included "a historical section" (chiefly in
the missionary discourses, Acts 2:22; 10:37-39; 13:23-25) to the
organization of the gospels. The scholarly community was divided
on whether "expansion" or "unfolding" of the kerygma could
be predicated of the gospels. What has chiefly lasted from German and English scholarship on the kerygma or gospel is its centrality.

In Pauline formulation, the gospel was born of the Easter experience (2 Cor 5:18-19). It was the message of reconcilation (2

Cor 5:19) which God "founded" (LXX Ps 77:5) in the apostolic witnesses of the risen Christ, whose God-given task ("ministry of reconciliation," 2 Cor 5:18) was to bring to the world the message of God-in-Christ reconciling the world to himself (2 Cor 5:18). This kerygma or gospel was no merely human word, but the word of God (cf. 1 Thess 2:13); in and through it God himself appealed to the world (2 Cor 5:20). The apostles were mere envoys on behalf of Christ. Here, as in the pre-Pauline kerygmatic, confessional, and liturgical texts, we find defined the bonds of meaning that held the Christian movement together.

The earliest evidences of the life of the Church are lapidary expressions of faith intending and confessing in the present a set of saving events from the past: "Christ died for our sins!" and especially, "He was raised on the third day!" What emerges from this kind of intending of events (present meaning hinges on past happening; past happening is attached to present proclaiming and confessing, not extrinsically but precisely as the object of the proclaiming and confessing) is that the entire tradition of faith-formulation is nourished on the memory of Jesus, whose life, death, and resurrection it attests as saving events—just as the gospels do *in flawlessly conservative accord with the earliest kerygma.* The rise of the gospel tradition, a distinctive kerygmatic didache, was an entirely natural outgrowth of this faith. The catechetical tradition of faith-formulations and the kerygmatic didache of the gospel tradition are parallel phenomena, regardless of whether the gospel tradition ought or ought not to be conceived as an "expansion" or "unfolding" of the kerygma.

Here let it suffice to refer to the consequences of this state of affairs for every new proposal on Christian origins, be it historical-Jesus research, Church history, Pauline exegesis, or what have you.

Recent research, for example, proposing reconstructions of a non-eschatological Jesus, unconcerned with the scriptures but keenly intent on social reform (e.g., radical egalitarianism in striking parallel with Cynic social reformers) and on preventing a disastrous war with Rome, has invited us to widen our perspectives and reconsider our presuppositions. Can any of these bold new proposals be brought into intelligible historical coherence with what we know of the faith of the earliest Church? It is a thorny question. I am not ready to say that they cannot; it would be reassuring if those who urge the new proposals—Marcus Borg, Richard Horsley, John Dominic Crossan, and others—would explain how they can.

The solid status and pervasive thrust of the faith concretized in early formulations, be they tight and lapidary or relatively loose (see below), attest a faith so pervasive in earliest Christianity as to pose a challenge to the following elements of the new proposals: a supposed immunity of Jesus to contamination by apocalyptic eschatology; his indifference to the legacy of classical Israel; disparity between the new proposals and the absorption of the world of Judaism surrounding earliest Christianity in themes of covenant and law, prophecy and messianism, remnant, restoration, and the like. All three factors suggest how problematic the claim to historicity is on the part of the new proposals.

The kerygma, on the other hand, illuminates and correlates much of the actually available data on the earliest Church. This raises the question of how non-eschatological social and political reforms, for example, fit into what we know for certain of early Christian faith and life. One uncircumventible reason for thinking that no swift dispatching of the question can carry conviction is that, while much of the work of continental and British scholars at mid-century calls for revision of accent and the like, there is no real prospect of undoing their basic ascertainment. There is no prospect of softening or reducing the resistance of the kerygma to proposals that would bypass it. It is massive and shatterproof.

If anything, scholars at mid-century underestimated the solidity, vitality, and pervasiveness of the kerygma in the life of the earliest Church. Current considerations relevant to the kerygma go in the opposite direction.

While we look forward to a fundamentally more satisfactory state of the question for the currently confused debate on "unity and diversity," we have been offered a promising new development. I refer to two articles of Eugene E. Lemcio. Both contest the claim of James D. G. Dunn's study of unity and diversity that a unifying core kerygma is an abstraction. The counterproposal of Lemcio is that there runs all through the New Testament a concrete kerygmatic core expressing the Church's self-defining allegiance. This recurrent core is thematic, but not formulaic. It concerns

(1) God, who
(2) sent [= gospels] / raised [elsewhere]
(3) Jesus.
(4) A response (accepting, repenting, believing and the like)
(5) to God
(6) brings benefits (variously specified).

Formulas and non-formulaic texts are easily accommodated to this specifically *theological* (as distinct from strictly christological) schema. The issue of the harmonization of categories, genres, motifs, has long been a distraction in the discussion since Dodd's study of the apostolic witness. The issue we are dealing with, however, is primarily religious, not literary.

Lemcio's analyses signify that the whole New Testament (no literary exceptions) attests God's saving act in Christ. Note the accent on "God" and the accent on "act." Lemcio rightly criticizes certain misleading accents—the primacy, if not exclusivity, of concern for themes of christological status; the "problem" of how the proclaimer became the proclaimed in the treatments of the kerygma by Bultmann, Cullmann, and others. The contributions of Lemcio's own two articles will have to be integrated into the still future synthesis that ought now to follow up on mid-century work. The kerygma theologians, when they insisted on the kerygma as the center of Christian faith, built far better than they knew.

3

Self-Reversals, Horizons, Dialectic

The Phenomenon of Self-Reversal

Spontaneous human functioning (we said early in chapter one) has a normative character. It is "the key to how to do the job." We remarked that perhaps the most fascinating and persuasive aspect of this normativeness is the phenomenon—negative in itself but with a potent positive impact—of "self-reversal": when I quite spontaneously operate in one way, but laboriously theorize in another, I am bound to find myself caught in a kind of schizoid doublethink.

In our ordinary living we cheerfully draw on the world in a thousand ways, yet in our formal philosophical efforts we may line up one reason after another against acting, against even the possibility of acting, in this way. As Richard Wilbur has it: "We milk the cow of the world, and as we do, / we whisper in her ear, 'You are not true.'" A concrete instance of spontaneous performance subverting thematic content is: "We cannot know what is really and truly so." The self-contradiction latent here can be swiftly rendered patent by making thematic *the act of affirming:* "I am stating what is really and truly so when I say that we cannot know what is really and truly so."

One may just as effectively play off denied content against the performance of denial. "Let me see if I get your drift. You deny the correspondence theory of truth because it fails to correspond to the way we actually think."

There have been thinkers ready and willing to complain about this ploy. Heidegger thought it trivial. Frederick Copleston calls it "slick." But you will notice how carefully everyone, or almost everyone, tries to avoid getting caught in the pincers of self-reversal. "Almost everyone," for Jacques Derrida seems to be aware (how *deeply* aware is, let's say, undecidable) of his repeated immersions in self-reversal without betraying much discomfort.

In fact, self-reversal is deconstruction's daily bread. In practice the theory supposes as a condition of its own possibility that we not only can, but do, operate in the manner it condemns. M. H. Abrams, a close observer and critic of deconstruction, noted that the masters of the movement are double-dealers in language, "working ambidextrously with two semantic orders—the standard and the deconstructed." That is, they construe in the ordinary way (though "provisionally"—as if, like medieval astronomers, "to save the appearances"), meantime moving ahead to the main task, that is, deconstructing. But the gap between performance and theory—a gap that keeps coming to light in function of the structured spontaneities of human intentionality—*wrecks the theory.*

Some theorists cling to the belief that it is up to them to decide whether this matters. He does not have to be right, says Stanley Fish, just interesting. That is one to ponder. Does he not have to be right about not having to be right, just interesting? If the answer is yes, his claim is false; if the answer is no, his claim is dropped. Self-reversal spins the mind, but the spin is worthwhile, positively therapeutic. If Fish does not have to be at least *possibly* right about theory and practice, his continuing to be "interesting" becomes moot, like the appeal of navel-gazing for non-navel-gazers.

Abrams has found the deconstructionists' cool acceptance of self-reversal among the more disconcerting aspects of the movement. There is no reason in the world, however, why we should allow the cool pose of the deconstructionist to diminish our confidence that self-reversal definitively wrecks the theory that is reversed. There is just no way to get around it: self-reversal is a crusher, and what it crushes is unsalvageable. It may be maddening, but you are not allowed to escape the consequences of cutting off the branch you are sitting on.

John Searle, in an article on the cultural wars as they affect the university, showed graphically that ordinary human linguistic practices so presuppose realism on being and knowing that even the most eloquent argument against it implicitly offers evidence that demonstrates it. It seems unfair, but there it is. Realism is not a thesis or theory, but

> the condition of having theses or theories or even of denying theses or theories. This . . . is a point about the conditions of communicating intelligibly. Falsehood stands as much in need of the real world as does truth.

In his short study of Nietzsche some years ago J. P. Stern pointed out that the modern masters of suspicion, Marx, Nietzsche, and Freud, thought of their own work as revelation pure and simple and of any opposition to it as an irrational conspiracy by vested interests. Every ideologist carries a single burning coal in the tongs of his mind, an explanatory idea meant to unlock the secret of how human beings function. But none of these masters, Stern noticed, was eager to apply the explanation to his own work. A way of reducing psychoanalysis itself to the sexual impulse might just possibly have been wrung from Freud, but Marx knew as well as we do that he had not written *Das Kapital* out of material interest, nor does the will-to-power explain Nietzsche's composition of *The Anti-Christ* and other monographs on the will-to-power.

Jean-Paul Sartre considered life itself chaos, but art and "the imaginary" he considered order. On the other hand, he acknowledged that literature owed its power to being somehow like life. He certainly knew that the chaos he affirmed of life he could not make work in a novel. An authentic Sartrean novel would be a shapeless muddle. But novelists labor under a first commandment, Thou shalt not be dull. If *La nausée* or *Les chemins de la liberté* are plotted and the characters convince, is it enough to say that he anticipated the contradiction and built it into his system? Or are we to conclude to the novelist's bad faith, on the basis that if the novel works, the philosophy does not and vice-versa?

Literary theory has found itself in a like dilemma. A few years ago Bernard Bergonzi pointed out that the followers of Nietzsche and Foucault were passionately persuaded that truth is no more than a rhetorical device employed in the service of oppression, and they said so at length. What then is the status of their saying so? Is it false? Or in the service of oppression?

Self-reversal, in short, is commonplace. Our cultural landscape is strewn with its debris. Some examples are concise, others haplessly elaborate, like Richard Rorty's four-hundred-page philosophic argument purporting to show the non-cognitive character of philosophy and hence the futility of philosophic argument. Since we are embarked on a philosophic enterprise, it may serve our purposes to see *why* self-reversal works as it does. The answer seems to lie in "the notion of being" and, still more specifically, in the cognitive phase of this disinterested desire. When we hear, "I am stating what is really and truly so when I say that we cannot know what is really and truly so," we are spontaneously struck by the speaker's two-gun act of doublethink: right-handed, shooting his left foot, and left-handed, his right. It is like humor and the experience of spontaneous laughter. One does not immediately know why one laughs, nor does it matter; humor is self-justifying. Catching on to self-reversal, however, can be enlightening.

The drive to know prompts wonder and inquiry; it triggers insight; it summons reflection and judgment. It structures every level of knowing. For example, it structures the intelligent level, charging wonder with hunger-for-intelligence and insight with the claim of satisfying it, a claim of relevance to some question-for-intelligence. A hearty "Yes, indeed!" is no answer to "Who, what, where, when, why?" To say that "Yes, indeed!" is a *mistaken* answer is insufficient. It is simply not in the running among answers. It is a kind of non-answer answer. It violates the inbuilt claim of a question-for-intelligence to a responding insight (not a responding judgment).

So too, the drive-to-know structures the rational phase of knowing, hunger-for-sufficient-evidence triggering the reflective quest for such evidence; moreover, it not only invests the act of judgment with a claim to objectivity and truth, it also summons the knowing subject to commit himself to it. Nietzsche would have much preferred that error be impersonal, the mere quality of an opinion, and he urged that the falsity of an opinion not be held against it. But the drive to know is both other and greater than that. The claim immanent in the process of cognitive intentionality is such that in erroneous judgment the error is personal and the subject mistaken. I who judge, I am mistaken. As Rochefoucauld put it, everyone complains of his memory and no one of his judgment. We suppose that we have little or no power over our memory, but we do not complain about our judgment, because that touches us too intimately. Rochefoucauld was right and Nietzsche wrong. And why Nietzsche was wrong about judgment and error is now evident. It is precisely because, having denied the inborn all-intending drive to know, he could not discern the spirits prompting the grounded, and inhibiting the mistaken, judgment. It remains, and remains as a fact of human intentionality, that in and through false judgment I myself am mistaken.

The repudiation—lightly offered in postmodernist circles—of objectivity or truth or the personal dimension of the grasp of truth, violates human experience, the experience of fully human knowledge in general, the experience of judgment in particular. This strikes at the root of our humanity. Without necessarily having any interest in figuring out why, we are all spontaneously aware of judgment as a personal verdict that lays claim to being true. Consequently, to say, "We cannot know what is really and truly so," contradicts the immanently rational structure of judgment, and making the performance of judging thematic renders this evident: "I am stating what is really and truly so when I say that we cannot know what is really and truly so."

What the phenomenon of self-reversal reveals is the reality of invariant structures in human intentionality. Their invariance cannot be on the side of the object being known, which is boundless in variety, ever changing, subject to revision. It must then be on the side of the active subjective principle: the conscious, disinterested desire or drive-to-know, Greek *noēsis,* not *noēma;* Latin *intentio intendens,* not the open *ad-infinitum* and ever-revisable *intentio intenta;* hence, the privilege and promise of the analysis of human intentionality and, in particular, of cognitional theory.

Systematic Exploitation?

Bernard Lonergan was adept at pointing out self-reversal. What is wrong with Hume's theory of the mind? Lonergan summed it up in three sentences: "Hume thought the human mind to be a matter of impressions linked together by custom. But Hume's own mind was quite original. Therefore Hume's own mind was not what Hume considered the human mind to be."

In a book review that must rank among the all-time unappealable counterstatements, he remarked:

> [The author] asserts an unbridgeable difference between the way in which God is in himself and the way in which he is in our knowledge. This, of course, while absolutely possible, is not possibly known within our knowledge, and so the reader may wonder how [the author] got it into his knowledge.

Self-reversal is a bleak, if instructive, spectacle. The bleakness makes one want to go on immediately to something else. It belongs to the instructive side, however, to wonder: would it be possible to reproduce on a larger scale the utter definitiveness with which self-reversal sinks mistaken theory? Is there a way of making self-reversal, which seems definitive but limited, pay off systematically? What if we were to come into possession of truth on fundamental aspects of human functioning? Would we not find ourselves in possession of a powerful instrument for discriminating, methodically and productively, among a vast range of major truths and errors?

Just such an instrument was an eighteenth-century dream, the dream of a science of human nature. Though Collingwood called it a relic of substantialism, the dream might well be transposed into the non-substantialist terms already suggested above: "invariant pattern." This is just how Lonergan conceived it: the invariant pattern of human intentionality.

We have hitherto discussed cognitive intentionality in terms of "sequence"; now we shall enhance sequence with the suggestive metaphor of level-by-level ascent. Level one of intentionality is empirical, connoting "consciousness" in the subject and "data" as object; moreover, since data come before the understanding of data, there also belongs to this empirical level the sum-total of all conscious human operations and their products *insofar as they present themselves*—to psychology, say, or to cognitional theory—as *data of consciousness*. The second level of intentionality is intelligent (wonder, questioning, and question-answering). To this second level belongs not only the quest of answers but their selective conceptualization, the working out of the significance of what we have understood, the logics and methods that permit us to do this. The third level is rational (questions-for-reflection, the collating and weighing of evidence, grasping it as adequate or not, and judging). Such is the level of true and false, certain and probable. Lastly, the subject finds himself spontaneously promoted to a new, fourth level by questions for deliberation, evaluation, decision. This level is responsible: we are here concerned with ourselves, our ends and means, our loves and hates, the courses of action open to us, and their likely results; here, too, we carry out our decisions or fail to do so. This, in a word, is the level at which the free subject emerges, engaged in producing "the first and only edition of himself."

This scheme is radically unrevisable. For, since any revision would have to appeal to data, it would have to allow an empirical level of operations. Since any revision would have to offer some better explanation of the data, it would have to allow an intelligent level of operations. Since any revision would have to claim that its better explanation is more probable, it would have to allow a rational level of operations. Lastly, since no one takes up the task of revision unless he considers it worthwhile, the revision must affirm or suppose a responsible level of operations.

The fact is that we human subjects do exhibit a set of structured spontaneities: attentiveness, intelligence, reasonableness, and responsibility. What subverts mistaken theories is the gap between the theory and these structured human spontaneities.

There is a passage in Lonergan where Aristotle is evoked as if having been present when (according to Plato's *Meno*) Socrates contrived to demonstrate the seemingly ignorant slave-boy's knowledge of geometry, and from it inferred the boy's contemplation, in an earlier mode of existence, of eternal mathematical forms. This stunning inference captured the wonder of Socrates' listeners—except for Aristotle, who was left pondering Socrates' diagram in the dust. Pre-existence? Hardly. From a diagram in the dust that kid had abstracted an intelligible form! Having (with Plato) problematized the conditions of knowledge and concluded to the need of intelligible forms, Aristotle figured out by inference how in fact we acquire them. There are several more or less reasonable arguments accounting for how we come into possession of ideas, but, *in fact,* how do we do so?

The test of the answer is the field of human performance. Once the pattern of human operations has been brought to light in radically unrevisable fashion, new possibilities heave into view: in particular the new possibility of systematically confronting theories of knowing with facts of knowing, theories of love or freedom with the facts of the human subject in love, freely disposing of himself. What we blithely call "the facts" are a normative pattern—empirical, to be sure, but not a slice of life.

Critical realism takes its shape from the experience, the facts, the patterns, of spontaneous human functioning. These facts are finally what reveal the will-to-power, the primacy of race, the indeterminacy of texts, the merely cultural character of gender-differentiation, to be among countless ideological aberrations ultimately subject to self-reversal. This leads us to the presuppositions of dialectic and to dialectic itself. Presuppositions: "dialectic" has to do with horizons; "horizon" evokes conversion; "conversion" is a change in the subject. Our thematic sequence, accordingly, will be: "subject and subjectivity"; "horizons and conversion"; finally, "dialectic and the choice of horizons."

Subject and Subjectivity

The human subject finds himself directed from within to the exercise of specifically human capacities, directed to fulfillment by an inner drive or desire. We find out about ourselves from our operations. Operations that consciously focus on objects are named "intentional"; in and through the selfsame operations the operating subject is "conscious." How should we distinguish between intentionality and consciousness?

First, we should examine the claims of a conception commonly found among naïve realists. Intentionality (knowing and willing) is direct (the subject knows an object) or reflexive (the subject knows himself). "Consciousness" corresponds to the second. It is accordingly a subdivision (the reflexive part) of intentionality. Lonergan has responded to this view. Consider, he says,

> the two propositions, John knows his dog, John knows himself. In both the subject is John. In the first the object is John's dog. In the second, the object is John himself. It follows that knowing is of two kinds: there is direct knowing in which the object is not the subject; there is reflexive knowing in which the object is the subject. Name reflexive knowing consciousness.

In this way one maintains the key stipulation that in consciousness the knower himself is known.

Nothing could seem simpler or clearer. It does, however, raise a problem. In knowing, it is the subject that undergoes change, not the object. (No one—no, not Heisenberg either—holds that anything or anyone is changed by the mere fact of being an object of cognitional activity.) If, however, consciousness is knowledge of an object (namely, oneself), and if the object of knowing is not changed by being known, some strange consequences follow. If without consciousness John has no psychological unity, then with consciousness (as knowledge of an object), John is simply disclosed to himself as having no psychological unity. Again, if without consciousness John cannot be the conscious subject of physical pain, then with consciousness (as knowledge of an object), John is merely shown to be incapable of pain. Again, if without consciousness John can function neither attentively nor intelligently nor rationally nor responsibly, then with consciousness (as knowledge of an object), John is revealed to himself as incapable of functioning attentively, intelligently, rationally, and responsibly.

These puzzles find a swift and complete resolution just as soon as one drops the simplistic notion that consciousness is the presence of the subject to himself as object (a presence that effects no change in the object known) and puts in its place the notion of consciousness as the constitutive presence of the subject to himself as subject. "Constitutive," for it is precisely this presence that makes the subject to be "subject," not just in any sense of the term, but in a psychological sense. This "presence" is a whole inner dimension, a living interiority and unity, a capacity not only for pain but (as intentionality is exercised) for attention, intelligence, reasonableness, and responsibility.

By consciousness the subject is known not as object, but precisely as subject. While this presence is genuinely cognitive, the "knowing" is inchoate, tacit, concomitant. It is a presence, both cognitive and constitutive, of the subject to himself in the act of being a subject. It is not fully constituted knowledge (which always implies inquiry, insight, reflection, and judgment), but it is experience having a cognitive dimension. Consciousness, so far from being a subsection or subdivision (the reflexive part) of intentionality, is the subject-constituting and subject-revealing dimension of all intentionality, whether direct or reflexive. As by intentional operations such as knowing or loving, objects are made present to the subject, so by consciousness these selfsame operations make the subject present to himself. If consciousness endows operations and their subject with a dimension of interiority, intentionality endows them with openness to worlds beyond the self.

A last observation on our intending of the world: we would not know it if we could not or did not intend it. But what sets fully human knowing of the world apart in kind from our sense-knowing of the world is *mediation*. Seeing is immediate to what is seen. Fully human knowing is an active intending—an *intentio intendens*—that comes to term in a mediating *intentio intenta*. This is not the reality of the world; it is that in and through which one takes cognitive possession of the reality of the world, on condition that the *intentio intenta* is grounded and grasped as such. Truth is meaning that consciously corresponds to its object. I propose X to you, counting on your *intentio intendens* and trusting that you will catch my meaning (= what I mean, my *intentio intenta*) and tell me whether in your judgment what I mean is so.

Until now we have used the words "consciousness," "subject," "subjectivity," and "intentionality" without defining them in terms of introspective experience. We shall henceforward use them all as technical terms defined in accord with the above observations.

Horizons and Conversion

"Horizon," literally, bounds one's field of vision. It is the line in the distance where earth and sky meet. Metaphorical use of the term is over a hundred years old in France and Germany, but has won a place in English dictionaries only in the relatively recent past.

Horizon, metaphorically, is the limit of what one knows and cares about. To begin with knowing: the "known" takes in the range of questions I can raise and answer. The "known unknown" is the range of questions I can raise, but cannot as yet answer. The "unknown unknown" is the range of questions I cannot raise, since they are meaningless to me, at least here and now. "Horizon" is the boundary between the second and the third.

Now consider caring: at the center of my field of vision are the persons and things I intensely care for or about. Then there is the wider circle of the persons and things that I am aware of, interested in, more remotely concerned for; finally, there is an outer circle of what I take in more or less passively, and this extends as far as the mind's eye can see. Its boundary shuts out the great meaningless unknown and unloved. (The truly meaningless to me is precisely what I do not ask questions about. If someone asks me about what is meaningless to me, I might possibly get interested; or again I might answer: I haven't a clue.)

Clearly, my horizons are the product of my life history. As a viewpoint is a habitual accumulation of insights, judgments, and decisions, so a horizon is a habitual accumulation of viewpoints, with greater or lesser coherence depending on how rigorously one has cultivated a concern for coherence.

The literal horizon changes with one's vantage point as one mounts or descends; similarly, one's metaphorical horizons are subject to change. The root possibility of such change lies in the orientation of human intentionality to the boundless All. Unrestricted, this orientation has for its goal what is, everything, being as true and good.

"Orientation" here is "conscious tendency and capacity." In its malleable cognitive phase, it is the drive to the intelligible, the true, the real, or to being as open to being known; in its complementary existential phase, it is the drive to the good, to value, to being not only as open to being loved, but as loving. It is the drive that sustains and finds expression in every human aspiration.

Horizon is structured. Every apprehension of data, Lonergan observed,

> involves quite naturally and spontaneously, a kind of selection, and every selection, in turn, includes an initial structuring, and every structuring prepares and, in a certain sense, anticipates future judgments.

Horizons are accordingly "the structured resultant of past achievement" and a conditioning limit on further development. This means concretely that we do change, but the changes are not arbitrary. We progress or decline, and movement in either direction bears the cachet and observes the logic of a personal history.

The vital importance of horizon emerges with the observation that what falls within it can make sense, and what falls outside it cannot. Inasmuch as it defines my field of vision, within it insight can be a bull's-eye, judgment true and certain, argument conclusive, and value authentic. Outside it insight seems erratic, judgment far-fetched and flawed, value alien and illusory.

Without some fusion or overlap of horizons, you and I cannot agree; we cannot trust one another; we can hardly be allies and certainly cannot be friends. Moreover, if a fusion or overlap of horizons is a condition of agreement, still even this is no pledge that our common horizons are consistently inclusive of the real order of things. We may be friends by pooling our illusions.

It can be sobering, even frightening, to realize that my horizons are without guarantee of thorough and stable grounding in the real. Why, come to think of it, should nature be bound to issue me a pledge that, whatever my upbringing, life-experience, and dispositions, I am in solid rapport with reality? "It just might be possible," wrote Augustine to Jerome, "that what you think is not the same as what the truth is." Oliver Cromwell to the Church of Scotland: "I beseech you in the bowels of Christ, think it possible you may be mistaken!" In time we shall take up the question of how it is possible to ascertain whether one's horizons have allowed one to be in more than intermittent touch with the real. For the moment suffice it to say that the drive to being— the disinterested desire to know and the deep drive to fulfillment in the good—is the root of intentional conformity with the real. Such is the premium on living in accord with intelligence, reason, a good conscience. Virtue pays, after all.

If horizon is a factor of fundamental importance not only for being in tune with the real, but even for being merely able to see eye-to-eye with anyone else, it is equally fundamental to rational approaches to disagreement and debate. You and I may disagree; but our disagreement might be resolved by my catching hold of just a fragmentary angle, a corner of the perspective that is yours. This often happens among friends, but is hardly possible among those whose differences are horizonal—that is, fundamentally different and significantly opposed.

It is yet another step to posit irreducibly opposed horizons. There are things on which X and Y are in secure and easy agreement, and other things—for example, moral aspects of political policy—on which they are radically, irreducibly opposed.

Even so, it would be mistaken to assume that radically opposed horizons are utterly immobilizing and signify the end of useful communications. Both X and Y can change their views not only by adjustments within their horizons, but also *by changing their very horizons*. This can happen in many ways. One of the ways, and one that is far from rare, happens when one arrives somehow or other at an ascertainment that cannot be accommodated by one's current horizons. Something will have to give. Of course, it might be the new ascertainment. On the other hand, it might be one's old, familiar, comfortable horizons. There may well be a struggle. Time and again, however, it happens that the new ascertainment will not be denied. It may even be welcomed as a liberation, a life-saver, a pearl of great price.

As intentionality evokes the theme of horizon, horizons evoke the theme of conversion. Today the term is chiefly used for change in the religious sphere. Here we shall stipulate its sense as a technical term for a change of horizons. Religious conversion is the all-pervasive change effected by allotting the habitual primacy in one's life to the love of God. Moral conversion is the habitual priority that one gives to values over satisfactions, when the two conflict. Finally, intellectual conversion lies in a clean break with picture-thinking, a set of ideas formed in childhood: knowing is like seeing. Intellectual conversion is the adoption, in place of a picture-thinking style of realism, of a realism grounded in the compound of experience, understanding, and judgment.

These conversions, when they take place in the same subject, offer an instance of *sublation:* a transcending that includes and enhances what is transcended. Intellectual conversion carries the subject past the naïveté of picture-thinking, wishful thinking, and peer-group thinking, to the facts of intentionality. Moral conversion neither cancels nor even distracts from this; in bringing the subject beyond the value, truth, to values generally, it stabilizes and maximizes devotion to truth and the sophistication of a truly critical hold on the truth-issue. Again, religious conversion sublates moral conversion, deepening it, making it less liable to unravel under pressure, setting it in new perspectives, charging it with new purposes, moving the focus from values to the ground of values. Here the subject is "grasped, possessed, owned through a total and an otherworldly love."

These sublations do not, however, establish the ordinary genetic order of conversion-events. Commonly, the order is the exact opposite. First, there is God's gift of his love. The eye of this love discerns the world of values. These include the value of believing the truths taught by the religious tradition, and in such belief and tradition lie the seeds of intellectual conversion.

Dialectic and the Choice of Horizons

Here "dialectic" refers to a deliberately contrived procedure meant to clarify—and ultimately to resolve—radical conflicts. The word "radical" stresses that these are not just any conflicts, but the most stubborn of all: those that arise from irreducibly opposed horizons. Many conflicts can be resolved by correcting misunderstandings, coming up with new information, commending new perspectives, and the like. Conflicts resolved in this way arise typically out of differences of perspective. But dialectic is concerned with conflicts that arise out of opposed ways of viewing and valuing the world. What X considers true and good, Y takes to be false and evil. Dialectic traces differences of this kind back to different matrices, grounds, horizons.

The diversity and opposition of horizons, however, are not the end of the matter. Horizons are liable to critique. The technique of dialectic aims, first, to differentiate between conflicts, with a view to locating those that are genuinely irresolvable. Such are the conflicts in which the opposing positions are reducible to horizons which are themselves irreducibly opposed. The possibility of productive dialectic hinges on an observable fact: *irreducibly opposed horizons may be tested for their claims to coherence with the facts of human intentionality.*

If both sets of horizons pass this crucial test, we are dealing not with a truly dialectical conflict, but with a lesser conflict resolvable by appeal to further relevant evidence. If, on the other hand, both sets of horizons fail this crucial test, we have taken a powerful step toward efficiency of argument and toward truth. What does *not* happen is that basic, irreducibly opposed sets of horizons *both* cohere with the facts of human intentionality.

It is clear that we are dealing here with a powerful tool. If self-reversal is converted into methodical dialectic—a technique grounded on the observation that fact is normative—we have found a way of settling what would seem otherwise to be irresolvable disagreements, those not resolved by appeal to rational argument, precisely because they include disagreements on rationality. They differ not on particulars within a horizon, but on horizon itself.

There is a rhetorical ploy often heard in argument on such topics as experience, truth, value: *whose experience? whose truth? whose value?* Whose, indeed? Dialectic is a way of finding out how to meet the challenge of such questions with answers that work. It is true that dialectic, the process of reducing seemingly hopeless arguments to rational form by locating the irreducibly opposed horizons of disputants, their wellsprings or generative matrices, does not take us the whole way to the truth. Dialectic is first and foremost a technique of clarification. But insofar as it does clarify, it allows us a significant choice. Furthermore, it allows us to discover true allies and true adversaries; and since birds of a feather flock together, dialectic is likely to instigate new alignments and entry into new friendships.

The reader should not be misled into thinking that here we have a technique that works so automatically that it can dispense with human excellence, in other words, with intelligence and virtue. It does not. It does suppose, however, that among the participants in dialectic there are men and women who truly exhibit traits of intellectual and moral authenticity, or conversion.

Particularly crucial in matters of theology (and by no means limited to such matters) is religious conversion. It is not enough to have some notion of which conflicts are basic and significant, which horizons have some claim to cohere with the ascertainable facts of human intentionality. Nobler, more ambitious than clarification, the ulterior goal is truth. The beauty of dialectic is that in making thematic the drive to truth and the complexity and subtlety of the obstacles to truth, it prompts birds of a feather to flock together, bringing the best into alliance, enhancing the prospects of truth in the group, the academy, the Church, society at large.

For men and women en route to self-determination in the spheres that count—religious, moral, intellectual—dialectic is an *occasion* of conversion. So far from being a dead end, it serves first of all to bring us to the point at which we cease to take our horizons for granted. Such changes, we noted above, often take place when we discover that the horizons hitherto habitual to us are unable to accommodate some new ascertainment that simply will not be denied. Another occasion, another way of setting oneself on the road of continuous personal growth, is the practice of dialectic. It thematizes "horizon," truth, the truly worthwhile. It not only thematizes, but promotes, conversion.

An Exercise in Dialectic

Actual practice of dialectic may be both long and laborious; here we shall offer an example streamlined for clarity. It is simply an effort to show how dialectic might concretely work. The example is the debate between language-analysts and cognition-analysts. Our example is an exchange between Edward MacKinnon (1968) and Bernard Lonergan (1972).

The language analyst begins with an observation. The meaningfulness of language is essentially public and only derivatively private. This is shown first by the role of usage in determining the meaning of words. Second, reflection reveals that if this were not so, language could not serve as a vehicle of communication among persons and among groups. A consequence of this state of affairs is that:

> The meaning of a word is not explicable by reference or reduction to private mental acts. The usual scholastic doctrine is that words have meaning *because* they express concepts. Meanings are primarily in concepts, private mental acts or states, and then derivatively in language which expresses such a concept.

The conclusion is that the way to clarity must lie in the task defined by Ludwig Wittgenstein, namely, the description and analysis of ordinary language and how it works. The way to clarity can hardly be thought to lie in cognitional theory or in the metaphysics of knowledge.

The critical realist response makes the point, first, that "mental acts" do not take place without a sustaining flow of expression (though the expression need not be linguistic).

Second, there is no denying that the ordinary meaningfulness of ordinary language is essentially public and only derivatively private. One does not learn a language without performing mental acts, but it is true that in learning one performs mental acts expressed interiorly and exteriorly, imitating the ways in which language is ordinarily used.

Third, what holds for the ordinary meaningfulness of ordinary language does not hold for the original meangingfulness of any language, ordinary, literary, or technical. All language develops, and the new elements are either discoveries of new uses for words already in existence or inventions of new words or a process of trial and error by which new discoveries and inventions are diffused.

> All three are a matter of expressed mental acts. The discovery of a new usage is a mental act expressed by the new usage. The invention of a new word is a mental act expressed by a new word. The communication of the discoveries and inventions can be done technically . . . or spontaneously. . . .

In any case, mental acts are indispensable to new meaningfulness.

The position of "ordinary-language philosophy" turns out, then, to suffer from a variation on Hume's problem. As Hume was unable to account for the novelty of his own epistemological position by appealing to knowledge as "impressions linked together by custom," so the ordinary-language philosopher can neither deny the fact of new meaningfulness in the constant development of ordinary language nor account for it by appeal to the public character of ordinary usage.

No matter what tack is taken by "ordinary language philosophy" in the face of the need for an explanation of *new usage,* which "ordinary usage" simply cannot provide, the final disposition and solution of this debate will depend on what precise position the ordinary-language philosopher takes. Let us suppose that he takes his stand on the exclusion of mental acts from his horizon. Does the horizon excluding mental acts cohere with the facts of human intentionality? How well does it cohere with the lectures, the articles, the books of the ordinary-language philosopher?

> How rare is the man that will preface his lectures by repeating his conviction that never did he have even a fleeting experience of intellectual curiosity, of inquiry, of striving and coming to understand, of expressing what he has grasped by understanding. Rare too is the man that begins his contributions to periodical literature by reminding his potential readers that never in his life did he experience anything that might be called critical reflection, that he never paused about the truth or falsity of any statement, that

if ever he seemed to exercise his rationality by passing judgment strictly in accord with the available evidence, then that must be counted mere appearance for he is totally unaware of any such event or even any such tendency. Few finally are those who place at the beginning of their books the warning that they have no notion of what might be meant by responsibility, that never in their lives did they have the experience of acting responsibly, and that least of all in composing the books they are offering the public.

Or, it may be that the ordinary language philosopher acknowledges the existence of mental acts but considers problems of meaning irresolvable by recourse to them. But the critical realist is in a position to account—by the occurrence of insight, of practical judgment, and of responsible decision—for the new meaningfulness that bids to enter and, in fact, is ever entering the resources of the speech-community. What can the ordinary-language philosopher do but systematically overlook the distinction between ordinary meaningfulness and the new meaningfulness that he cannot account for, but that the critical realist can?

What accounts for the horizon that excludes the existence, the operation, the utility of mental acts such as wondering, inquiring, supporting with evidence, judging, evaluating, deciding, and the like? Surely the answer is clear: failure to break with picture-thinking and failure to swing round completely and coherently to new criteria of knowing the real: intelligent grasp and reasonable affirmation.

The exercise of dialectic thus highlights the relevance of intentionality analysis and, within it, of horizon-analysis, the difference of positions from counterpositions, the role of thematic coherence with the spontaneously self-imposing traits of intentionality in vindicating the former and, no less important, the role of incoherence with performance that burdens the counterposition: for example, for those who deny the existence or relevance of "mental acts," the failure to explain to one's listeners and readers that in the lecture or text to follow there is no claim implicit or explicit to offer the fruits of such mental acts as questioning, insight, reasonable or responsible judgment, all of them having been excluded in principle from the position of speaker or writer.

At its most authentic, human subjectivity is defined by a three-fold break with the conventionally modern and postmodern: the break with picture-thinking, the break with the primacy of gratification, and the break with the great dogma of the secular, or of the this-worldly as ultimate horizon. Later, closer to the realities of New Testament scholarship, we shall at least indicate how dialectic may serve to help us discern ideological illusions that bid to undermine (or are already undermining) the field.

PART II

ROOTS OF HERMENEUTICAL CONFLICT

Our supposition is that conflicting views in the field of New Testament studies are rooted in prior conflicts on more general and fundamental issues: objectivity, truth, reality, the good, history, cultural values, and criticism. In the phrase "conflicting views in the field of New Testament studies," the views intended are not disagreements grounded in the limitations of evidence, which yield forthwith as sufficient evidence comes to light; they are disagreements grounded in disparity of horizons, which rarely find a resolution without some change of horizon.

Such differences feed cultural competition and conflict. In view of what have virtually become cultural wars, it is a worthy ideal to try to treat disputed issues in a manner at once fundamental, competent, and civil, setting aside the tactics of those who are convinced that inquiry cannot lead to truth and so must lead to pressure groups and political muscle. We wish, on the contrary, to pay some attention to truthfulness as an element in the quest of truth. This does not necessarily call for the avoidance of disagreement, but it does commend honest and civil disagreement.

Cultural battles are fought today in political arenas once relatively (or was it only seemingly?) free of cultural politics, for example, in the now politicized humanities and social sciences. The situation is unambiguous. The battles are part of a new Thirty Years' War that broke out in the middle 1960s, though its roots are older. Ideological, like most wars in our century, it has engaged Marxists, Freudians, Nietzscheans, sociobiologists, structuralists, deconstructionists, historicists, new historicists, and many others. This has not left New Testament studies untouched. The conflicts are especially of an epistemological, religious, moral, and political kind. Happy the university department not undermined by the vices that often accompany overt and covert conflict.

New Testament scholarship once mostly reflected confessional and theological differences; now it registers ideological movements largely, though not exclusively, derived from non-religious sources. In considerable measure these have supplanted theology as guide to textual interpretation, historical-Jesus research, early Christian history. Theological discourse has subsided; ideological discourse has taken over; ideological enmity has replaced *odium theologicum.*

Critical realism has several contributions to make in this context. First, it offers a newly exigent and precise account of human intentionality. Second, it illuminates the epistemological issues, for it entails a break with the cognitional myth that is the mother of epistemological confusions. In locates in intentionality itself the radical orientation to intelligibility, truth, reality, goodness, beauty. It locates the explanatory ground of this orientation in the rational affirmation of God and of the divine attributes: infinite wisdom, goodness, and power. Closer to interpretation theory, critical realism defines a role of basic importance for horizon-analysis, insists on objectivity (in a non-positivist sense) in interpretation and history, rehabilitates the primacy of interpretation over analysis, the intended sense as intrinsic to the text and as the primary object of interpretation. Finally, with reference to values, this philosophy offers a non-ideological way of dealing with alienation, one that aims not at rationalizing, but at relieving and dissipating it.

Second, critical realism, as we shall see, has something to offer in the sphere of Christian theology. This will be implicit in the three chapters of Part II and explicit in Part III.

4

Critical Realism and the True, the Real, the Good

To enter into "critical realism" is to do more than adopt a philosophic opinion: it is to undergo a conversion. The negative side of this conversion-experience is the break with picture-thinking, thinking that depends on the sense of the real acquired in childhood and confirmed ever since by the all-but-overwhelming persuasive power of the senses. This is why the break entails an "upset of crisis and conversion"; the upset is "needed to purge oneself of one's childish realism. . . ." The positive side is the act of "swing[ing] round completely and coherently" to the new criteria of fully human knowing. It is the recognition—at some point a stunning recognition—that whereas reality is delivered in and through truth, truth is delivered not by the senses, but by acts of intelligent grasp and reasonable affirmation.

Objectivity, Truth, Reality

Lonergan illustrated the issues involved in the break with childish realism, or the myth that "knowing is looking," by the example of Jack and Jill.

> Jack or Jill is invited to raise a hand and to look at it. The hand is really out there; it is the object. The eye, strangely, is not in the hand; it is some distance away in the head; it is the subject. The eye really sees the hand; it sees what is there to be seen; it does not see what is not there to be seen. That is objectivity.

61

There follows the naïve generalization that any cognitional act that is sufficiently like seeing must be objective, whereas any cognitional act that is very different from seeing cannot be objective. The power of the paradigm of ocular vision is such that even should introspection discover no intellectual activity that resembles seeing, still some such activity really must exist; otherwise our intellectual acts would be merely immanent—and the idealists would be right! But, as violators of common sense, the idealists have got to be wrong. And if they are wrong, their premise—that there is no intellectual activity like seeing—must be equally wrong. Thus was born the neo-Scholastic "intuition of being," and naïve realism, making modest adjustments, became dogmatic realism.

The idealist is not impressed with this effort to support the claim to "see" being and truth: to look, by superlook, at the correspondence between looking and the looked at (between knowing and the known). No, says the idealist, here something has been *over*looked: the difference between reality and appearance. And he makes clear that by "appearance" he means not some sort of hallucination, but simply limitation to precise description. What do Jack and Jill know when each looks at the hand a dozen or so inches in front of their respective faces? Here is how the idealist sizes up the situation:

> Jack may say that his hand *is* out there in front of his face, and Jill may say that her hand at least *seems* to be out there in front of her face. . . . When Jack says "is," he is not reporting what he knows by sight alone; he also has made a judgment. . . . When Jill says "seems," she is limiting her report to what is known by sight alone.

Again, the idealist, like the naïve realists above, can generalize. Not just seeing, but hearing, smelling, tasting, and touching, are a knowing not of reality, but of appearance. And what holds for the reach of our outer senses holds equally for the reach of imagination and, indeed, for every cognitional act respecting what is sensed or imagined.

As the idealist was unimpressed by the naïve realist, so the critical realist is impressed by neither the one nor the other. Against the naïve realist evoked above, he denies that the objectivity of human knowledge is given in the act of seeing. Human knowledge adds to sensing the experience of wondering, the shaping of wonder in questions, the effort to answer them, the further effort to find out how good any given answer is. Since fully human knowing is irreducible to seeing, so is its objectivity: partly that objectivity consists in experienced data, partly in the normative requirements and enablements of intelligent insight and reasonable judgment, lastly in bringing all these together: the data, the normativeness immanent in insight, and the normativeness immanent in judgment. Objectivity is a state of mind to which the empirical, the intelligent, and the reasonable have all made their contribution. Syllogistic reasoning ("If A, then B; but A; therefore, B) provides an analogy. The normative components proper to intelligence and reason correspond to the major proposition; the empirical component, to the minor proposition; the syllogism (like reflection leading to judgment) brings these together, and the conclusion that follows corresponds to judgment, objective and true.

Intellectual operations, the critical realist points out to the naïve realist, are not like seeing; on the contrary, they are what seeing never is, immanently intelligent (as in relevant construal) and immanently rational (as in grounded judgment). And going back over the idealist's exposition, he further points out that not only was Jack adding judgment to seeing when he said, "My hand *is* out there in front of my face," so was Jill when she said, "My hand *seems* to be out there in front of my face." It is as much a matter of judgment to hold that an object is not real but apparent as it is to hold that an object is not apparent but real. "By our senses we are given, not appearance, not reality, but data."

The Jack-and-Jill story is one of those parables that has more than one point. First, there is a notion so solidly founded on sense experience as to seem simple as sunlight, clear as crystal, inescapable as death and taxes: human knowing must be some sort of seeing. It must at least be very like seeing, a sort of high-class intellectual seeing.

If understanding were to have this character, observes the critical realist, "judgment" would be merely an added grace, an optional extra. In fact, however, this simple, clear, inescapable idea is a counterposition, that is, a philosophic compass-error. It might seem at first to suffer merely from being approximate, a bit imprecise. But it is not just a little off. It is flatly mistaken. Furthermore, compass-errors are rapidly magnified by one's following their mistaken direction. Second, we notice the naïve realist's fierce determination to nail down objectivity without delay and at any cost. Third, there is the perfectly correct acknowledgement that the idealist accords to intellectual acts other than and different from seeing. But there is the same idealist's failure to observe that among these acts is wondering, spontaneous and unrestricted, already an intending of "the real." Fourth, critical realism relates to idealism not as a subtraction, but as a set of additions: wonder as immediately intending the real; questioning as the thematizing of wonder, and insight or answer as "answer *to* question" inasmuch as question and answering insight have the same object; the relevance of reflection and the quest of sufficient evidence; the grasp of sufficient evidence (or grasp of those conditions on which the solidity of some insight depends, and of their fulfillment or non-fulfillment); judgment as the personally posited verdict that puts one, in one's conscious intentionality, either into conformity with or into difformity from the real state-of-affairs or simply "the real."

The critical realist, we have said, charges naïve realists and idealists alike with "picture thinking." What, concretely, does the charge amount to? The answer lies in themes that we have considered already: the long primacy in the life of the human subject of sensing and feeling and of the corresponding world of bodies immediate to the senses. Why do naïve realists and idealists tie "objectivity" to perception? Because their world is a world of bodies, a picture world.

> If their world were the universe of being, they would agree that the original relationship of cognitional activity to the universe of being must lie in the intention of being. But their world is a picture world; the original relationship of cognitional activity to the picture is the look; and so it is in looking that the naive realist finds revealed the essence of objectivity, and it is in *Anschauung* [perception] that the critical idealist places the immediate relation of cognitional activity to [its object]. There exists, then, something like a forgetfulness of being. . . .

Before leaving Jack and Jill, we should add some last comments on how the Kantian type of idealist described above *differs from* the naïve realist, while also aligning himself with the naïve realist on the issue of "the real" as a picture world.

To be "real," the object sensed (here, "my hand") must be made to belong to the sphere of "that which is." Jack, a naïve realist, does not hesitate to say that it does. If his hand were not real, how could it be there to be sensed? (At some later point he might be inclined to posit a suprasensory act of "seeing" in what he senses, the existence otherwise merely supposed.) The idealist says, "No, the matter of whether the hand actually *is* out there now is held in suspension until judged."

So the idealist here differs from the naïve realist on one point relative to *how* the real is ascertained. Jack, when he said, "This hand in front of my face is real," went beyond seeing to judging. But the idealist does not differ from the naïve realist on *what* is being ascertained. For both of them, "the real" is the-already-out-there-now. (Already: that is, given prior to raising any question about it. Out: that is, an object of consciousness extraverted to the world of bodies delivered to the senses. There: like sense organs, so sense objects are in space. Now: the time of the sensing is the time of the sensed.)

If for both the naïve realist and the critical idealist the real is the same, namely, the-already-out-there-now, the question of its reality is simply whether we can predicate existence of it. To this Jack says, "Yes, of course"; the idealist finally says, "Certainly not," for sense does not pronounce on the real, and he knows no cognitive act *immediately related to its object* other than sense-perception *(Anschauung)*. That is, he knows no suprasensory act that immediately relates him to being/reality.

Furthermore, he betrays his concessions to and alignments with the naïve realist in his failure to see that Jill's positing of "appearance" is just as much a matter of judgment as was Jack's positing of "reality." Still under the spell of childhood's simple sense of "reality," the Kantian idealist supposes that to get to the real, one merely adds "existence" to the-already-out-there-now; or, if existence cannot rightly be added thereto, this already-out-there-now world is just a world of appearances.

What the idealist does *not* do is *to redefine the real in terms of intelligent grasp and reasonable affirmation*. By noting (apropos of Jack) the need of judgment to pronounce on "the real," the idealist was momentarily en route to a fully coherent realism; by failing "to swing round completely and coherently" to new criteria for fully human knowing, by stopping short instead at the naïve realist's referent of "the real" or "the-already-out-there-now," he staked out the ground for idealism as half-way house between naïve and critical realism.

Reflective Confirmation of the Critical Realist Conclusion

Let us now make our way back to the common-sense starting point of the naïve realist and his sense of *the real as the immediate*. As we insisted above, this simplicity is steadily commended to all of us by the long dominance in our lives of senses and feelings and, correspondingly, of a world of bodies, the immediate world, the only one known to the infant. This powerful primacy accounts for the naturalness of the equation of "the real" with the-already-out-there-now, and this *sense* of the real hangs on long after the many transitions to adulthood have occurred, long after the entry into language and linguistic competence, the move into "story," the addition to the world of immediacy of ever wider and more engaging worlds mediated by meaning.

The transitions that stimulate this growth take place more or less naturally and forgettably. Accurate objectification of human intentionality is difficult and rare. We attain to truth, for example, to the truth of empirical statements like, "Ah, the postman is late today," with utter ease, but it is only with great effort that we arrive at an accurate hold on this observation's easy attainment of truth. (What are the fulfilling conditions? Well, they include the memory of what time the postman usually comes . . . and so on.)

We have thus far come to some elements of a satisfactory epistemology and now wish to confirm definitively what progress we have made. If one equates the real with the-already-out-there-now, it follows that animals—so we outsiders to the animal-world observe—live in a real world. But they themselves do not project the horizons of the real. They do not wonder about the real nor do they affirm the real in judgment. They accordingly do not live in the world as "real"; they merely adapt to their environment. A kitten will perceive the difference between a saucer of milk and a realistically painted saucer of milk by not finding in the second the satisfactions of the first. All of us began by operating in infancy and childhood somewhat like that.

As we grow, however, we human beings *wonder* about the real. And if in our use of the word "real" (meaning thereby the-already-out-there-now) we draw on the inheritances of childhood, we are at least in good historical company. We may know better, but it is still hard not to sympathize with Dr. Johnson for having, in a fit of impatience with Boswell's opinion (Berkeley was wrong but irrefutable), delivered a powerful kick to a rock, crying, "I refute him *thus!*" Before and contemporary with the days of Johnson and Boswell:

> When Galileo pronounced secondary qualities to be merely subjective, he meant that they were not "already out there now real". . . . When Descartes maintained that material substance must be identical with spatial extension, his material substance was the "already out there now real." When Kant argued that primary and secondary qualities are merely phenomenal, he meant that for him the "already out there now real" was mere appearance.

For the critical realist, on the contrary, the issue of the real is posed for the first time by wondering about it—an act of intelligence. The issue, moreover, is resolved only by converting the wonder into a focused question, finding a promising answer, asking how good the answer is, and determining that it is good as gold. The real, that is, is grasped in and through true judgment. But this holds not just for one or another case, but with full generality, and so for the real as such. The real is what first of all is wondered about and finally is reasonably affirmed. (Lonergan preferred the formula, "The real is the intelligently grasped and reasonably affirmed.")

The economy, economists, and economic theory, insofar as they are understood intelligently and affirmed reasonably, are real (and in some respects a more serviceable paradigm of the real than "the tree" or "the hand in front of my face"). But neither Galileo nor Descartes nor Kant defined the real coherently and consistently in terms of the drive to know and the goal of knowledge. Hence the almost paralyzing sense of difficulty and complexity, and the recourse to qualifying abstractions, that the question of "the reality" of, say, the economy, or "the reality" of economic theory seems to impose, especially on naïve realists (neo-scholastics, empiricists, behaviorists), but also on idealists (Kantian and neo-Kantian, Hegelian, Crocean). No problem for the critical realist. For him the-already-out-there-now world of immediacy is the data we wonder about and will pronounce on in the light of grasped evidence. Insight is not a passive registering, but an active construal. The "objective" is not what registers without distortion, but that for which there is sufficient evidence. The real is not bodies plus existence, but the intelligently grasped and reasonably affirmed.

There is an exquisite irony in the charge of picture-thinking levelled by a picture-thinker, Richard Rorty, against two non-picture-thinkers, Aristotle and Aquinas. Rorty blames misleading imagery (the mind as mirror) for inducing mistaken accounts of knowledge. Unhappily, his own hold on Aristotle and Aquinas fails here. He overlooks the intention of being; he mistakenly supposes that insight, for them, is a grasp of principles of being (the forms, substantial or accidental, of objects of knowledge). He rightly attributes to both the thesis of knowledge as intentional identity but understands this in hermeneutical rather than metaphysical terms. The imagery of "eye" added to "mirror" is ill-calculated to make the theme of Aristotelian identity clear. The crucial point is that one breaks with picture-thinking by focusing on and grasping the alternative to the "real" as the-already-out-there-now. Here Aristotle and Aquinas were impeccably deft, and Rorty is out of touch with both.

There are many reasons for rejoicing in the clean break with the picture world, for it liberates the human subject from several illusions. The first illusion has to do with an old debate on objectivity and subjectivity, and the new form it took in New Testament studies at mid-century (see below, on Bultmann's essay on hermeneutics).

The most common philosophic stance is naïve realism in some "rigorous" form: positivism, sensism, pragmatism, behaviorism, and the like, with their view of subject and object, subjectivity and objectivity. The latter pair are like east and west, and never the twain shall meet. Why not? In virtue of a conundrum begotten of sense-knowing as the paradigm of fully human knowing. If one conceives "object" on the model of the object of ocular vision, and "objectivity" on the model of the objectivity of the senses, what can subjectivity contribute except error? This is no doubt the secret of why so many discussions in New Testament scholarship, if they touch on some matter that has to do with knowing, for example, the question of criteria of (or better, of indices to) the historicity of gospel data, fall all over themselves in condemning "subjectivity." Or, alternatively, the writer takes what seems a more sophisticated tack, and dismisses "objectivity" with contempt.

Once we are cured of the supposition that the paradigm of knowing is looking at one's hand to see what is there, while most carefully avoiding seeing what is not there, a new and second way of dealing with object and objectivity presents itself.

> "Object" in the context of elementary knowing is simply the term of extraverted consciousness: whatever is seen, heard, touched, tasted, smelled. The condition of the objectivity of such knowing is the proper functioning of the senses. But "object" in the context of fully human knowing is whatever is intended by questions and known when the questions are satisfactorily answered. The objectivity of this kind of knowing is accordingly complex. An experiential component lies in the givenness of data. An intelligent component lies in the demand expressed by a question and met by a [relevant] answer. A rational component lies in the further demand that the answer be true, met by the assembling of evidence and the reflective grasp of it as sufficient.

There are many variations on the naïve realist conception. Perhaps the most obvious shortcoming of all these variants lies in what Lonergan called "The Principle of the Empty Head," which is simply naïve realism applied to interpretation:

> According to this principle, if one is not to "read into" the text what is not there, if one is not to settle in a priori fashion what the text must mean no matter what it says, if one is not to drag in one's own notions and opinions, then one must just drop all preconceptions of every kind, attend simply to the text, see all that is there and nothing that is not there, let the author speak for himself, let the author interpret himself. In brief, the less one knows, the better an exegete one will be.

Views like this one are just what is likely to awaken an inquiring mind from its dogmatic slumbers and lead it straight into idealism. The supreme example, Immanuel Kant, had a direct and indirect impact on nineteenth- and twentieth-century New Testament studies. Further, the absolute idealisms that appeared in Kant's wake and were correlated systematically by Hegel also impinged on New Testament studies, beginning with the generation of Strauss and Feuerbach. In the Kantian and Hegelian camps the criterion of truth was *coherence*. The extentialism of twentieth-century kerygma theology in Germany was always under remote control by Neo-Kantian immanentism, and never got beyond a criterion of consistency—a state of affairs that for decades baffled and frustrated naïve-realist Catholic and Protestant conservative critics of Bultmann.

It was a dialogue of the deaf. Bultmann's conservative critics found fault with—naturally, what else?—his subjectivity. Bultmann responded with a crusher, an essay entitled "The Problem of Hermeneutics," which flatly repudiated (though in other words) "the Principle of the Empty Head."

> Nothing [he wrote] is sillier than the requirement that an interpreter must silence his subjectivity, extinguish his individuality, if he is to attain objective knowledge. That requirement makes good sense only in so far as it is taken to mean that the interpreter has to silence his personal wishes with regard to the outcome of the interpretation.

So, for decades the debate went; that is, it went nowhere. Eventually, Bultmannian existentialism, incisive within its limits, but exceedingly limited in both resources and themes, simply died out for having said what it could and having no more to say. Until that happened, Bultmann's critics could only bewail his unwarranted subjectivity; Bultmann and his allies could only counter with the painfully inadequate epistemological resources (coherence) of Neo-Kantian idealism.

The problem lay in disparity of horizons. It is a problem that reaches a critical point in philosophic and religious texts. Empiricists, idealists, and critical realists operate with diverse horizons. They may all speak of objectivity and subjectivity, good and evil, progress and decline, etc., but each understands every term in his or her own way. It is pure illusion to suppose that philosophers can successfully read philosophy and biblical scholars the Bible by relying on good sense, good will, and honest effort. It just does not work. For seven hundred years scholastics tried to read Aquinas through conceptualist lenses, and failed at the crucial points. For two hundred years exegetes have tried to read the New Testament through idealist, then romantic, then positivist, then existentialist, and all along through common-sense naïve-realist lenses, and failed even more conspicuously.

Last of all, in attempting to confirm not merely by pragmatic reference to the experience of conscious intentionality, but *definitively,* the objectification that we call critical realism, we should face the most radical issue of all. It deals at once with the final vindication of critical realism both as critical and as realist, and with its power to deal with the crippling alienations of Western society in our time. Until now the warrants we have offered for critical realism have been, first of all, its positive capacity to lay bare elements of human experience and to make them understandable. We have furthermore assessed a telling correlation, that between the natural spontaneities of intentionality and the critical-realist account thereof (together with its flip side, the phenomenon of self-reversal undergone by alternative views). But as any critic steeped in metaphysics (a traditional Thomist, let's say) might point out, we have not offered a definitive explanatory vindication of our claim to "correspondence" as mediating the real in and through the true. There remains a final nagging question. Why should the answers that satisfy the intelligence of the subject yield more than that, more than just satisfaction? We assume that they do, and we can point to the fact that, again and again, this assumption is confirmed by its fruits. Still, we have not offered an account of how intelligibility, truth, the real, the good are ultimately *grounded.*

True affirmation and the grasp of the real in and through true affirmation do not themselves yield *an explanation of the groundedness* of the intelligible, the true, the real, the good. The grasp of the real takes place, but its explanatory vindication is still lacking.

The issue is most pointed, or at any rate most dramatically pointed, respecting the good. We are occasionally conscious of a kind of undertow toward moral authenticity, a pull of both feeling and judgment. We hear the voice of conscience. But there is also the voice that asks, is it worth the candle? Though we praise progress and denounce decline, we can also ask:

> But is the universe on our side, or are we just gamblers and, if we are gamblers, are we not perhaps fools, individually struggling for authenticity and collectively endeavoring to snatch progress from the ever mounting welter of decline?

Below we shall deal with the good, the structure of society as a quest of the good, with the moral virtues, and with practical wisdom as a kind of counterpart, in the existential sphere, of objectivity in the cognitive sphere. But here we shall plunge without further ado into the existential question that has gripped Western thinkers especially since mid-century. Does the quest of the good attune us to the real order of things (the universe) or set us in laborious and futile opposition to it? Can we rule out the radical alienation of men and women who strive for the good and struggle to live a responsible life in a world utterly indifferent to their struggle? Those familiar with Ernest Becker, a compelling young North American philosopher-anthropologist who died in the middle 1970s, know the struggle reflected in his thought. If, as Becker feared and thought, our world is just what it appears to be—a shining planet spinning meaninglessly in space—and if we are simply weak and frightened animals staving off our fear of death by choosing one or another illusory hero-role, what is the point of the true and the good? To the end Becker remained mesmerized by the question; he could confront it but not resolve it.

Unless there is a moral agent responsible for the world's being and becoming, Lonergan argued, the world cannot be said to be good in that moral sense. But if not, then there is this choice: the subject might keep up the moral struggle, only to discover that whatever success attended it would alienate him from the world. Or he could renounce the moral struggle, drift into the "now seductive and now harsh rhythms of his psyche and of nature," so ending in moral failure and alienation from his own nature.

The dilemma, alienation in either case, is resolved only by a moral agent responsible for the world's being and becoming. Is man himself this moral agent? Only in the most painfully limited way. For we find ourselves pushing for an answer to the question not of whether, despite everything, we ought to do what we can in a morally neutral world, but of whether the world really is not morally neutral, but good; whether it is on the side of those who hunger and thirst for righteousness. This question, moveover, has its counterpart in the related issues of whether there is an ultimate grounding of intelligibility, truth, reality.

These dilemmas—is the world, its intelligibility, truth, reality, and goodness, ultimately rooted or grounded?—are not dissipated until the question of God, his existence, omnipotence, and goodness, finds an answer. In its full scope, to be sure, the issue falls outside the immediate limits of the present inquiry; but since it is too important to leave untouched, we take it up in an appendix. Only if the question is resolved by the affirmation of God will the following issues likewise find resolution: (1) Is critical realism both critical and realist in an unrestricted sense? (2) Is the world not morally indifferent, but enlisted in the cause of the moral good and destined to arrive at the good? (3) Is the story celebrated by the New Testament positively believable and to be believed? And, depending on the answer, is the turn of the West away from its foundations a turn toward life or death?

The second and third questions we hold in reserve for the moment. On the first question, the reader may have immediate recourse to the appendix that states the issue of God precisely in terms of intelligibility and truth, and goes on to the affirmation of God as infinite in goodness, knowledge, wisdom, and power. The dilemma as stated above is: if the moral struggle is sustained against all odds, does not the human subject run the risk of ending in alienation from the world? If the moral struggle is abandoned, does not the human subject run the risk of ending in alienation from him- or herself? Happily, this dilemma *is* dissipated, for the question of God—raised by inquiring into the possibility of fruitful inquiry, by reflecting on the nature of reflection, by deliberating on whether deliberation makes sense—finds an answer in *rational affirmation of the existence, omnipotence, and goodness of God.* It follows that the universe *is* intelligible, true, good, beautiful, holy by vocation and destiny. These traits ultimately depend on God as the source and end of creaturely intelligibility, truth, goodness, beauty, and destiny.

These reflections belong by right to a philosophy of being, which has its role in the cultural wars of our time. As Sartre set out to draw *all* the conclusions that a perfectly consistent atheism authorized, so the critical realism that finds its ultimate justification in the rational affirmation of the existence, omnipotence, and goodness of God consistently sets out to draw the full range of hermeneutical conclusions from the contrary premise. As Sartre argued (perfectly coherently) that there were no natural essences, since there was no God to know them creatively, to bring into

being the divinely intelligible, so with equal consistency we infer
(in Part III, chapter seven), based on the contrary premises of
God's existence, omniscience, and omnipotence, that God knows
every dimension and facet of "the problem of evil"; that, as all-
wise, he knows many solutions; that, as all-powerful, he can effect any of them; that, as all-good, he has effected some one of
them. The dilemma of the goodness of the universe is resolved
by inferring that God has chosen a solution, that he has made
this solution somehow available to mankind, and that to a theist
and specifically to a critical-realist theist it cannot be that evil
should infect mankind as simple miasma, a simply dispiriting,
simply destructive and unappealable fact. In short, "the problem of evil" *must have a solution,* and our concrete existential
problem lies in finding out what it is.

Desire for the Truly Good

We have considered the desire to know; now we consider the
desire to be. It may be variously named. Lonergan called it "the
notion of value." It is conspicuously the crown and completion
of the notion of being, for here the notion of being takes the form
of desire for the truly good, which is simultaneously the drive to
fulfillment or happiness. Of course, nothing is clearer than that
human intentionality does not offer any automatic pledge respecting what the truly good, what happiness and human fulfillment,
might consist in. Apparently, God left that to human persons to
figure out for themselves. Human intentionality, one might suppose, must surely include resources fully equal to the question.
History tells another story, infinitely colorful, a record of folly
and frustration. Human beings have proven to be anything but
adept in the pursuit of happiness. Half the time, it is a meander-
ing voyage on a ship of fools.

What the inquiry into intentionality does show is how human
beings function in fact. First, they are oriented to knowing. This
is not the part of life to which most give maximum attention. Beyond the sphere of knowing (but by no means unrelated to it) there
is the hunger for personal fulfillment and the efforts, often fran-
tic, to appease it. Here we enter the sphere of ends and means,
of loves and hates, of human success and failure.

To get hold of conscious intentionality as existential, it is worth our while briefly to reconsider its anticipation in judgment. The grasp of the virtually unconditioned brings cognition to the brink of realized conformity with reality. The acts by which the knower has brought himself to this point, so far from being an alienating experience, constitute a certain self-realization. The seeker finally enters, by true judgment, into possession both of himself and of some part of the real.

The transition that we call "the age of reason" takes place far more easily than its existential counterpart and completion. As children, we moved haltingly but successfully out of the confines of immediacy into the larger world, qualifying our sense of the real. Within our range, we entered the world mediated by meaning. The appeal to belief, qualified by many vagaries, wore thin; partly it was forced to yield to "reasons."

The age of reason is likewise the age of conscience. Approval and disapproval, no longer coming only from outside, offered guidance from within. Although guidance from within is insecure (the child, by comparison with non-rational animals, is instinct-poor), it is capable of extraordinary development. Here the role of feeling is paramount. We distinguish among feelings (1) non-intentional states and trends and (2) intentional responses. "States" are exemplified by fatigue, irritability, ill-humor; "trends" by hunger, thirst, sexual appetite.

> The states have causes. The trends have goals. But the relation of the feeling to the cause or goal is simply that of effect to cause, of trend to goal. The feeling itself does not presuppose and arise out of perceiving, imagining, representing the cause or goal. . . . Intentional responses, on the other hand, answer to what is intended, apprehended, represented. The feeling relates us . . . to an object. Such feeling gives intentional consciousness its mass, momentum, drive, power.

Feelings of the latter sort mainly regard two classes of objects: the agreeable/disagreeable and values. The first class of objects is ambiguous. Satisfactions do not necessarily belong to the category of the authentically good for me. Values, on the other hand, are grasped with reference to the fully human subject, and include *vital values* (such as health and physical wellbeing), *social values* (such as the good of order, which conditions the vital values of the community, and which are to be preferred to the vital values of individuals), *cultural values* (such as art and letters), *personal values* (persons as loving and being loved, as originators and models of values), and *religious values* (which relate persons to the ground of all meaning and value).

The desire to know the truth is extended by the desire to realize the good. When one asks, "What is the truly good?" one does not know but already intends the reality of what would be known if one knew the answer to this question. The very posing of the question sets one's face toward the reality of the truly good. Such is the nature of intending. The radical, natural desire of the good, which extends the natural desire of the true (or the drive to know), continues to promote the subject from stage to stage, and continues to reveal itself empirically as immanent norm. As the drive to truth summons the subject to act in accord with intelligence and rationality, so the drive to value rewards success, and saddens failure, by the voice of conscience.

All our value judgments, simple or comparative, reflect, express, reveal the natural, conscious, unlimited drive to the good. Our quest of the good, like our quest of the true, is precisely a dimension of the drive, appetite, desire, quest of *being*. The whole of human experience insistently instructs us on how steep the demands of the moral life are. Traditionally, we set "the age of reason" at about seven. But we do not hold the human being fully responsible for his or her actions until about age sixteen, or eighteen, or twenty-one. There are minimal age-requirements for holding public office, a requisite that makes excellent sense.

By harsh experience of failure, we learn how difficult it is to achieve habitual self-restraint; and how it is even harder to sustain the habitual without failure over the long haul. Experience shows how provisional self-control is, how unreliable people are. We find ourselves unable—faithfully, dependably, consistently—to follow the voice of immanent norms inviting our attention, intelligence, reasonableness, responsibility, and summoning us to sustain such performance over the long run. It is no surprise that virtue, though natural, is not commonplace; that civility is sporadic; that courtesy cannot be counted on. Authenticity defined by norms internal to human intentionality cannot be taken for granted; it must be laboriously cultivated; and that may not suffice.

Experience brings sobriety. Human authenticity is not a serenely possessed quality, but

> consists in a withdrawal from unauthenticity, and the withdrawal is never a permanent achievement. It is ever precarious, ever to be achieved afresh, ever in great part a matter of uncovering still more oversights, acknowledging still further failures to understand, correcting still more mistakes, repenting more and more deeply hidden sins.

Apropos of knowledge, we said that objectivity is the fruit of authentic subjectivity. But pushing beyond the cognitive to the existential sphere, how are we to arrive at authenticity, if even laborious cultivation barely suffices to generate discontinuous, imperfect achievement? Certainly, we ought not to underestimate the human experience of contact with persons who have made their way to the good and somehow installed themselves in it. It is not treatises on virtue that set us on fire. Fire passes from torch to torch.

Even this suggestive allusion to the power of personal contact—"all real living is meeting"—is not a fully satisfactory answer. Among further answers there is inevitably that of "religion." We might dispense with the appeal to religion if, for example, the human-potential movement could come through on its promises of self-realization; if we could achieve ultimate meaning without reference to religion or, simpler still, get along without ultimate meaning.

A part of the human-potential movement is distinctive. Those groups that, following in the line of the "twelve-step programs" pioneered by Alcoholics Anonymous, do offer a kind of spirituality for a secular age. It is generically religious. A large body of experience lies behind it. This is the experience of finding that we cannot make our way entirely on our own. We cannot do without God, for we cannot persevere in living intelligently, reasonably, and responsibly without some hold and some reliance on ultimate context. "To live intelligently, reasonably, responsibly, an adult has to form some view of the universe," argued Lonergan. Moreover, he added, the same adult must form some idea of his place and role in the universe along with his fellow human beings:

He may do so by appealing to myth, or to science, or to philosophy, or to religion. . . . A mythic solution will do only for the immature. A scientific solution is impossible, for science methodically and systematically refuses to consider the issue. A philosophic solution is out-of-date, for philosophy has become existential; it is concerned with man in his concrete existing; and there the issue is authenticity.

But, the argument continues, the human being exists *authentically* in the measure in which he or she succeeds in self-transcendence, which has its *fulfillment* and its *ground* in God's gift of his love to us. Religion reveals itself as a generally and finally indispensable resource for human authenticity.

If this seems a turn away from the challenge of modernity to take refuge in tradition, a parallel situation in antiquity—the duel of Socrates with the sophists—may throw a different light on it. The power of the historical sophists can still be discerned today, thanks in part to the Platonic dialogues. The sophists were up-to-the-minute intellectuals who offered *aretē*, "competence, success," to the Greeks as citizens and private persons. In reality they offered something more and something less. More, for the sophists promoted a whole *view of life,* new, modern, contemporary. Less, for their view of life concealed a destructive element, one not easily pinned down. In the analysis of Josef Pieper, it was a readiness to meet life's challenges with the offer of rational technique. Socrates, a man of the city (for him the country was mere refreshment) was, as inquirer, a modern like the sophists. He differed from them, however, at the crucial points. He was a conservative on customs and traditions, and a delver into them when they touched on themes such as cosmic origins, the primal state and fall of man, judgment after death.

What Socrates offered, by contrast with the sophists, was knowledge and virtue, and especially knowledge of virtue. When at the beginning of the *Symposium* one of his interlocutors (now over twenty-three centuries ago) brought up what we call the cardinal virtues—justice, courage, measure, practical wisdom—he was citing an *already* age-old tradition. As then, so today, some context is supposed by and attached to the theme of virtue: the structure of the human good in the concreteness of a social order and ultimately of a comprehensive world order.

This structure of the human good can be variously treated:

as implicated in the discussion of virtue (in particular of justice, as in Plato, or indeed in such modern treatises as those of Pieper himself) or in the discussion of political philosophy (as in Plato, or in Yves Simon's *Philosophy of Democratic Government* on the functions of authority) or as a preliminary, independent question raised in the context of analysis of intentionality (Lonergan on the reciprocal dependence of person and society in the quest of goods). All these treatments exhibit major points of convergence. A major point of divergence, as Hans-Georg Gadamer has noted (in agreement with Aristotle), is the gap in Platonic idealism between the Idea of the Good and any cultivated orientation to or ambition of good action. The gap is filled by practical wisdom *(phronēsis),* a theme to which we shall have occasion to return.

The main convergence in these discussions is at the reciprocal dependence between person and society, between ethics and politics, between the quest of particular goods and of the common good. Thus, Lonergan's "good of order" (the functioning or malfunctioning of concretely related individuals and groups in society) effects, among other things (when it functions well), a steady flow of particular goods. "My dinner today is for me an instance of the particular good. But dinner every day for all members of the group that earn it is part of the good of order."

Lonergan's schema may be reproduced here:

Individual		*Social*	*Ends*
Potentiality	*Actuation*		
capacity, need	operation	cooperation	particular good
plasticity perfectibility	development skill	institution role, task	good of order
liberty	conversion	personal relations	terminal value

The point of the schema is to specify the main factors in the operation of society as a quest of the good. Since the good is not static, the fourth column designates goals of choice and action. Particular goods meet the needs of individuals; the good of order meets common needs, including (as noted above) the stable supply of particular goods to individuals. "Terminal values" are objects of choice, true particular goods or a true good of order.

Individual good breaks down into potency and act. In the first line, reading across: capacities and needs prompt operations, which actuate capacities and meet needs; moreover, human operation is largely cooperation: for example, that among individuals in the quest of particular goods that everyone needs. The second line: plasticity and perfectibility allow for growth, the development of skills that meet societal needs and correspond to tasks variously institutionalized to contribute to the good of order. (Here we interrupt to draw attention to the third column, which suggests frameworks of cooperation: the family, the business enterprise, the economy, the church or sect, the state.) Finally, the third line is meant to suggest the themes central to human intentionality as existential: liberty (= self-determination, including above all the choice of horizons) and the possibility of authentic existence, the kind of human living that, if shared, contributes to *progress* and, if isolated, cannot prevent *decline*.

Those contemporary ethicists who are intent on rehabilitating the theme "virtue" are doubtless reinventing the wheel, but for an eminently practical reason: we cannot do without it.

Justice is indispensable. Bound by natural necessity to live together, human beings cannot achieve human purposes without cooperating and without the quest of social goods. Reciprocal dependence obtains between these quests as well as between the goods quested after. Individuals cannot achieve their own purposes, we say, "apart from organized society"; in the concrete this means "apart from duly contributing to and duly receiving from society," and without each rendering to his neighbor and fellow citizen what is his due. "Duly" and "due" say justice.

Courage is indispensable. Without it, justice can neither be achieved nor sustained. Without courage, the individual person cannot maintain his own quest of the good, nor can society achieve the common good: the good of order and its effective apportioning to individual persons the good appropriate to them.

Measure/temperance/self-control is indispensable. Without it, we do not have the free disposition of ourselves, whether to reach the development that allows one to find a place in society or to cooperate when such a place has been found or to operate freely on the existential level (compare with the third line listed above).

Because justice, courage, and temperance are indispensable, so is practical wisdom, for without it to define the mean that is justice, the mean that is courage, the mean that is temperance, these indispensable principles of operation could not come into being. Are we here involved in a vicious circle? Without justice, courage, and temperance/self-control, it is hardly possible to arrive at practical wisdom. No, the circle is not vicious, for feelings that respect values occur; practical insight *(phronēsis)* into the difference between real and merely apparent good occurs; good judgments occur; and right choices occur. Because they occur, one can and does plant and build. To change the figure, the subject does advance, spiral-fashion. Progress replaces routine.

A further word on practical wisdom (what the Greeks, Aristotle in particular, called *phronēsis,* what the scholastics called *prudentia*): this distinctly practical cognitive and moral habit approaches, in the context of existential intentionality (the human drive to the good), a structural analogy to the role played in purely cognitive intentionality by objectivity. The analogy is imperfect, for objectivity is a component internal to cognition, intrinsically conditioning every true judgment. Practical wisdom does not thus intrinsically condition every good act. As an acquired habit, however, it has a role to this extent comparable to objectivity: it specifies the mean of virtue in every virtue, so making habitual good acts possible. Without it a habitual attainment of the good could not happen.

This wisdom, with its hold not on the transcendentals, but on the concrete, *the way to* the transcendentals, is necessary by a necessity of means to attaining true virtue, as objectivity is necessary by a necessity of means to attaining true judgment.

Aquinas, on the distinction between the two forms of wisdom, noted:

> It is not the function of prudence (= practical wisdom) to concern itself with the highest things; that is the function of wisdom. But prudence commands in the sphere of what is ordered to wisdom, namely, in the "how to arrive" at wisdom. Therein prudence is accordingly . . . wisdom's handmaid.

Practical wisdom is the kind of wisdom that allows the human being to make his way to fulfillment in the good, to happiness. As Aquinas also says, it is the supposition of moral excellence.

Modernity as Change in the Cultural Superstructure

There is much in the discussion above—on objectivity, truth, reality, and desire of the good—that has passed intact from one cultural era to another. The so-called cardinal virtues have been a thematic constellation for millennia in Greek culture, in Jewish wisdom, in Christian moral doctrine. The survival of such themes is the more impressive in view of the radical nature of the changes undergone by civilizations and cultures from Hebrew and Greek antiquity to the present. Here we shall deal with a single epochal change: the continuous evolution of modernity from the late seventeenth century to the present. (We take "postmodernity" to be one among many contemporary efforts to give final definition to an era that has hitherto resisted fixed contour.)

Let the "social" signify a way of life, and the "cultural" the meanings and values that sustain it. Culture in this sense has an undifferentiated spontaneous dimension; at the same time there are bound to grow up more differentiated modes of consciousness that are reflective and critical. The result: a cultural superstructure peopled by men and women who make it their business to submit social meanings and values to scrutiny, evaluation, criticism. Arts and letters summon the entry of interpreters and critics onto the scene; craftsmen and artisans are supplemented (or supplanted) by scientists and technicians. Specialties proliferate: in the human sciences, philosophy, theology.

Herbert Butterfield traced the origins of modern science from 1300 to 1800. There came a moment in this history when scientific insight reached critical mass and the framework bequeathed by Aristotle to Arabic and European civilization could no longer accommodate it. This time was circa 1680, after the Renaissance and post-Renaissance astronomers and mathematicians, and on the threshold of the Newtonian high tide. Aristotelian conceptual structures—above all a metaphysics given concrete determinations by natural science and mathematics—yielded at last to an empirical physics that did not depend on metaphysical and religious underpinnings. It depended on the rule that the Royal Society would formulate: all questions are excluded from consideration that cannot be settled by the appeal to observation or experiment.

This movement of liberation belonged to the period (1680–

1715) that Paul Hazard called *la crise de la conscience européenne*. How might this change in the European cultural superstructure be summed up today?

> To put the matter summarily, necessity was a key notion for Aristotle but today it is marginal; in its place is verifiable possibility. Causality was a key notion for Aristotle, but today, in effect if not in name, it is replaced by correlation. The universal and abstract were normative in Aristotelian science, but modern science uses universals as tools in its unrelenting efforts to approximate to concrete process. Where the Aristotelian claimed certitude, the modern scientist disclaims anything more than probability. Where the Aristotelian wished to know things in their essences and properties, the modern scientist is satisfied with control and results.

The first and foundational change, then, was a change in the conception of science. Having triumphed on this battlefield, the break with Aristotle carried over into the quest of human self-knowledge. So long as the metaphysical framework stayed in place, the adepts of perennial philosophy contemplated an objective universe and understood themselves within it in terms of the same objective categories. Once the framework began to be felt as an obstacle, inquiry sought and settled on the empirical focus: concrete, contingent, and historical, the mass of data kept within generous limits of relevance. The classicist conception of man had been framed in terms of "nature": changeless form, essential, necessary, universal, normative. It abstracted from the human subject as actually acting, as conscious and intentional, as bright or stupid, virtuous or vicious, located in this rather than that historic, geographic, civilizational, social, and cultural context.

Out of these new inquiries emerged the self-orienting, self-determining "subject," transposed in the course of the present century from a cosmological to an anthropological context (what is first studied is not the universe but the human subject), and the claim to define the culture and its future hinged on how this subject was understood. The new terms of understanding in any case were concrete. Leading categories included the phenomenological, the existentialist, and the personalist.

The modern era has shown what the sciences liberated from the heavy furniture of Aristotelian structures could envisage and accomplish, and what the new view of the incarnate person, freed from every temptation to obscurantism (where system failed), could achieve as well. Lonergan understood the sources and resources, and he appreciated the elemental strength, of classicist culture; at the same time, he grasped in the light of actual developments its glaring weaknesses as well, and how they have been or might be overcome. He has provided an example of what Collingwood required of a historian who would point to "progress" from point "a" to point "b"—here, from classicist to modern, or empirical, culture. He understood both: the needs/problems that classicist culture met; the new needs/problems that it could neither grasp, sympathize with, nor meet—which led it, in time, to perish. Lastly, he understood what losses modern culture itself sustained in letting the gains of classicist culture go, and what might now be done to maintain the successes of old and new alike.

This is quite different from the critiques mounted by scholasticism. In the wake of the age of Aquinas there had been a sharp falling off from the heights. Variant forms of conceptualism presenting themselves as "Thomism" could neither sustain nor further Aquinas' achievement. Among the traits of scholasticism from the fourteenth century on was a besetting tendency to construe basic conflict in voluntarist terms. Since reality was directly and easily accessible, the deep divisions of the worlds that succeeded one another from the fourteenth-century decline through the sixteenth-century break-up to the eighteenth-century Enlightenment—their often irreconcilable perspectives and obsessions—had their roots, so the scholastics thought, mostly in bad will. Lonergan offered an alternative to the aloofness of this brooding conservatism. He understood disagreement in terms of diversity of horizons, and the projection of horizons in terms of lived intentionality. The scholastic instinct had been not to understand and come to terms with the world created by unmetaphyical science, but simply to hang on to the heritage (*depositum custodi,* 1 Tim 6:20).

The theologians, Lonergan observed, having painted themselves into a dogmatic corner, began reassuring one another about their certainties. His own alternative was a way of keeping the legacy of the past and integrating it into distinctively modern scientific and cultural achievements in accord with the motto of Leo

XIII, "To enlarge and enrich the old with the new" *(vetera novis augere et perficere).* He was able to transpose an ancient heritage to an open-ended post-Kantian context and to set it on a course of discriminating renewal and growth.

Lonergan's work went far beyond Kant, as is evident from its thoroughgoing and distinctively un-Kantian valorization of the scholastic adage, *ens per verum innotescit* (being becomes known through the true). Reality comes to light not as a known-unknown through use of a limiting concept (Kantian idealism), but through the act—and only through the act—of judgment made objective by antecedent grasp of the virtually unconditioned. Reflective intelligence thereby climaxed the discursive and laborious process of trying to find out what was true. This account of judgment brought to light a human consciousness that was simultaneously empirical, intelligent, and rational, for judgment proceeded from a reflective grasp on *evidence* that revealed a given reading of *empirical data* to be not only *intelligent,* but *reasonable.*

The critical components in the state-of-affairs defining modernity were, then, a new conception of science in rigorously and methodically empirical terms, and a new conception of the human sciences in similarly empirical terms. In the latter disciplines the data were not of nature, but of meaning, so gradually making clear and guaranteeing the centrality of history and hermeneutics. These changes, positively motivated and justified by their fruits, still contributed (quite apart from any and all deliberate efforts to secularize) to an explanation of the absence of God from modern culture. The absence of God from modern culture could not be reduced to a mean-spirited conspiracy of libertines; it was the corollary from a new conception of science as simply empirical, unsupported by metaphysics. Science, whether of nature or man, could not deal with questions that fell outside the scope of its methods (and so, in the words of Laplace, "had no need of that hypothesis," that is, of God). It could not deal with the questions that Christian classicist culture had considered the most crucial of all. There were neither any data on God nor resources for dealing with the purported data on human destiny.

For the most part, scientists themselves were aware of these limits. For the most part, therefore, they systematically refused to entertain questions that transcended the scope of empirical method (God, religion, the conduct of human life, etc.). There are certain questions, however, that, though they transcend the limits of science, do so in ambiguous fashion: for example, the question of what kind of knowledge science is. Moreover, the unparalleled prestige of scientific knowledge can mislead (and has misled) scientists and others into supposing that the limits of science and the limits of knowledge simply are coterminous; such, for example, is the logical positivist view that non-empirical statements are meaningless.

Second, there has in fact been added to the crucially defining role of science liberated from philosophy a further movement, not scientific but ideological, that would define modernity. It is the thesis of unrestricted human autonomy. The thesis took shape in conjunction with the rise of the historical consciousness and the recognition that culture is man-made. It takes its stand on a pretention to concern for the future and for the shaping of the future exclusively by autonomous human purpose. But concern for the future, Lonergan has pointed out, if it is not just "high-sounding hypocrisy," supposes rare moral attainment.

> The future will belong to those who think about it, who grasp its real possibilities, who project a coherent sequence of cumulative realizations, who speak to man's longing for achievement more wisely than the liberal apostles of automatic progress and more humanly than the liquidating Marxists.

This sets the stage for the presentation in the next chapter of the rudiments of critical realist theory of interpretation and of history, and for their confrontation, in chapter six, with alternatives, some of them clearly ideological in a negative sense.

5

Theory of Interpretation, Theory of History

We begin with a reprise of the opening description of "reading as paradigm of knowing," setting it in the context of three views of insight; second, we survey, in a critical-realist perspective, the rudiments of interpretation theory and leading elements of the theory of history.

Reading and Insight: Three Views

In the opening pages of this primer we referred to three views of reading: two extremes and a third position occupying the entire space between them. There is the view (grounded in naïve realism) that, merely by converting signs into words, the reader straightforwardly allows the already fully constituted meaning of the text to register or imprint itself on his mind. Again, there is the bolder, Nietzschean view (though our example appealed to the form it took in Northrop Frye) that reading is a creative assembling of elements within one's own resources and the projecting of this meaning onto the text—Frye's "picnic to which the writer brings the words and the reader the meaning." Finally, there is the critical-realist view that reading not only assembles elements of meaning from within one's own resources and ascribes it to the text, but does all this under the controlling guidance of textual warrants, so as (in the best-case scenario) to assemble and ascribe to the text just those meanings that the writer intended and managed to express in and through the text.

The first corresponds to the Scotist conception of understanding: an intellectual act, but oriented like eyesight to the outer world. It is, in short, extroverted intellectual intuition. In the full form of Scotist theory this is preceded by an act that, though unconscious, is inferred on metaphysical grounds: the abstracting of an "intelligible species" from a phantasm or image. The central act of intelligence follows: an intuition, intellect registering the abstracted intelligible form just as a sound eye registers the image of a colored, lighted object. This is itself followed by a third moment: the comparison of concepts to see which are compatible, which are connected by necessity, etc. This view of understanding (we focus on the second of the three operations above) we shall call the fallacy of insight as pure reception.

The second (Nietzschean) view, or Northrop Frye's picnic theory, expresses an ideal of free and creative intelligence. "Reception" of some sort is supposed but not described. The heart of the matter is the ascribing to the text of the meaning that the reader has internally assembled. It is a synthesis of what has been taken from the text with the experience, wit, tact, fancy, imagination, and will concocted by the reader. There is no way of isolating the contribution of the text (it might well be minimal) and no way of deciding whether the reading is "accurate." Maximizing its main trait, we name this view the fallacy of insight as pure projection.

The third, in-between account corresponds to the grasp of understanding that runs from Aristotle through Augustine and Aquinas to modern critical realism. When the geometer understands a circle, he grasps in the image or phantasm not only roundness, but the reason why the circle must be round. At best the phantasm presents this "reason why," this "must," concretely and imperfectly, for "reason why" intrinsically surpasses any and all images. Understanding the circle as a round plane curve determined by perfectly equal radii from a single point is new (not actually and integrally preexistent in any phantasm). Its creativity is limited, however, for the contribution of the image or phantasm is essential: it has teased intelligence into bringing this intelligent construal into being. As Aquinas put it, whenever anyone tries to understand anything, he forms images for himself *in quibus quasi inspiciat quod intelligere studet,* "in which he inspects, as it were, what he is trying to understand." Notice the *quasi.*

One does not literally see, look at, inspect a reason why. One inspects an image with a view to finding a reason why at the level of intelligent construal.

Each view has its ethos. For the fallacy of insight as pure reception, it is the scrupulous concern to see what is there to be seen and to avoid reading into the object (e.g., the text) elements supplied exclusively by one's own subjectivity. Its ethos is objectivity as flight from the subject.

For the fallacy of insight as pure projection, the richer the reserves of the subject, the better the reading. Its ethos is prodigality.

For critical realists, the richer the reserves of the subject, the better the reading, *provided that textual warrants are allowed to define it.* Its ethos is responsibility.

For sharers in the fallacy of insight as pure reception, the problem is to figure out what brazen intrusion by subjectivity might have led to a misreading. For sharers in the fallacy of insight as pure projection, there are no misreadings, only readings more or less bright, more or less rich or witty or humanly helpful. For critical realists the problem of reading is to measure up to the challenge of the text: are the horizons of the reader broad and deep enough to accommodate the meaning of the text? Has he sufficiently attended to details of the text? Has anything been overlooked, underestimated, or exaggerated? Which readings can be profitably brought together? Which can be excluded as flatly mistaken or probably inadequate?

Earlier, apropos of "reading," we raised the issue of whether texts mediate meaning to us, or we merely ascribe meaning to texts. It is evident that partisans of the fallacy of insight as pure projection ought to, and for the most part do, answer that we ascribe meaning to texts. This answer, ambiguous with respect to mistaken readings, is flatly false with respect to accurate readings. For the fact is that we sometimes understand in what we hear or read just what the speaker or writer intended us to understand—an experience that theory should not only not overlook, but should acknowledge and build on. Meaning may be "creatively" projected; it may also be and sometimes is accurately recovered. In practice, laws against plagiarism acknowledge that we do catch on to other people's meanings and that we are not allowed to pretend that our every reading is our own creation.

The tendency of the fallacy of insight as pure projection is to overlook this experience, as a banal, negligible accomplishment.

Partisans of the fallacy of insight as pure reception may seem here to be on the side of the angels. But it was their simplistic view of understanding and dull-witted underestimation of what is required to come up with an adequate reading that in the late 1970s called into being the reader-response movement, many of whose leaders promptly installed themselves in the fallacy of insight as pure projection. Moral of the story: virtue is a mean between extremes.

Theory of Interpretation

The positive human need of communication, dramatically shown in the baneful impact on individual human beings of cutting them off from communication with others, is at the root of activities such as reading and writing. There can be no doubt about the primacy of language among the resources of social intercourse.

Language, an encoding resource shared by a speech community, is both conventional and instrumental: conventional inasmuch as its ordinary meaningfulness is established by common usage, and doubly instrumental inasmuch as it is used to express meaning, and the expression of meaning itself serves ulterior human purposes. Both the classical view of language (namely, that it is the vehicle of thought) and the Leibnizian view of language (namely, that it is the determining medium of thought) are true as affirmations but false insofar as either is made to negate the other. The two are reconciled in a higher viewpoint, which permits the distinction between ordinary linguistic meaning (language as a determining medium) and original linguistic meaning (language as a vehicle of thought). "All men," said Alfred Whitehead, "enjoy flashes of insight beyond meaning already stabilized in etymology and grammar."

We should indicate what "interpretation" adds to "reading," namely, formality in response to difficulty. Interpretation is a methodically mounted effort to read a text that does not yield its sense immediately. Some texts—TV commercials, cartoon captions, and other jokes—do yield their sense immediately. Otherwise, they are failures. Clearly, not all texts require interpretation in this technical sense. Indeed, the contrary view is self-reversing.

If all texts needed interpretation, every interpretation would require its own interpretation, and so *ad infinitum*. Those that do call for interpretation pose a certain kind of difficulty, not abstract difficulties connected with understanding the referent, like those associated with Euclid or Einstein, but concrete difficulties connected with understanding the text, like those associated with Pindar, Dante, Shakespeare, Goethe, Hopkins, Rilke.

The act of interpreting is not an intuition and ordinarily does not come into being in a single flash. It is a deliberately contrived three-step procedure that consists in (1) working out an understanding of the intended sense of the text; (2) judging whether this understanding is probably accurate; and (3) stating what one regards as a probably accurate understanding of the intended sense of the text. The first two steps involve a kind of spiraling into the sense of the text through the various hermeneutic circles.

There is, first, the circle of whole and parts. "I understand the whole in virtue of understanding the parts; I understand the parts in virtue of understanding the whole." Logically, the circle is vicious; actually it is broken open by insights that, alternating between part-and-part and between parts-and-whole, mediate an ever firmer grasp of the text in its parts and as a whole.

There is, second, the circle of things and words *(Sache und Sprache)*. "I understand words by understanding the things they refer to; I understand things by understanding the words that refer to them." The first limb states a fundamental insight: "whoever does not understand the things cannot draw the sense from the words" (Luther). If I have had no independent access to what the text is about, the text is likely to be obscure to me. The second limb states how one moves through a grasp of words to a firmer grasp of things: the interpreter understands things, with the writer, by means of his words.

There has been a strenuous effort in the last two decades to rid interpretation of "the referent." This is an error deriving from a confusion between the analytic approach to language and the interpretative approach to discourse. Contrary to some criticisms of Ferdinand de Saussure, there was no need for him to involve the referent in his analysis of sign, since the analysis regarded the requirements of linguistics, not those of interpretation. A proper analysis of the object of interpretation will reveal that what is sought is unique meaning: there is, as Lonergan has put it, only one Hamlet; hence the relative pointlessness of generalization and the universal, except as contribuing to a context in which Hamlet is shown in its uniqueness. Hold on individual or intended meaning presupposes the reader's independent access to the referent (one born blind is bound to find a treatise on "color" obscure); and an appreciative hold on this meaning supposes, further, some vital, personal relationship *(Lebensverhältnis)* to the referent. The need of attention to the referent accompanies interpretation from start to finish (the relation to the referent is part and parcel of what Emerich Coreth calls "the dialectic" of *Sache und Sprache*). An exercise memorably relevant to this ascertainment was Valentine Cunningham's demonstration that even James Joyce, that grand master of intertextuality, could not be properly read without the play of referents. Obviously, attention to referents is utterly indispensable to the critique following interpretation.

A third circle is that of reader and text: "I understand the text in virtue of understanding myself; I understand myself in virtue of understanding the text." The second limb is richly empirical, for literature contributes to insight into ourselves, helping us to know what we have in common with, and what sets us apart from, given elements of the world. And the first limb? Texts that characteristically call for the deliberately mounted three-part effort we call interpretation are not texts that could as well be put in other terms, not texts in which language is severely functional to abstract meaning, as in mathematics, the natural sciences, and those modes of social science that approach the natural sciences as closely as they can. Given the nature of those texts that summon the effort of interpretation, human self-knowledge is a prerequisite of and a continuing factor in the process of interpreting.

Self-understanding is an element of one's enabling "horizon," a condition of the understanding of poems, plays, novels, and other literary, religious, philosophic, and theological texts, especially eminent texts, classics. This bears on the existential dimension of interpretation and interpretation theory. It may be that the self-understanding of the interpreter is simply inadequate vis-à-vis the text. One suspects something of the sort when told, as we are told by Walter Savage Landor, that the *Inferno* is "the most immoral and impious book that ever was written" and Dante "the great master of the disgusting." It may be that the problem of the interpreter is not met by resources such as encyclopedias, handbooks, Oxford Dictionaries of one kind or another, and that what is needed is neither information nor the solution of a problem but the cure of a blind-spot, which might be massive. The cure might lie (it often does lie) only in a conversion—religious, moral, or intellectual. The inadequate interpreter probably will be unaware of the need of conversion; so the conversion may never be forthcoming. A Ph.D. might be a union-card of sorts, but it does not guarantee that its holders are able to measure up to the texts of the New Testament in the sense that they are able to figure out what such texts mean and how they mean it, or (if others have figured it out) to catch on to what others say such texts mean.

We attempt to work out a solidly grounded understanding of the sense of the text so as to encounter text and implied author in their true selfhood. This personal contact with and response to the work is the nexus between interpretation and critique, and the most existential moment of critique is the report it offers on personal encounter. The variously enriching encounter with great literature is among the experiences that lead ordinary readers to become interpreters.

The existential is in many respects the most crucial as well as the least immediately educable dimension of interpretation. A good graduate program might supply the prospective interpreter with the linguistic, philological, literary, and historical resources for meeting the texts; what it might well fail to supply is a realistic hermeneutics, one that focuses on subjectivity, on the existential point and purpose of interpreting, which reflects the existential dimension of life in general.

This dimension, personal but not private, raises a further issue, intrinsically formidable and socio-politically delicate: the state of health of the various traditions to which interpreters find themselves heir. To begin with the fact of tradition: "The classics," says Lonergan, drawing on the riches of Gadamer's *Truth and Method,* "ground a tradition."

> They create the milieu in which they are studied and interpreted. They produce in the reader through the cultural tradition the mentality, the *Vorverständnis,* from which they will be read, studied, interpreted. Now such a tradition may be genuine, authentic, a long accumulation of insights, adjustments, reinterpretations, that repeats the original message afresh for each age. . . . On the other hand, the tradition may be inauthentic. It may consist in a watering-

down of the original message, in recasting it into terms and meanings that fit into the assumptions and convictions of those that have
dodged the issue of radical conversion. In that case a genuine interpretation will be met with incredulity. . . .

This, evidently, is a central theme for any hermeneutics that, like
critical realism, focuses on key issues of subjectivity, personal,
individual, and social.

Traditions, like horizons, are simultaneously enabling and
limiting. Since we can alter and purify both, neither is imposed
on us like a fate. Those most fruitfully responsive to tradition
are also great purifiers of tradition. Lonergan's performance as
critic of classicist culture—conceptualist, spuriously "eternal,"
normative not only within limits, but to the point of pretention—
was also a purification of Catholic tradition, since the Catholic
Church was among the last great social institutions to modify its
ties to this culture, once cultivated by all Europe and Byzantium.

The object of interpretation has been a much-confused as well
as much-disputed issue. We define it as *the intended sense of the
text*. Here the accent must be allowed to fall on "the text," for
the object of interpretation is not any sense or intention that is
extrinsic to the text; it is not (contrary to E. D. Hirsch, Jr.) what
the poet had in mind but was unable to put into words. In a text,
whether of prose or poetry, what counts is what the author both
intended and managed to express. So, to interpret a poem, go
to the poem. (Such was the advice of the New Critics, dominant
from the 1930s to the 1970s, and in this they were surely right.)
If interpretation is what you are after, do not go to the diaries,
notebooks, and letters, but to "the poem itself." The *intrinsic*
determinant of the text is what counts, and this (though the theorizing of some New Critics on this point was confused) is precisely the intended sense. As form is to matter, the two together
constituting the composite which is the living organism, so the
intended sense is to language, the two together constituting discourse (the speech or story or poem or letter).

Here we should make clear that "the intended sense" is an
inclusive term. It does not barely cover the conceptual content
yielded by even a good paraphrase, for even good paraphrases
cannot be expected to capture the "how" of the meaning. The
intended sense, however, includes *how what is meant is meant*.
This is the root and the point of hermeneutics. As Lonergan on

one occasion insisted, there is a correspondence between the act of meaning, in all its modalities, and "what is meant." "For the root of hermeneutics," he argued, "and the significance of literary forms lie precisely in the fact that the correspondence between meaning and meant is itself part of the meaning and so will vary with variations in the meaning." The intended sense, as inclusive of the how of the meaning, includes, for example, the *tone* that qualifies the meaning, the affirming of what is meant, and *the limits of the affirming* of what is affirmed.

Again, texts differ by genre. In one genre the rhythm in which what is meant is expressed may be unimportant; in another, quite important. It may be a main index to tone, or to the level of affirmation, and so forth. And what holds for rhythm holds in general for whatever enhances meaning: phanopoeia (sharp visual imagery), melopoeia (orchestration of sound), logopoeia (implied allusion to words, images, motifs, that writer and reader hold in common memory).

So, insistence on the intended sense should give no comfort at all to fundamentalists, who, all indications to the contrary notwithstanding, insist that, unless otherwise specified, texts should be read in accord with the proper sense of the words. On the contrary, the intended sense is an unknown-to-be-known. We do not know in advance whether what is intended is a proper sense, a figurative sense, a symbolic sense, or what. If the text calls for interpretation, we do not know its intended sense at one stroke or at first glance. It becomes known piecemeal, progressively, by close concentration and repeated effort. It is not turned into a known by any programmatic interpretative assumptions to which given readers are committed. It is turned into a known through the interpreter's dedicated attention to textual particulars.

It seems probable to me that the failure to keep in mind the above qualifications on "the intended sense" led, historically, to the now widespread error of supposing that intention/*mens auctoris,* etc., are not, or ought not to be, factors in interpretation. The "error" is explicable. Consider, for example, the passage where C. S. Lewis has Screwtape instruct Wormwood, "The Historical Point of View, put briefly, means that when a learned man is presented with any statement in an ancient author, the one question he never asks is whether it is true." Hans-Georg Gadamer has with great effectiveness appealed to the bond between the bracketing of the claim to truth and the act of explicitly assuming or adopting what Screwtape calls "the Historical Point of View." If you and I are not engaged in an effort to come to an understanding on something, or if our efforts to do so have failed, and we have lost the will to keep trying, the moment has arrived at which both of us adopt something akin to "the historical approach" to one another's view. When I am no longer open to what truth there might be in your view, I become "historical" about it in Screwtape's sense of the term: how, I wonder, did you get that way?

There is no doubt that Gadamer has seized on a psychological factor of hermeneutical significance. Why do some read Plato, learning nothing, whereas others read him excited by the experience of learning constantly from him? Talent is not an adequate answer. Disposition, on the other hand, might well be. Some expect to learn, are disposed to do so, and learn. Others expect to learn nothing, are disposed to learn nothing, and learn nothing. The latter, in Gadamer's view, read Plato from "the Historical Point of View."

The moral that Gadamer draws is plausible, but not the only moral that can be drawn. Here is another moral: expecting truth to be accessible is part of the interpreter's ideal "openness" to the text. Ideally, the interpreter is dealing with a text to which he finds himself "connaturally" related; that is, the interpreter's ideal should be to enter as far as possible into this connaturality with the text. In significant measure interpreters positively constitute their attitudes, expectations, and purposes. It would certainly be a vice or flaw to entertain toward the task in hand the truncated expectations of a Plato-reader who does not expect to learn from Plato.

When we speak of "the intended sense" (the object of the task of interpretation) we understand it to include tone, nuance, affirmation—in other words, the whole of textually realized intention. What must not be overlooked is that *affirmation—and so truth-claim—is integral to the intended sense* of all texts to be interpreted, be they contemporary or no. True, ancient texts may pose special problems and call for special efforts; but the age of the text should not be allowed to alter the task of interpretation.

The poem or speech or story or letter—the text that the interpreter is engaged with—belongs (as we have said above) to the category not of "language," but of "discourse"; now we add that the reason for this is precisely *the intended sense.* That a poem, even an only moderately successful poem, is not just a chunk of language is attributable to this and to nothing else. Linguists implicitly acknowledge this when, with Ferdinand de Saussure, they distinguish between *langue* (linguistic system) and *parole* (utterance, actual use or exercise of linguistic system).

We should add to Saussure's binary pair two further useful distinctions: that of E. D. Hirsch (who attributes it—so far as I can determine, mistakenly—to August Boeckh) between "sense" (the originally intended sense) and "significance" (new, added senses that accrue to a text in the course of time and tradition); and that of Gottlob Frege between "meaning" (the intelligible content of an expression) and "reference" (a relation of predicability: the meaning applies to or is predicable of such and such objects).

So far as interpreters are concerned, the study of "language" is for the sake of understanding "utterances"; the interpreter's prime concern is with "sense," though "significance" is a resource for the quest of the sense as well as an object of interest on its own; finally, the quest whether of sense or of significance breaks down into the effort to grasp "meaning" and "reference."

The so-called "intentional fallacy" defined by two New Critics (W. K. Wimsatt, Jr., and Monroe D. Beardsley) by way of opposition to the approach to literature through biography and other factors extrinsic to literary texts, is thus a misnomer. It is perfectly true that the object of interpretation is not the intention of the writer as in the writer, in other words, as extrinsic to the text. But the definers of the so-called intentional fallacy overlooked the far more basic issue of intention precisely as *intrinsic to the text.* The discussion that followed explored every available or imaginable cul-de-sac. Partly the problem lay in conceiving intention only in terms of extrinsic causality (the writer as efficient cause, bringing the poem into being—a topic of no further interest to interpretation once the poem is born). Many New Critics, on the other hand, simply in virtue of their conceiving the object of interpretation as "the form" of the poem or play, thereby achieved the grasp of intended sense (without the distractions that "intention" seemed to them inevitably to entail). Does this prove the superfluousness of our thematizing "the intended sense"? The best answer, perhaps, is to experiment with a counterquestion: is "the implied author" (that voice that inhabits and speaks through the whole work) a serviceable or a superfluous hermeneutical component? Whoever chooses the former option should ask himself "why?" He may find himself surprised to discover that, in answering, he has *eo ipso* found the rationale of insistence also on the intended sense.

There are distractions that derive from mistaken theory and they are indeed irrelevant, but the intended sense is not among them. The confusion unhappily bequeathed to literary students and scholars by the failure of New Critics to differentiate between the relevant and the irrelevant sense of "intention" has hung on for forty years like an unshakable neurosis. From Gadamer's dismissal of the *mens auctoris* as alien to interpretation to the vagaries of recent and current literary theorizing, it has been a peculiarly resistant confusion, enough to baffle interpreters and theorists alike. (One recent and successful effort to state the matter clearly and justly is that of Meir Sternberg, in *The Poetics of Biblical Narrative*.)

It does not follow from the foregoing that the intended sense is a priori deeper or truer or more interesting or humanly more significant than senses that accrue to the text in the course of its journey through time. The original mythological text from Ugarit (Father 'El and Ba'l the storm-god) on which the scene in Daniel 7 is based is not necessarily superior to Daniel 7 (God and Michael, angelic champion of Israel); Daniel 7 is not in every respect superior to the Son-of-Man traditions in Matthew 25 or Luke 17 and 22. What does follow is the need to differentiate these senses so as to do justice respectively to the text, to the history of its impact and transformations, and to the ties—be they slight, fragile, fortuitous or firm, intrinsic, and intricate—among them. This capacity to differentiate, incidentally, is new: it is among the achievements emergent in modern philologically and historically guided interpretation, which could not come into being prior to the rise of the historical consciousness with its many new instrumental resources.

We now turn aside for a moment from interpretation, which focuses on intended meaning, to other forms of construing texts. They are extremely various and sometimes highly specialized. The parent of a kidnapped child reads the ransom note for its intended sense. The police detective reads it for what it might unintentionally reveal of the sender. The first reading is interpretative; the second, analytic. Again, when a social historian of antiquity reads an encomium, his first reading is interpretative: he wants to catch the intended sense. His second reading is analytic: he wants to know what the encomium reveals, intentionally and unintentionally, of the world of the encomiast, the positive meanings and values as well as the limits, biases, and illusions shared by the encomiast, his subject, and his audience. Much is revealed intentionally, and even more is revealed without being intended *(praeter intentionem)* or contrary to intention *(contra intentionem)*.

The important point is that interpretative reading is primary and indispensable. It is only by rightly understanding the ransom note as a ransom note that there is any point in examining the ransom note for what it might unintentionally reveal of its sender. It is only through understanding the encomium on its own terms and in accord with its intended sense that the social historian can use it as a resource for reconstructing the semantic network, the horizons and field of vision, the social world of the encomium.

Of the extremely various kinds of analytic reading, some are prior to and for the sake of interpretation (e.g., text-critical analysis, designed to determine exactly what was originally written; linguistic analysis of dialect or idiolect; literary analysis of form or genre). Other modes of analysis (like the social historian's analysis of the encomium) suppose interpretation. Unless the interpretation is right, analysis of this kind is almost bound to be wrong. Many years ago Cleanth Brooks and Robert Penn Warren, in an early, now out-of-print edition of their *Understanding Poetry,* suggested a fascinating interpretation of Robert Herrick's "Horatian Ode Upon Cromwell's Return from Ireland." It is clear that any use of the ode to establish a historical thesis on sentiments of support for Cromwell in any group of which Herrick was a part would first have to decide how to settle the subtlest matters of tone in the ode. Clearly, then, interpretation enjoys an unqualified primacy over the kinds of analysis that follow and depend on it.

There are still other forms and styles of reading, all not only legitimate, but more or less indispensable to the life of literature. There is, for example, ascription, in other words, the tricky business of ascribing new meaning to old texts; there is a rich variety of modes from parody to ideology critique. Finally, there is a further issue raised by Lonergan's extension of explanatory science to the task of interpretation. Interpreters usually know that those for whom they are working out an interpretation have no difficulty in grasping X (a particular part or aspect of the sense of the text) but great difficulty in grasping Y. The particulars will differ for a different audience having different resources. What Lonergan calls "scientific" or "explanatory interpretation" does not deal with parts or aspects of the text in relation to a particular audience; it deals with them in their relation to each other and to the totality of meanings. This kind of interpretation represents a real possibility and has a variety of uses. But it also supposes a readership (not that of a primer) which is already technically prepared by the mapping of the whole of intentionality, to profit from it. We shall accordingly not deal with it here, but shall simply refer the reader to a brief account in the Glossary under the heading "Comprehensive (or Universal) Viewpoint."

There is at present a very powerful tendency in New Testament studies to prefer analysis to interpretation. We noted above that analysis either precedes and prepares for interpretation, or follows and depends on it. Both kinds of analysis are indispensable. What we do *not* need (and often get) is *substitution of analysis for interpretation*. This has especially characterized the work of psychological and social-scientific interpreters and structuralists. For example, a psychological reading or analysis of myth material in the early part of Genesis may greatly enrich the interpretation of these chapters; but, however fascinating, it is no substitute for an interpretation. What holds for psychological readings holds also for social-scientific, historical, and even theological readings, regardless of their merit otherwise. No such reading substitutes for interpretation. Reading/interpreting, precisely because it has its own integrity, allows others to address us in and through the text, and so differentiates itself from every use of the text as occasion and stimulus for reflection independent of intended meaning, even the most charged with this or that kind of wisdom.

A brief word on analytic work of the first kind (that which prepares the way for interpretation): it cannot so much as get started without some provisional, preliminary construal of the text. Form critical studies are of this kind. But the preliminary reading is quite consciously provisional; it is held in brackets, revised, tested, while the form critic persues his specialized, technical analysis of how various stereotypical elements work together. Hans-Joachim Held's study of the miracle stories in Matthew can serve as a model of how to do this kind of analysis.

Take another sort of analytic work that is essentially prior to interpretation (though the analyst, once again, is constantly dealing with interpretations along the way): the effort to figure out how, when, where, why, and under whose auspices the orally transmitted stories analyzed by the form critic took shape. This is a topic about which the texts themselves are, for the most part, silent. Still, Luke 1:1-4 offers a set of clues. The question is: how are we first of all to interpret this intriguing Lukan text, and then to analyze it historically? Much depends on the analysis. Is Birger Gerhardsson (or those who offer variants on his theory) right on the interpretation and analysis of the Lukan text? The analysis must range far beyond the text itself. It is a challenge of enormous proportions, with many aspects, and a significance for later literary and historical work that can hardly be exaggerated.

By and large, we place history after interpretation. Nevertheless, as the name "historical-critical interpretation" is enough to indicate, historical ascertainments of many kinds also come before interpretation, and are among the interpreter's resources.

In accord with what is said above about the difference between "reading" and "interpretation," a final word on interpretation in the concrete. "A Dante interpreter" is not a mere reader of Dante. He has read not just the *Commedia,* but all of Dante, many times. He has lived with the texts that he undertakes to interpret. He knows many by heart, has read them in sundry editions and several languages. A medievalist entirely at home in his Latin Bible, in medieval history and literature, he is an adept of Bernard, of the Lombard, the Schoolmen, and Aquinas. He is equally a *Sachkenner* of the ancient world, the Latins in particular, Ovid and Virgil above all. He can talk Dante with anyone from fellow Dante interpreters to school children. He has "encountered" Dante at the existential level of interpretation, and the encounter has subtly dissipated his biases and transformed his critique. He knows Dante in his vices and limits; it is the knowledge that spouses have of one another, having passed through enchantment to disenchantment to re-enchantment, deeper, stronger, less illusory.

Theory of History

Among the modes of analysis that follow interpretation we must accord pride of place to history. "Analysis" by no means covers the whole of the proper activity of historians, but for our purposes, we distinguish it from interpretation in token of several analytic traits. The goal that the interpreter has laboriously arrived at—a probably accurate statement of the intended sense of the text—is a mere starting point for history. Many interpreters go from interpretation to critique: they deal with issues of art and artistic orchestration of resources, with truth, with social significance, and the like. Nevertheless, interpretation is itself an integral act. Though interpreters may go on to critique or evaluation, they are satisfied, as interpreters, with settling on what the writer means (and the level at which he means it). The historian is not.

To dramatize this, the historian understands the intended sense, but he is not a believer in testimonies. He is an analytic examiner of testimonies, intent on finding data possibly relevant to the questions that he, the historian, has framed entirely on his own. He is not, then, a mere analyst of "early sources" (despite the contrary practice that mulishly hangs on among many biblical scholars), but a questioner of all sources. Later sources may serve his purposes as well as, or better than, earlier sources. So, he is no mere "historically inclined" interpreter.

A better and closer model for (at least the Rankean type of) historian is the detective. Detective stories, as Collingwood brilliantly showed by his own example of the genre in the course of presenting his theory of history, can serve as excellent models of some aspects of historical thinking. Without good interpretation— that is, without a grasp of the virtually unconditioned (= sufficient evidence supporting a hypothesis that answers an interpretative question) to lay a viable groundwork—good history is impossible. And of course by "good history" we mean, once again, grasp of the virtually unconditioned (= sufficient evidence supporting some hypothesis that answers a historical question).

It is possible to practice a kind of preliminary criticism of data, by directly interrogating relatively isolated data on their probable antecedent claims to historicity. Numerous patterns of inference thus come into play. They are often misleadingly called "criteria of historicity," despite the fact that there is no single pattern or combination of patterns invariably requisite to passing a solidly probable judgment of historicity on some datum or data. These patterns are more modestly and far more accurately named "indices to the historicity of data." With particular reference to gospel research and historical-Jesus research, these indices include: *discontinuity* with the tendencies and practices of the transmitting Church; *originality* vis-à-vis Judaism; *multiple and multiform attestation* (e.g., datum attested in more than one of the quasi-independent streams of tradition, or attested in both sayings and narrative form); *irreducibly personal idiom* (Jesus' distinctive use of words, idiom, turns of phrase, images, stylistic devices, etc.). Of these indices it should be noted that attestation (whether multiple or multiform, or both together) is not enough to warrant a solidly probable judgment of historicity; that irreducibly personal idiom does not by itself secure the particular saying in which it occurs; that whereas discontinuity regularly, and originality in many cases, might well secure historicity of data on their own, the proper procedure is to look for convergent and cumulative evidence. It is here that all the indices are relevant. In general one learns from the masters. On personal idiom, for instance, the masters have been Dalman and his successors, among whom Joachim Jeremias has so far proven to be "easily first" *(facile princeps)*.

Historically nuanced judgments on the data in general are at least as significant as particular considerations of isolated data. If the classical form-critical views on the origin of the stories and sayings of Jesus are solidly reliable, the best indices will have to be applied in gingerly fashion, tending to reduce rather sharply the pool of usable data. If, on the contrary, the original form critics' views on the origin of Synoptic materials are ill-grounded (as the present writer holds), and if alternative views (those expressed, for example, in the opening hundred pages of Rainer Riesner, *Jesus als Lehrer*) are much better grounded, the indices to historicity will be usable and important.

Historical-Jesus research involves not only critical history, but the capacity to distinguish between its applicability to our grasp of context and its non-applicability to the mentality of specific figures within that context, for example, Jesus. It is amazing how often this fundamental discrimination is violated. Apropos of the sense of Old Testament texts on the pilgrimage of the nations,

Jeremias well observed that a true view of how Jesus read these texts "can only be arrived at by ignoring all the questions and conclusions of modern historical and literary criticism of the Old Testament, for such questions did not exist for Jesus." (Similarly, no ancient Jews disposed of modern hermeneutics; for us, their various hermeneutics are so many unknowns-to-be-known.)

Again, it has often been rightly observed that the estimate of data is likely to find revisions and refinements in the course of actual historical investigation. Historians who settle the critique of data prior to and independent of an actual inquiry and follow this by a new effort of correlation (likely to yield at best an extremely modest reconstruction) betray either a singular lack of ambition or, more probably, an inadequate theory of history. The same holds for those who think of history as limited to settling matters of pedestrian fact. Such were the many critics who, apropos of the "new quest of the historical Jesus," felt betrayed by their fellow-existentialists. Bultmann wavered, but soon took his place among them, warning that we could not know whether Jesus in the last hours had "suffered a collapse" (and in the end was dragged kicking and screaming to the cross). This line, as Marjorie Chambers pointed out, drawing quite effectively on philosophic resources of a limited kind, might and ought to have been modified by reference to voice, presence, character, etc., of the *dramatis personae,* chiefly Jesus himself.

The prejudicial limitation of history to pedestrian fact, not uncommon among continental scholars writing in the first half of our century, was bound up with a marked recoil from the "psychologizing" of the nineteenth-century liberals. But the "baby" of human subjectivity is not the "bath-water" of groundless psychological conjecture. A service rendered by the Bultmannian "new quest" was to weaken and qualify both prejudices.

What the style of pedestrian-fact-oriented history can and does do in New Testament scholarship is not utterly valueless, but it is very schematic, akin to the phenomenon disparaged above, in other words, the reduction of the historian's task to examination of "the earliest sources"; and, like that reduction, it is a holdover from positivism. Good exegetes can be very bad hermeneuts. This is certainly true of those who—keenly conscious of adopting a stance of "rigorous standards"—are always warning us of the limits of history, of how it cannot do this or that, cannot deal with the inner secret of human intentions, and so must leave us outsiders to everything of interest and everything that counts. How dull. And how haplessly ignorant.

Real historians are not crippled by such inhibitions. First, they frame their own questions as strategically as they can; second, they work by hypothesis; third, they make the sustained effort to verify their hypotheses. In the process they go well beyond the criticism of isolated data. They ground the probable historicity of both data and "facts" (in the Collingwoodian sense: historically verified answers to questions; in other words, hypotheses verified as solidly probable). So, whereas unambitious history practices scissors-and-paste reconstruction, real history involves what Johann Gustav Droysen called the process of *forschend verstehen,* coming to understand as the process of inquiry continues, and thus, for example, changing the status of data in accord with their role in hypotheses verified as historically probable.

Historical thinking and historical knowing are dynamic; the thinking comes into being precisely as inquiry—with its "cool ecstasy" of growing insight. The "knowledge" comes of verifying the thinking. It just will not do, therefore, to survey in advance the mass of data, freeze-dry, package and label it, merrily go on to so-called reconstruction without further worry about historicity, and call the whole "critical." Or even an advance in method!

If ever the theme of "horizon" is relevant to inquiry, it is exceedingly relevant to historical inquiry. Positivists are, no doubt, the worst offenders, but not the only ones who think they can get along without reference to "horizon" and horizon analysis. Horizons make a difference. Consider epistemological horizons.

> Empiricism, idealism, and realism name three totally different horizons with no common identical objects. An idealist never means what an empiricist means, and a realist never means what either of them means. . . . What are historical facts? For the empiricist they are what was out there and was capable of being looked at. For the idealist they are mental constructions carefully based on data recorded in documents. For the critical realist they are events in the world mediated by true acts of meaning.

There are phases and kinds of history. To begin with the phases "historical interpretation," though the term is used quite legitimately in many different ways, may be taken to designate the effort to answer the question of what historical *dramatis personae* were after, what their goals were. This effort, to be sure, has a certain completeness in itself; but since it leaves open a major further question, it may be taken to be a first phase of historical inquiry. The question left open is answered by "historical explanation": the effort to explain why what happened happened, and why it happened in the way it did.

This way of using "interpretation" and "explanation" seems quite satisfactory. Historical interpretation, as the quest of purposes informing actions, corresponds to what Collingwood called seeking "the inside of the event," the meaning that charges it and makes it a specifically human action. There are, of course, other good uses of the term. Droysen, in an effort to break the positivist philological prejudice in favor of modelling history on textual criticism, proposed in its place the modelling of history on the understanding of textual meaning. Under "interpretation" he accordingly included not only the effort to discern the aims of historic figures, but to grasp the interconnections of events, their dependence on the situation that was their point of departure, as well as the realization of purposes and ideas that resulted.

If, however, we stay with our own initial distinction between interpretation and explanation, we can illustrate the difference between them by the inquiry into the aims of those involved in a revolution (interpretation) and the inquiry into the revolution itself. A revolution might well fail to correspond to what anyone intended.

> It is certainly not what the old regime intended and it may be only more or less, if at all, what the revolutionaries planned. Historians inquire not only into the intentions of all concerned but into the unpredictable interaction of these intentions and so into "the meaning of the revolution." Since the revolution is not a subject of intending acts, its "meaning" lies in the interaction of the totality of intentions and in the impact of this interaction: the changes wrought in the field of social possibilities, the new situation with its new set of orientations.

Historical explanation answers the question of why this went forward and that did not, and why this went forward in the way it did.

If interpretation and explanation serve to distinguish phases of history, fact and value may distinguish different kinds. There are historians whose resources orient them toward Ranke's ideal of rediscovering "how it actually was/happened"; and there are those whose interests orient them toward Burckhardt's ideal of history as a revelation of values. We should distinguish the latter kind of history, which is just as demanding as, indeed is more demanding than, the Rankean type, from the pre-critical history with which it shares a keen interest in values.

Pre-critical history may serve in a citizenship booklet to exalt and enhance American or Canadian or Swiss values by recounting the national history in a way that serves the national interest. This kind of history is neither false nor spurious.

> It is *artistic:* it selects, orders, describes; it would awaken the reader's interest and sustain it; it would persuade and convince. Again, it is *ethical:* it not only narrates but also apportions praise and blame. It is *explanatory:* it accounts for existing institutions by telling of their origins and development and by contrasting them with alternative institutions in other lands. It is *apologetic,* correcting false or tendentious accounts of the people's past, and refuting the calumnies of neighboring peoples. Finally, it is *prophetic:* to hindsight about the past there is joined foresight on the future. . . .

Obviously, this kind of history may be well or badly done. Even when it is done with self-restraint and respect for data and facts, it is distinct from the evaluational history which regards the past from a normative standpoint and pronounces on the legitimacy and illegitimacy of developments. Here just as much as in Rankean history, anachronism and archaism are among the possible illusions of the historian. Anachronists find the seeds of all welcome developments in the indefinitely early past; archaists regard as corruption any development not unequivocally discernible from the beginning.

The nineteenth-century theorists who worked so hard to place history in the ranks of authentic and distinctive disciplines were especially intent on the differences between history and science. Both are methodical inquiries, but not only do the methods differ, the way the methods impinge on the subject, or subjective pole of the inquiry, differs. Why? Because the growth and development of historical understanding do not admit systematic objectification as do mathematics or physics. But it is only in our time—most clearly and unequivocally in Lonergan—that history is recognized as a sophisticated extension of the understanding that grows in and by day-to-day living, an extension of common sense. The historian does not start from some set of postulates, but from the sum-total of himself and his horizons.

> The more intelligent and the more cultivated he is, the broader his experience, the more open he is to all human values, the more competent and rigorous his training, the greater is his capacity to discover the past. When an investigation is succeeding, his insights are so numerous, their coalescence so spontaneous, the manner in which they complement or qualify or correct one another is so immediate and so deft, that the historian can objectify, not every twist and turn in the genesis of his discovery, but only the broad lines of the picture at which eventually he arrives.

We thus conclude not to relativism, which has lost hope of the attainment of truth, but to "perspectivism," which stresses the complexity of history and the approximate and reformable character of the knowledge of even the most exigent historian. He can work toward perspectives that take account of many angles of vision, but in the phrase adopted above, he is limited to recovering "broad lines."

The scientist can be a fool without the embarrassment of his folly showing up in his science. The historian has no such protection. There is, however, a flip side: scientific achievement is not calculated to make the scientist a wise man, whereas the impact of sustained historical insight tends to make the historian wise. (Such generalizations are not guarantees; contemporary historians have exhibited spectacular lapses by their forays into journalism, on Hitler's "diaries," for example; fine work on the seventeenth-century scene is not proof against talking nonsense on Stalin.)

The historian operates in the light of his whole personal development. Naïve realists are most likely to overlook this, for they above all habitually overlook the fact of horizons. Hence the utter improbability of the recent proposal for arriving at the kind of history of Jesus, objectively ascertained, that "all reasonable people" may embrace, by the device of locking up four informed and honest historians—a Catholic, a Protestant, a Jew, an agnostic—until they come up with a consensus view of "the historical Jesus." This, first, is a return to the pre-Droysen, textual-criticism model for history; indeed, it is not far from how the

Nestle text of the Greek New Testament took shape, in other words, by following wherever two out of three critical texts led. Second, it betrays a simplistic supposition—the counterpart in history of the Principle of the Empty Head—that objectivity is arrived at through the subtraction of subjectivity. This is at an opposite pole to critical-realist theory: objectivity is the fruit of authentic subjectivity. Third, it rejects, without adverting to, the fact that historians operate in the light of their whole personal development. Let us say that miracles, messiahship, and "resurrection" are grasped in their implications by all four arbiters. If these are actually realized in the history of Jesus, the reduction of Christianity to a mere one among several models of salvation is flatly ruled out. Then will not the Jew and the agnostic determine how to deal with the historical evidence of Jesus' self-understanding, actual mission, and fate? Are "all reasonable people" expected to go along with this?

Before we take up in swift succession salient hermeneutical issues relative to history, we offer here a comment on historians' presuppositions and on the open-endedness of historical knowledge to ulterior goals. As already noted, the critical a priori of history is the historian himself; his horizons, preferences, tastes; the sum of his life history. Histories differ partly in token of the object of inquiry: the boundless complexity of events and their openness to a very wide variety of questions. But they also differ in token of the diverse horizons of the historians. Now, horizons are established, grow, and contract in accord with the life-history of the inquirer. Historians may or may not have reached clearly articulated views of knowledge and reality. They will surely have had diverse life-experiences. They will have operated in several patterns of human experience and so will exhibit consciousnesses diversely differentiated, which may or may not include literary competence, social sophistication, the scientific spirit, or flair for philosophic reflection. Historians differ in intelligence, in imagination and temperament; in their curiosity and alertness, their personal interests, tastes, sympathies; in how habitually exigent they are with respect to evidence and, in general, in the sum of their virtues and vices, intellectual and moral.

The object of historical inquiry is to produce a narrative that interprets and explains the past. But the object of the narrative itself is knowledge, even wisdom. For such narratives tell us, the readers, as well as the historian himself, what man has done, and therefore what man can do; what man is and what he might be; what I am and what I might be. History, in a word, mediates the encounter with possibilities of human existence. There are, no doubt, further values that attach to historical achievement; given any value, historical interpretation and explanation are proximate and open goals. Positivists may argue otherwise, but not with real coherence. The motives, values, uses, and ulterior purposes of history, be it ever so critical, are metacritical factors. They are not generated by method. They arise from the historian's moral being and in the end they account more fundamentally and adequately than anything else for the kind of history he produces.

Salient Hermeneutical Issues

Do historians have philosophic commitments? Do they work by analogy? Do they employ ideal-types? Do they serve social and cultural goals? Are they detached from bias, and is their work value-free? Do they truly know, or merely believe? Here we present Lonergan's handling of these questions.

First, when "philosophy" is used to refer to that part of philosophy that deals directly with history, the answer to the first question is yes, for the methodical tasks of history relate, as particular to general, to "transcendental" or "generalized empirical" method. This "transcendental method" is, first of all, the implicitly or immanently normative way in which human knowers know. It is how, in his conscious intentionality, the human subject operates, namely, on four levels: empirical, intelligent, reasonable, responsible. Central to these operations is the notion or drive to being-as-true (intentionality as cognitive) and being-as-good (intentionality as existential). "Transcendental method" is, secondarily, the objectification of this intentionality in the spontaneous mode. Intellectual, moral, and religious conversion thus merely objectify—and so, radically accord with—human intentionality in its spontaneous, self-assembling, immanently normative dynamism. Historians may or may not be aware of this relation of historical method to transcendental method. If they are, so much the better; they can profit from bringing their work into more fully conscious conformity with their own immanent norms. If they are not, then they are like M. Jourdain, who exclaimed, "What? When I say 'Nicole, bring me my slippers and give me my nightcap,' that's *prose?*"

Second, do historians work by analogy with the present? They do, clearly; but "analogy" is a weasel-word. That is analogous which is simply different and in some respects the same. The past is to be assumed to be analogous (in the sense of similar) to the present except insofar as there is evidence of dissimilarity. How well do we, historians or not, know our own age? In general, less well in terms of rounded knowledge than historians will know it in a generation or two. Besides, much in the past is settled beyond reasonable doubt, even though it falls outside the personal and collective experience of today's historians. New Testament scholars in particular should know, apropos, for example, of miracles, their possibility, etc., first, that there is a radically new state of the question for scientific laws of the classical type, and second, that Ernst Troeltsch's "all-levelling" rule of analogy, "the uniformity in principle of all historical happening," is a dogmatic piece of relativism expressing a philosophic inadequacy.

> Finally, while each historian has to work on the analogy of what he knows of the present and has learned of the past, still the dialectical confrontation of contradictory histories needs a basis that is generally accessible. The basis we would offer would be transcendental method extended into the methods of theology and history by constructs derived from transcendental method itself.

Third, do historians employ ideal-types? Good historians, who grasp the limits of ideal-types, do use them, and effectively. But the limits are severe. Ideal-types are not historical descriptions, but theoretical constructs. Loose and general ideal-types do not generate much explanatory power, whereas the more detailed and promising they are devised to be, the less applicable they are, and the more subject to diminishing returns.

Fourth, do historians serve social goals? Are they free of bias and is their work "value-free"? They may well work in the service of social causes in a broad, remote sense (as proposed above, where history is open to ulterior, metacritical goals) without being liable to the objection of writing propaganda. But social and cultural causes should not be their direct and immediate concern. For the social or cultural cause would thereby cut into the properly historical task (e.g., the establishing of historical fact) and occasion the risk of corrupting the historical project. Theology may have this kind of corrupting influence; so may the social sciences; so may the ends of interfaith dialogue; so may a secularizing philosophy. In fact, we have no lack of examples of all these.

Detachment from bias is of the highest importance, far more for historians than for mathematicians and scientists. Bias, no doubt, pertains to the human condition: the bias of unconscious motivation (brought to light by depth-psychology), the bias of individual egoism, the still blinder bias of group egoism, and the general bias of common sense, which takes itself and its own limited practicality to be omnicompetent. It is blind to long-term consequences and instinctively suspicious of all theory. This fourfold challenge is met radically by conversion, intellectual, moral, and religious. Lonergan's formula is "a continuous and ever more exacting application of the transcendental precepts. Be attentive, Be intelligent, Be reasonable, Be responsible."

Is history value-free? Yes, in the sense that it is not directly and immediately concerned to promote social and cultural causes. These causes are incarnated values subject to bias and all its distortions. If they are allowed to affect historical inquiry directly, they will undermine the investigation. Insofar as the historian attempts to settle matters of fact, history is, in a sense, value-free. Value judgments, however, can be pressed into the service of empirical inquiry.

> Finally, history is not value-free in the sense that the historian refrains from all value-judgments. . . . The historian ascertains matters of fact, not by ignoring data, by failing to understand, by omitting judgments of value, but by doing all of these for the purpose of settling matters of fact.

Without value-judgments, the Rankean style of history would not be equipped to fix on worthwhile questions. Such value-judgments allow history to be (in Friedrich Meinecke's words) "the content, the wisdom, and the sign-posts of our lives." Moreover, the Burckhardtian style of history is not only not value-free; it is positively value-charged. The intrusion of subjectivity so feared by nineteenth-century positivism is realized not by the historian's exercise of value-judgments as such, but by false value-judgments, such as those dominant in ideologically-driven history. This may include Marxist history, Nietzschean history, old historicism (in the manner of anti-philosophical "scientific" historians), new historicism (the style commended in the works of Michel Foucault), and pre-critical, apologetic rah-rah nationalism, partisan religious history, and the world of uncritical commitment to "tradition" that J. H. Plumb called "the past" in *The Death of the Past*. But there are true value-judgments as well as false value-judgments; in Lonergan's view they are the achievement of a moral objectivity or self-transcendence. They are by no means antithetical to or subversive of true judgments of fact and the cognitive objectivity that made them possible; rather, as the product of moral self-transcendence, they presuppose and complete true judgments of fact.

Our last question is whether historians believe. One aspect of the question is already settled: historians regularly meet testimonies not to compile those they believe and drop in the waste-basket those they do not, but to see how the mass of testimonies (even if all of them should be false) might serve to answer their analytic questions and to contribute to critical reconstruction. But it would be utterly unrealistic to suppose that historians can get along exclusively on the basis of critically generated and personally controlled ascertainments. They depend on others and cannot do without "suppositions under remote control." There is belief and belief. When Dalman and his succesors tell me that a given form is rare but attested, I have reason to believe them. As belief is part of all collaboration (not just philology, but physics, biochemistry, and statistics), and all networks of collaboration, so belief is a factor for historians who depend on other historians. No one can share in the work of historical collaboration and maintain the Enlightenment fiction that he lives without belief.

6

Alienation and Illusion

There are a thousand auspicious avenues to cognitive and affective engagement with the real. This is what allows us to know the real as a deep, rich order of persons and things, and to make realism connote heights, depths, variety, plenty, access to a luxuriant, yet finally coherent, order. Our inner drive is to the real in its concrete totality. Historical—individual and social—grasp of the real, however, is limited, and this allows realism itself to change from era to era and generation to generation.

"Realist" should hardly connote recoil from the marvellous; Aquinas, following Aristotle, took the marvellous to be the common object of philosophy and poetry. Applying to literature the view of realism that we have been dealing with in this primer, we can illustrate the connotations of realism by non-reductionist writers.

Evelyn Waugh's great gifts included an eye for the hilariously incongruous at the heart of modern chaos. Recoil and disgust did not quell, but whetted his curiosity and added to his vision of a world out of joint. From *Decline and Fall* to the great *Sword of Honour* trilogy, Waugh's enduring fictions make up, in the mode of a fierce and idiosyncratic social and religious conservatism, a monument to social, cultural, moral realism. Not that Waugh had any interest in the philosophy of critical realism. But his vision of things was discriminating and (in our sense) realist. So critical realism warrants celebration of the Waughvian "vision" and the brilliance of the books that embody it. The same realism stands, to be sure, in a comparable relation to Waugh's variously opposite numbers: Cocteau or Claudel, Orwell or O'Faoláin, Solzhenitsyn or Silone or Lowell or Larkin or Walker or Wilbur. . . .

There is no critical-realist hermeneutical bias favoring any particular manner. What realism favors is the inventiveness and precision of response to the real: wonder, wit, and imagination, insight and judgment, decision and love responding to infinitely angled, densely layered orders of being. Critical realism is as connatural with fiction as with fact, has no preference for sobriety over gaity, stays alert to the common nonsense in the slogans of common sense, and while cherishing Western civilization, privileges no particular culture as normative. It celebrates the whole world of the true and real, what is good, beautiful, perfect.

Here, however, we shall take up programs and projects that, we shall argue, are to some degree or other out of touch with the real order. The task is a challenge to discernment. At this point our resources include a hold on intentionality, its objectification in transcendental (or generalized empirical) method as well as in the epistemology of critical realism; with a hold, in particular, on the existential level of intentionality; and with a basic grasp of how this realism finds expression in methods of interpretation and historiography.

The stamp of twentieth-century critical realism lies in its alertness to the strategies and devices of the flight from understanding. Lonergan was convinced that to disregard any place of refuge for this flight was to invite a prompt counteroffensive from the base thus left intact. His keen interest in the analytic account of intentionality was accordingly matched by an equally keen interest in dialectic. He recognized that the empirical-scientific culture dominant since the nineteenth century all too casually dismissed the *normative* significance of the self-assembling structures of intentionality, so burdening itself with a radically uncritical mentality. Hence the open invitation of the nineteenth-century scene to a festival of fads and ideological movements. Kierkegaard, who long in advance of its apogee intuited its power, called it "the howling madness of the higher lunacy."

Since resources for meeting it head-on were not ready at hand, one generation after another witnessed the realization of a grim prospect: that Europe should install itself in illusion and folly. In such limited spheres as science and technology an illusion-free realism could claim ascendancy. By contrast the new chase after empire and imperial wealth flowered in two World Wars. The price of illusion was high. We are better equipped today, however, than we were a hundred years ago for the examination of the sources of illusion, notably including ideologies. We shall begin not with hermeneutic particulars, but with introductory reflections on ideology.

Ideology: Nietzsche, the Modernist and Postmodernist Impasse

"Ideology" has numerous senses. Here it is used in a markedly negative sense: the rationalization of alienation. We begin with the central factor in the rise of nineteenth-century ideologies, that is, the secularization of Europe and the cresting of atheist humanism. Nietzsche caught, as few if any others of his time did, what it meant to have done what a mass of Europeans in the years 1830–1870 had done, namely, dropped further worry over God and religion. He applauded the apostasy, reconceptualized it as the "death of God," and undertook to work out a personal view of its implications. Like Kant, who wrote a critique not of pure reason, but of Scotist reason, Nietzsche repudiated the Scotist scheme of "being and God" as mediated to his time via Renaissance scholasticism, Gottfried Wilhelm Leibniz (1646–1716), and Christian Wolff (1679–1754). Nietzsche dealt with "being" in different ways at different times, sometimes as the Parmenidean rejection of becoming and motion (= "life"), more often as the Scotist "reality" added "lyingly" to the-already-out-there-now. With Scotus he posited the concept of reality as *least in comprehension* or content, *most in extension* or predicability. So "being" is least in content. But God is Being. Therefore God is "the last fumes of evaporating reality." The "last, thinnest, emptiest" becomes "the first," in other words, *ens realissimum*. Once the real world is banished, the apparent world can be banished, too. Both are the-already-out-there-now, waiting to be replaced by something better.

Nietzsche is a model ideologue—precocious and passionate, an angry, ill-balanced loner—but he stands out from the pack by the sheer brilliance of his *aperçus* and language. Endowed with a flair for subsurface connections and strategies, he grasped more clearly than his contemporaries the foundational status of the cognitive drive to the real, and did his utmost to undercut it. With admirable clairvoyance he saw that if the spontaneous drive to know were not challenged and discredited, his own attack on objectivity and truth, on accuracy in interpretation and history, on the goundedness of the philosophy of being, would lack plausibility. Reading could not be reduced to the creative importation of meaning to the text being read. But that was among the defenses erected by his ideological rhetoric. "Reason" in anything having to do with language was "a deceitful old woman."

Philosophers before, contemporary with, and after Nietzsche were ready to insist on the impossibility of extracting an "ought" from an "is." Nietzsche added to the dissociation of "ought" from human intentionality a new *tone:* brightness, cheer, gaity, serenity *(Heiterkeit).* The tone at times had a familiar ring. It was a little like Luther's style: the Lord says thou shalt not covet thy neighbor's wife, and some wily Transalpine theologian says this means only, thou shalt not do so *voluntarie* (voluntarily).

> Let us consider what naïvety it is to say "man *ought* not to be thus and thus!" Reality shows us an enchanting wealth of types . . . and does some pitiful journeyman moralist say at the sight of it: "No! man ought to be *different"?*

"Ought" is illusory; "ought" is against "life." In other words, there ought not to be any ought.

We can pause here: we already have food for reflection. The power of Nietzsche, though it reaches beyond rhetoric, lies above all in the rhetorical enhancement of the human hunger for what he promises: spontaneity, vitality, freedom and might; the natural and beautiful, the elegant and noble; Mediterranean blue in preference to Königsbergian grey; joy not duty, life not thought, gloom, death. . . .

Nietzsche was among the most prominent forces of "the second enlightenment," which fastened on aspects of the existential subject and effected a reversal of tone respecting "subjectivity." Like truth, it was now applied more to people than to propositions. The new focus was on "the truth by which one is truly human, truly a brother or sister, truly a friend," etc. "Authenticity" became a watchword.

There can be no doubt about the unique beauty of authenticity, even of the limited authenticities by which one is an authentic scientist or technician, an authentic builder or banker. From the time of Nietzsche's death (1900) for the avant-garde, and from mid-century for the rest of the West, a new, wholly persuasive and decisive hold on the unique status of "the authentic" has set in. The era of positivism (which, however, has never wholly lost its grip on our society) had once succeeded in making "subjectivity" a boo-word; it has since become a hurrah-word. For all its claim to truth, however, the new convention runs a danger:

> The danger is that the values of subjectivity in its more recent sense will be squandered by subjectivity in its prior and pejorative sense. Unless the two meanings are sharply distinguished, praise of subjectivity seems to imply a condemnation of objectivity. But condemnation of objectivity induces, not a merely incidental blindspot in one's vision, but a radical undermining of authentic human existence.

Value for value, objective knowing falls short of authentic living; without objective knowing, however, human living can make it only as far as Nietzschean intensity, not as far as authenticity. Freedom and love, it is true, are the *peak* of intentionality, but they are also the peak of *human* intentionality, the peak level of human operations that are first empirical, intelligent, and reasonable, and if the human subject is not all these, neither will he/she be responsible, authentic, true (= truly human).

There is a further consideration. The Nietzschean abolition of "ought" that accompanied the abolition of God has a side that Nietzsche dismissed with too casual a wave. It is a down side. We have lived to see where Nietzsche's hailing of instinct and "the blond beast" can go. Nietzsche looked for free spirits who would rejoice without second thoughts in his light-hearted *"There are no moral facts whatever."* What is the likely future for those aristocrats of the spirit, sickly intellectuals like Friedrich Nietzsche? They will be among the first up for liquidation. It is remarkable that Nietzsche was not entirely unaware of this. It did not keep him from cheering the future and its brutality toward the weak. Remotely akin to Nietzsche's "noble Teutons," post-Nietzschean men who affirmed with sour satisfaction the lack of moral facts set up extermination camps and energetically wiped out millions, weak and strong. (Nietzsche in other respects was far removed—farther than Heidegger—from Nazi ideology. An admirer of Jews, he claimed, mythically, a Polish aristocratic ancestry.)

The modernist impasse is the failed effort to combine two incompatibles: the pure creativity of historically conscious man (we choose for ourselves what we ought to do) and escape from the nihilism of an oughtless world (I should not kill you? Says who?).

Since Nietzsche we have had a hundred years of effort, without success or the prospect of success, to render the incompatible compatible. So long as we are dealing with no more than the imagery of Mediterranean blue and the rhetoric of life, freedom, nobility, and the like, so long as we are taken up with the joyous errand of proclaiming rights and do not have to bother with the obligations that they correlatively impose, all goes well with the ideology of the oughtless world. But the minute we decide that we must submit the whole to intelligent questioning and reasonable reflection, we are brought up short at the modernist impasse: the incompatibility between choosing our own norms and avoiding the nihilist abyss.

What are our options? There is an option of accepting and living with the impasse. This is ultimately nihilist. To accept the impasse is to get along equally without the "is" of truth and the "ought" of goodness.

Respecting how this is done, we may distinguish modes of awareness: first, the drifters, who think as everyone thinks and do as everyone does. They advert neither to their own horizons nor to those of others. They easily find themselves mirrored in soap opera and, in that limited mode, their lives are dramatic. Second, the enterprising, who intend to take their lives into their own hands and live modernity commonsensically. They do not count on the "is" of truth; the "ought" of obligation they find alienating. The lady next door, culturally alert and engaged, on the side of a few angels (contributor to Greenpeace and Amnesty International), a cheerleader for abortion and euthanasia, would not describe, or even recognize, herself as a nihilist, but that is what she is. The third group, from whose allegiances she perhaps differs not one whit, nevertheless has a different vantage point. They are clear, for example, that all issues are political. Is this the politics that comes out of the barrel of a gun? Precisely. Such is the honest, conscious nihilist, no sinister figure darkly lurking alone, but a bright young academic worried over tenure and his mortgage, and conscious of having to fight for his rights, for they cannot be rationally vindicated.

Some have constituted this nihilism for themselves. Many others have not; they have inherited it and remain in it for lack of contact with resources alternative to the specific traditions of modernity. They find themselves in a universe without plan or purpose. They are not apostles of the modernist impasse, but they are indistinguishable from their more deliberate, fully committed nihilist allies in living parasitically on the dwindling capital of the West.

Second, there is the option of breaking with the impasse. The break is a repudiation, as neither reasonable nor responsible, of the claim to total autonomy under the heading of "historical consciousness."

Here, too, there is a difference of awareness respecting how consciously and adequately the break is made. There are those aware, but unthematically aware, of the normative factor immanent in human intentionality (the inner call to operate in accord with the self-assembling structures of intentionality, the summons to attention and intelligence, to reasonableness and responsibility). They find satisfaction in inquiry, feel the pull toward reason, hear the voice of conscience. They are unaware, however, of that further dilemma we considered earlier: that of the man who does not know whether or not the moral struggle puts him in tune with the world. (If he maintains the struggle, will he turn out to be a fool, in alienation from the world? If he abandons it, will he end up a knave, in alienation from himself?) Those who have not felt the force of such dilemmas are typically baffled by their modernist neighbor's view of the world as of a vast panorama of meaningless motion; Becker's shining planet spinning meaningless in space; an evolutionary process not only random where it must be random, but utterly, absolutely random and mindless. They have experientially found the "ought" that comes precisely from the "is" of the drive to the good. The idea of pondering the need to ground *ultimately* the intelligibility, truth, goodness, that they have productively affirmed in and by their lives has not (yet) occurred to them.

Lastly, there is a fully conscious break with the premises of the modernist impasse. Religious conviction may be the root of this sanity. Moreover, there are those who add to this a clearly worked out philosophic critique. Among the latter are critical realists, who invoke the rock of human intentionality and its philosophic objectification. Many are able radically to disqualify relativism's lost hope of distinguishing true and false as well as behaviorism's lost hope of distinguishing good and evil.

In this view, it is the modernist impasse that lacks critical grounding. Those who know this and whose hold on this knowledge is clear and firm owe it to themselves and to their neighbor to tell the truth or make the point directly and unabashedly. Heirs and representatives of relativism and other modernist traditions may never have been shown an exit from modern (including postmodern) nihilism. They have no idea that there might, for example, be a way superior alike to the simple but pretentious philosophies that compete for their fealty, to all ideologies (religious or secular), to fideism, fundamentalism, and secular surrogates, a way that might intelligently and definitively ground the difference between true and false, good and evil.

Before quitting this line of thought on the impasse between total autonomy and the sometimes inarticulate yearning to escape an ever emptier modern/postmodern nihilism, we may pause to consider a recent example of clarity on the modernist impasse with a nonetheless unresolved and hence troubled consciousness. Phillip Johnson, a legal scholar who deals with philosophic issues, has recently described the way that the late Arthur Leff of the Yale Law School dealt with the dilemma of modernity. Leff recognized the need of "an ultimate evaluator" if the distinction between good and evil were to hold, if values were to be coherently affirmed. But the situation of modernity, in Leff's view, is such that an ultimate evaluator is unthinkable. So Leff ended his eloquent reflections with a longing to affirm the good together with the pained realization that it could not be done. Concretely, in Leff's words:

> Napalming babies is bad. Starving the poor is wicked. Buying and selling each other is depraved. Those who stood up and died resisting Hitler, Stalin, Amin, and Pol Pot—and General Custer too—have earned salvation. Those who acquiesced deserve to be damned. There is in the world such a thing as evil.
> [All together now:] Sez who?
> God help us.

Leff was among those who, like Becker and countless others, grasped and articulated the dilemma, never solved or resolved it, but lived and died with it. Their honesty warns against cheap resolutions. Their failure to crack this hard nut is a warning, too—against resignation, and even more, perhaps, against any secret conniving with an illusory Camus-like or Hemingway-like Bogart-looking hero role in the existentialist manner. As Johnson observed, one who like Leff genuinely affirms the moral order can and should dismantle the dilemma: "When impeccable logic leads to self-contradiction, there must be a faulty premise." In fact, Leff's logic was impeccable: if we ourselves are the ultimate evaluators, no values hold; but; therefore. So far, no contradiction at all. But we find we must add: values *do* hold. The only authentic and coherent move at this point, the only intelligent, reasonable, responsible move, is to acknowledge self-reversal and go back, more carefully, over the premises. Some premise must be, and is, wrong. The voice of human intentionality directs us to reconsider the death of God (the very term whispers, "illusory") and the arrogant illusion of *total* creativity in man's authentic making of man. (A perhaps overscrupulous final comment on Leff: his theme of "ultimate evaluator" is generically valid, but open to misconstrual as voluntarist. A more exact exposition would take care to show that moral norms immanent in human intentionality mediated an ultimate source, i.e., divine law, or God.)

Nietzsche has unwittingly fathered the postmodernist option, too, as the inspirer of both Michel Foucault and Jacques Derrida. This "option," according to Jean-François Lyotard, *penseur* and cultural politician, is the condition of incredulity vis-à-vis meta-narratives, in other words, big claims for truth in narrative form, like the words of YHWH: "Man sees what meets the eye, but the Lord sees the heart" (1 Sam 16:7) in the stories of Saul and David. By meta-narratives we especially mean views like "the whig interpretation of history," the struggle for and fated victory of freedom or the POST TENEBRAS LUX on the wall of the Reformation in Geneva or the news of an act of God's salvation, on behalf of every human being, in the death and resurrection of Jesus, made Christ and Lord. The postmodernist is no ranter like the village atheist. He is a pluralist in upper case: the stories are all fine until they become "totalitarian," until they claim a privileged place in the sun. The kerygma in particular is fine. It might even make a fine contribution to a post-Christian religion for the whole world. (The phrase "whole world," however, rings a little thin. Postmodernists are Western academics, another avant-garde of the alienated bent on rationalizing their "condition.")

Variations on the Fallacy of Insight as Pure Reception

Naïve realism may take the tack of putative "rigor" not only in positivism, but in Humean empiricism, American pragmatism and behaviorism, and so on. Of variations on the fallacy of insight as pure reception, however, positivism is the prime exhibit and will be our main interest.

The movement reflected a simplistic nineteenth-century cult of science, an act of deep obeisance to science that philosophy felt obliged to pay after the pantheistic idolatries of idealism had passed. The result—bad science, worse philosophy—is best studied in hermeneutics, for example, in any number of handbooks on the method of history. *Introduction aux études historiques,* C. V. Langlois and Charles Seignobos (1898), in English translation since its appearance in France, is a handy example. The effort was to bring history as close as possible to the conditions of natural science. This was not easy; on the contrary, it was very hard, for no matter how carefully the positivist formulated the rules guiding analysis and synthesis, the pitfalls of subjectivity were everywhere. (Langlois in later life, instead of writing history, contented himself with reproducing selected documents.)

> With Langlois and Seignobos, then, there emerges a clear-cut distinction and separation between the determination of historical facts and the determination of their interconnections. This distinction and separation has its ground, it would seem, in notions of natural science current in nineteenth-century positivist and empiricist circles. But in those very circles there were bound to arise further questions. Why add to the facts? Must not any addition that is not obvious to everyone be merely subjective? Why not let the facts speak for themselves?

If it is true that 190-proof positivist theory, with its fixation on "facts" and tunnel-vision quest of connections among them, is today as defunct as the dinosaurs, it is equally true that in vaguer, gauzier form and untheoretical practice it is as current as computers. Apart from the scattered left of the avant-garde, and hold-overs from Kantian or Hegelian idealism, and a few centrist schools, such as critical realism, it remains an untheoretical but leading hermeneutic mentality among editors and learned socie-ties. The impact of positivism has been felt over a large part of social institutions and movements. In New Testament studies the area where erratic blocks, remnants, and catch-phrases of positivist theory and practice are ubiquitous, is historical-Jesus research, for example, in the mini-treatises on "criteria of historic-ity" or in efforts to deal with such non-public or "esoteric" tra-ditions as the Last Supper and the so-called "words of institution." Here the flight from the subject and the dread of subjectivity, bugbears that haunted Langlois and Seignobos, con-tinue to flourish, frighten, and inhibit.

The words Lonergan used to hit off the positivist mentality are helpful. Over and above "the facts," "*must not any addi-tion that is not obvious to everyone be merely subjective?*" One need only check the book-review section of a few middle-of-the-road journals to find out whether positivist fears and inhibitions have been allayed in our time or, on the contrary, are still alive among those who think of themselves as solid sober folk. They phrase their doubts about "what is not obvious to everyone" in self-effacingly timid terms: "Many will not find it easy to follow X in thinking that. . . ." In technical matters they have left their nineteenth-century forbears far behind; it is the lack of interest in theoretical issues that allows them to maintain the positivist orientation of their predecessors, notably fear of "subjectivity" in themselves and chronic suspicion of it in others.

The present century, however, witnessed the collapse of the prestige of positivism as such in the wake of the First World War. Ever since, the avant-garde in humanistic pursuits generally (and, among them, in New Testament studies) has been unsympathetic with the idiom of positivism, though they too have unconsciously and incoherently kept remnants of positivist patterns of thought—once again, not for lack of alertness respecting philo-logical, literary, and historical method, but for lack of specifi-cally philosophic sophistication. Meanwhile, in markedly conser-vative circles too positivism has hung on, and here too this has been less a conscious choice than a comfortable legacy from the past.

There is an irony in the subsurface longevity of positivism. Whereas twentieth-century positivism is an omnium gatherum of old-fashioned remnants, the whole point of positivism had been to be above all up-to-date, scientific, modern. The movement was an invasion of philosophic terrain by the prestige of "the norms of natural science." Admittedly, these "norms" are not only obsolete today; they never truly represented scientific method. They were as spurious in the nineteenth century as they are now, the mere product or progeny of ideological secularism, naïve realism, and scientific "status."

An instance of positivist remnants hanging on incoherently in the avant-garde: in mid-century Bultmann and his school maintained such remnants cheek by jowl with immanentist Neo-Kantian views of knowledge (as well as an existentialism derived from Kierkegaard and Heidegger). Looking back on the Bultmann era (in a 1984 Festschrift celebrating the hundredth anniversary of Bultmann's birth), John A. T. Robinson recalled:

> George McLeod, leader of the Iona Community, then one of the most prominent communicators of the gospel on the British scene, who "blessed Bultmann for every risk he takes," playfully accused him of "knocking his grandmother's religion with his grandfather's science."

There was more than a little substance in this accusation, playful or not. Bultmann did not investigate how much of the three-story universe that he attributed to traditional Christianity belonged among *thematic* Christian affirmations at any time. On the other hand, what Bultmann called the "modern world view" was largely nineteenth-century scientism—pseudoscientific ideology given to sweeping generalizations on "reality." Scientism's standard stage furniture featured nature as a mechanistic determinism and history as "a closed continuum of cause and effect," both conspicuous parts of Bultmann's "modern world view." All this Bultmann regularly attributed to "modern man." How widely it was ever shared is moot.

Caution tinged by positivism, international and ecumenical, is taken by many critics as fatally fused with "historical-critical method." This set of methods, with its putatively permanent bond with positivism, is too often burdened by another vice: a seeming preference, even when dealing with Pauline and Deutero-

Pauline texts that are allusive, rich in timbre, charged and poly-phonic, for dull, cautious, monophonic textual interpretation.

All of the interesting historical issues in New Testament scholarship touch items "not obvious to everyone"; so opinions on them fall under a priori positivist suspicion. Such, for example, are questions about the horizons and controlling perspectives of John the Baptist, Jesus, Peter, James, and Paul. We have had a body of solid contemporary work on all these issues. This has not changed our general situation: decade after decade, year after year we are greeted by a flood of monographs and articles that divide into two streams, with plentiful dry land between them.

The one stream is the mass of positivist-tinctured works—sober, cautious, timid—sometimes meant to shore up religious assurance; the other stream, reminiscent of the "chatter and con-tradictions of what is falsely called knowledge" (1 Tim 6), is up-to-the-minute, indulgent toward bright ideas, original and hun-gry for acknowledgement as such, tempted to be all-explanatory. The large middle ground of dry land between these streams ought to be flooded with the work of an international, interconfessional community of scholars, products with a plausible claim on being acknowledged as intelligent, reasonable, and responsible. The ascertainment that this is far from true should prompt our best efforts to bring about improvement and progress.

This ideal "middle ground" between the extremes, since it cor-responds to "insight" as analyzed and acknowledged by critical realism, is, as it ought to be, an attractive option both in itself and by comparison and contrast. Its competing alternatives are grounded in fallacious notions of insight. Both of them, though from opposite points of vantage, overlook the need of objectivity and judgment. The fallacy of insight as pure reception understands itself to be *already* objective, the job already done. And, as we are about to see, the partisans of the fallacy of insight as pure projection assure us that there *is* no job to be done. Some (there are many unambiguous examples from the days of Northrop Frye and other modernists on biblical literature to a younger genera-tion of postmodernists) instinctively recoil from the definiteness, the "closure" implied by grasp of the virtually unconditioned, by judgment with its commitment to "true/false," by belief, with its danger of religious conflict, heresy, war. (Frye was old-fashioned enough to have an alternative, a utopian "community of vision''; the postmodernist alternative has set refutation aside in favor of a boundless pluralism.)

Variations on the Fallacy of Insight as Pure Projection

We shall begin by discussing the view that reality is not of itself structured; whatever structuring it has is the product of human subjects. We shall take up two forms of this view, both philosophic, but the second applied simply to historical events.

The first is a view propagated by Nietzsche and widely shared among twentieth-century philosophers. We shall concentrate on the form it takes in the work of Jean-Paul Sartre, who plays his own views off against scholasticism. In the standard scholastic view corporal beings are hylomorphic (composites resultant from two principles of essential being, namely potency and act, or prime matter and substantial form). Composite beings are necessarily quantified and qualified and, as such, analyzable in accord with Aristotle's (linguistically based) predicaments: substance, quantity, quality, relation, place, time, position, condition, action, passion (= passivity to action). Man, the model case, is defined by genus as "animal," by specific difference as "rational." No other hylomorphic species, however, is definable (despite the view found in run-of-the-mill scholasticism that insight is an intuiting of substantial or accidental forms). Lastly, all finite beings, simple (spirits) or hylomorphic composites (animals, be they rational or not) exist in function of causality exercised by a self-subsistent cause of essence and existence. They do not bear within themselves "sufficient reason" for existence; essence and existence in them are distinct. They are contingent and caused.

The "absurdity" for which *La nausée* is famed is Roquentin's sudden realization that the roots of the chestnut tree before him, and everyone and everything around him, and he himself, and the components that make him up are all contingent. They might as easily not be as be. In this sense they are *de trop*—superfluous, "in the way"—and that is their absurdity. Moreover, they cannot be counted on to function suitably, reliably, predictably, for (contrary to scholasticism) they have no form, no nature, no essence. The contrary would have required that there be a God to think them creatively. Their lack of inbuilt structure combines with their absurd and superfluous contingence to yield a world without meaning, except for whatever intelligibility the human being might project onto it.

This touches a question that the existentialists posed but that found no answer among them: how is it that knowing should be endowed with the capacity to accord with the real? The structuring of the drive to know, the *intentio intendens* and its altogether non-arbitrary self-assembling structure (summed up in the formula "experience, understanding, judgment") must have its "reason," its point, in an equally and isomorphically structured to-be-known. This, however, ultimately implies a source of essence and existence in both knower and known: an utterly transcendent Creator, the very idea of which Sartre passionately repudiated. Here he stood in impeccable coherence with himself, for at the root of his view of the absurd and superfluous there lay a rock-bottom double-thesis: no God, no structured world. If there was no God to think the world creatively, there could be no objectively structured intelligibility.

The critical-realist position may be put succinctly. If one defines "being" heuristically, as the goal of the pure desire to know, the object grasped intelligently and affirmed reasonably, then one must affirm the intrinsic intelligibility of being. Otherwise, one is reduced to a counterposition unequal to the facts of conscious human intentionality. (Remember Jack's realism naïvely affirmed on the basis of sense, and Jill's idealism mistakenly thought to reflect rigorous description. The first erroneously identified the "real" with the-already-out-there-now; the second identified it with the noumenon lying beyond the horizon of the-already-out-there-now. The only view impervious to correction is "intelligent grasp," which implies an intelligible object, and "reasonable affirmation," which co-affirms this implication.)

It is perfectly true that Sartre would swiftly (and quite rightly) urge that a finally satisfactory account would entail a further— in his view, impossible— move, a rational demonstration that God is. (Nevertheless, that God must be and is, and that the contradictory view is self-reversing is rationally demonstrable.) So much for the first form of positing the unstructured.

It is worth adding a few words on a second form, an idealist-tinged theory of history to which Lonergan devoted close (and mostly positive) attention: Karl Heussi's 1932 study, *Die Krisis des Historismus*. Heussi's work is significant for its main point, namely, that early twentieth-century positivism with its simplistic conception of objectivity had prompted a backlash and brought about a crisis in historical studies. Heussi's own realism about the limits of historical knowledge is exemplary, and helps account for his many shrewd observations on historians and history. His error lay in locating the root of "historical perspectivism" in a conception of the structures of historical happening as indeterminate and subject to variation with the passage of time. This would make "the past" comparable to the "standing" of poets and novelists, which rises or falls in accord with the many contingencies of ongoing literary history. Lonergan affirmed Heussi's main point ("perspectivism"), but corrected its cognitional-theoretical explanation. The early twentieth-century error was not the assumption that the structures of the past were fixed, but the failure to realize that these same structures were too rich and complex to be recovered except in approximate fashion. "The past is fixed," Lonergan asserted; "its intelligible structures are unequivocal." But the past that is so fixed and unequivocal is the enormously, almost boundlessly complex past that historians know only in the most incomplete way. What is it, then, that gives rise to perspectivism? The answer must be: incomplete, approximate knowledge of the past. No one will ever know all that happened at the battle of Leipzig (October 16–19, 1813).

The error corrected here is not dead. It is repeated by literary and historical critics who, for reasons irreducible to any single pattern, imagine that historians produce from their own resources not only their opinions, but the data on which they claim to base them. The "looseness" typical of perspectival judgment, however, ought not be allowed to detract in principle from the strand of objectivity, distinct in kind from the other strands, which is *empirical* and consists in the givenness of data.

So much for two forms of the mistaken thesis that the real is unstructured. At this point we shall take up in turn reader-response theory, deconstruction, the new historicism, and the new pluralism.

Among the achievements and virtues of reader-response theory are three clean breaks: the break with naïve realism and the supposition that texts, of themselves and "already," in other words, in advance of the reader, yield fully constituted meaning; the break with "the personal heresy," the approach to literature through the life and times of the writer; and the break with the so-called "affective fallacy," for the theory of reader-response (or of reader-reception—though the latter term can refer to study of the responses of successive historical readerships) unambiguously favored taking account of rhetorical devices designed to elicit responses.

The first break was the most fundamental. The reader-response group recognized that, confronted by a text, one had a job to do as reader: namely, to draw actively on one's own resources so as, out of the curious signs that constitute the text in its minimal sense, to constitute the text's meaning. Since this clearly called for a considerable exercise on the part of subject and subjective intentional acts (acts of subjectivity), there was little sympathy among reader-response critics for any residual positivist shrinking from subjectivity. This allowed reader-response critics to adopt a lively, free-spirited approach to imaginative literature.

At the same time, it is equally beyond doubt that most reader-response theory is defective. Though it has rediscovered and made more explicit the New Critics' occasional oblique acknowledgement of the *implied* author (and added the correlative "implied reader"), it has also clung to the same critics' misleading "intentional fallacy." Misled thereby on "intention," reader-response theory failed to conjure up an alternative object of interpretation. This is how it arrived at the dead end of claiming not to be "right," just "interesting." There was no place in the theory for the marshalling and weighing of evidence and equally, of course, no place for that crucial increment of knowledge which is mediated by well-grounded judgment.

Reader-response theory has been a vital movement, with as many credits as debits. It is not deep. It has elicited from its adepts some talk of epistemology, but no effort to root "reading" in a full-blown cognitional theory. This has allowed basic defects to go uncorrected, despite the generally good sense and productive, as well as "interesting," work of its practitioners.

The contrast with critical realism consists in this, that the latter specifies a coherent set of definite tasks: to work out an understanding or construal of the sense of the text, to judge how probable this understanding or construal is, and to state what one judges to be a probably accurate understanding or construal of the text. The sense of the text is understood in terms of intentions textually objectified; it is supposed that to understand the text the interpreter must understand more than the text. This "more" includes not only objects or referents, but the author and the interpreter himself. And under "author," the critical realist means what William Barrett means:

> If we are readers of poetry, we do not read only isolated, single poems, we read a sizable body of the poet's work. . . . He becomes an individual and continuing voice to us, a poetic presence, a poetic identity. This poetic identity is not altogether the same as his identity as an actual person; in life the poet may have had rough edges, concerning which the poetry might leave us unsuspecting. But poet and man are not altogether unrelated; the poetic voice . . . is after all a part of the total identity of that human being.

The more reflective among reader-response theorists (granted, a minority) share this view of the author. But, as among New Critics, the movement has been of two minds on "the author" and appears not to possess the analytic resources requisite to settling the matter satisfactorily.

Whatever may be the hesitations of the reader-response group, Barrett is surely right about the need to know the author, in all his work and in all his developments, in order fully to know the poem, play, or novel. Barrett's main interest in this discussion has had to do with the absence of "consciousness" and "the subject" from modern philosophic discourse; this context helps account for the sharp definition, the accuracy and penetration, of his reflections on theorizing burdened by "dispensing with the author."

"Poetic identity," as delineated above, is inevitably missing from examples of poetry designed to show the non-necessity of the author, for example, poetry produced by computer. The computer cannot be minimally programmed (so retaining some claim to anonymity) and still exhibit the "poetic identity" that is integral to excellent poetry. (Barrett added that the theory in T. S. Eliot's earlier criticism—authentic poetry entailed the "extinction" of the poet's personality—is far removed from Eliot's own *oeuvre,* which everywhere bears the stamp of a most distinctive mind and sensibility.)

Deconstruction is as mixed in tendency as reader-response theory, but we shall deal only with the authentic extremism of hard-core theorists. They are, we mentioned above, more or less aware of being involved in self-reversal, but are careful not to let this daunt them. Jacques Derrida, Paul de Man, Hillis Miller provided stimulation, wit, and a certain disarming reading pleasure for many years. The movement has survived both self-reversal and scandal. What more can a mere refutation offer?

It offers, in any event, an occasion on which to repeat that what counts is not poise in the face of refutation, but a satisfactory defense or response. This deconstruction cannot offer. For a movement not loathe to claim prestigious status in the world, it is oddly ill-equipped to support its leading theses. Linguistics, Saussure taught, deals with language *(langue),* the speech-resources shared by a speech-community, which differs from the utterances *(paroles)* or discourse, in other words, actual use of language. A kind of mid-way position between the two is occupied by the purely phatic act ("the cat is on the mat"), an expression "competent" in that it observes the rules of language, but otherwise anonymous, relatively indeterminate, open to many senses. It is reasonable to hold that whoever wishes may treat utterances as if they were merely phatic acts open to new determinations—as if, that is, their status as *paroles* had not, by the definiteness of actual discourse, lost the general traits or multivalence that it had had as mere language *(langue).* But this possibility is by no means and in no sense imposed. It is not a necessity. It is a free choice that will be justified or not by what comes of it.

There is no advance guarantee that efforts to ascribe new meaning to old texts will succeed with readers and critics, or deserve to succeed. The success of "ascription" is conditional, for (humor apart) some *positive* relation to the original text is indispensable. What claim does a reading have that runs roughshod over the original solely in the service of some new meaning willed by the ascriber? (An instance of successful ascription: Origen's and Augustine's allegorical reading of the parable of the Good Samaritan; an instance of failure: Hegel's reading of Abraham as the type of alienation from nature.)

David Lehman, in his book on deconstruction and the fall of Paul de Man, and M. H. Abrams, in a series of lectures and articles, have each in his own way shown how naked and unarmed the movement is, how shallow its resources, in the face of reasoned objection or disagreement (and yet how stolidly unaffected it affects to be). Lehman's review of the movement in North America amounted to a thorough refutation, with sharply formulated arguments of his own and a rehearsal of the critiques of many others. Some critics pointed to internal contradictions in deconstructive theory and practice; others evoked the inevitable and unacceptable results, if the theory were followed with any semblance of rigor. Denis Donoghue, in his protest against the dehumanizing of literature, pointed out a telling phenomenon: Paul de Man, dealing with the confessions of Rousseau, hears the voice of someone

> talking about his own experience, accusing himself, justifying himself, and so forth. De Man can't bear to hear that voice . . . : he wants to see a machine working without human intervention.

This critical tack, Donoghue argued, would demolish in advance the entire range of questions raised "in morality, ethics, politics, and psychology." The dehumanizing tendency—the gaping hole where conscious human subjectivity and intentionality ought to be—is conspicuously and perversely operative in the proposals and practices of the deconstructionists.

Abrams' conversations with and about the deconstructionists are particularly rich, owing to the close attention he has paid to deconstructionist proposals and practices, and to his detailed accounts of exchanges between deconstructionists and their critics. Abrams offers too cool a dismissal of the cultural damage that deconstruction has done. He is also inhibited by the flat-out attack of "newreaders" on suppositions otherwise universally accepted; that, for example, in oral and written communications we can and do understand one another. Abrams is nonetheless loathe to say that deconstruction can be proven wrong.

> The skills that we ordinarily and unreflectively bring into play when interpreting the language we hear and read are remarkably subtle and sure; yet—despite the fact that their sureness is supported by a lifetime of interplay with other users of language, and by our ability to recognize and correct our errors—our confidence in these skills is vulnerable when subjected to a determined assault by a radical linguistic skepticism.

The reason why we feel vulnerable is that we cannot easily avail ourselves of a knock-down proof that everyone will accept.

This honest reflection, however, overlooks the fact and issue of horizon. We should not expect that hermeneutical questions are resolvable in the sense that all will catch on and agree, and only the flat-earthers be at a loss. This is most unlikely. Mankind in the mass does not and will not register complex arguments, even those that can lay claim to knock-down status. If the topic is the least bit beyond the grasp of common sense, if it calls for some sustained effort in order to put oneself in the position to see the power of even a devastating refutation, it will not gain the whole world. Themes of human functioning, conscious intentionality, its objectification, its application to the meanings and truth-claims of philosophic views on literary and historical questions—all of these are far too special for the general public. They are red meat only for the keenly interested. This is not a conversation everyone can join.

We certainly cannot require of every valid "proof" that it win the assent of "all reasonable people" (unless that term is adjusted to refer exclusively to those who are thoroughly informed on the issue and have brought themselves to the point of being morally and intellectually ready to make their way, on this issue, at least, to the truth). This seems too much to ask of ordinary people and ordinary language. There are great swathes of people who, reasonable in general, are nonetheless unable to discern why one argument for the existence and goodness of God is valid and another not. There are those, including some of the best and the brightest, ready to accept the invalid argument but not the valid one; others to accept both; still others to accept neither. In this context horizon is a factor both relevant and of signal importance.

The debate on deconstruction brings to the fore the fact that some principles—for example, the human mind, which in its own way is a principle, that is, that from which something (such as inquiry, insight, grasp of evidence, judgment, argument, logic, method) proceeds, do not need proof, for there is nothing more fundamental than them to appeal to as providing it. "Proof" *supposes* mind. So, the assaults of "radical linguistic skepticism" (deconstruction) on those remarkably subtle and sure "skills that we ordinarily and unreflectively bring into play when interpreting the language we hear and read" are utterly futile and irrelevant. They are also self-reversing: the assaults themselves make use of, depend on, presuppose, performatively acknowledge what is under assault, what they thematically deny.

Gratuitously to accept from the deconstructionists the ground rules for the debate over deconstruction is simply muddleheaded. Are we to extend comparable courtesies to all forms of nihilism? But this groundless gambit is the sole basis on which to conclude that deconstruction is irrefutable. As self-reversing, it supplies its own refutation, which the critic need merely make thematic and acknowledge.

This naturally prompts us to shift our attention from the now evidently disqualified rationalization which deconstructionist theory is to the more human, humanly sympathetic and challenging state of alienation that the theory rationalizes. Rationalization in this instance is shallow and alienation deep. It is alienation from basic aspects of the human condition and vocation. It calls for the return to the evidences of the notion of value, in other words, that aspect of the notion of being which culminates in appetite for the good.

What is there about "the good, value, the worthwhile" that is a turn-off? How is it that the hunger for wisdom is tempted by the nurture of nihilism? Recall for a moment the long reign of positivism and of "the principle of the empty head" (objectivity in the world of immediacy simple-mindedly applied to the world mediated by meaning). Who would not wish to get out from under the spurious burdens of objectivity in this sense? What man or woman of intelligence is not drawn to question the whole apparatus of objectivity?

Add to positivism the dead weight of nineteenth-century moralizing; conjure up the high price paid for "the stability of the family," for example, by generations of its victims (mostly women). Suddenly one hears the siren song of deconstruction inviting the burdened into a gravity-defying condition of weightlessness. Even the atheism of the nineteenth-century wore a deeply furrowed brow, as de Lubac's *Drama of Atheist Humanism* unforgettably detailed. By comparison, deconstruction is lighthearted, not taking on the burden of the world, alternating repudiation and an entertaining pooh-poohing of contrary claims. Literary circles in particular are attracted by a number of pleasing traits: the theory is fresh, bright, modern, foreign, radical, menacing, liberating, stylish, ahead of the curve. . . .

Well in advance of its appearance on the scene of history, Josef Pieper described it. Above we referred to Pieper's analysis of historic Greek sophistry and its advent in the fifth-century world of Athens. Pieper took sophistry not only as a historic, but as a durably recurrent phenomenon. The force of his study lay in two revelations. The object of the major one was Socrates' recognition of the hostility of forces whose hostility was hidden, and the shrewd tactics of his duel with this destructive, hard-to-pin-down phenomenon. The struggle did not play itself out in a single dialogue. Pieper mainly studied the first half of "the Phaedrus"; but the struggle was ongoing. What in the end Socrates found himself wrestling with was a view of *life as manageable by mere rational technique.* The second, lesser revelation bore on the attraction of sophistry for the young of Athens. They let the nihilist side (e.g., Lysias' discourse on love) pass almost without notice; what caught their attention—and this still holds for youth the world over—was that it was new, live, bold, and bright.

The sophists offered "success"; the deconstructionists offer freedom. Rational technique is once more the great solution, called on this time to dissolve the total apparatus of enslavement not only to tradition and all its sanctions, but to every claim on responsibility. To those who feel themselves somehow "outsiders," it is a magic sword-and-cape.

Years ago, as contemporary ideology was just beginning to take hold in literary studies, Lionel Trilling remarked that those who at the time were hailing madness as a superior form of sanity *did not plan to go mad themselves.* Eventually, this was recognized as a glaring gap between theory and practice, and fatal to theory. Being, in the end, has an incalculable advantage over its parasitic contraries. By nature we all stand in coherence with it. We can hardly help ourselves, for we are oriented from our depths to the real—at one moment maddened, perhaps, but at another enchanted by being as we know and live and love it, by its density and poignant beauty. Many who involved themselves in deconstruction not long ago—in full flight from being—are now coming back to the real, to what Philip Larkin called that "million-petalled flower / of being there."

This orientation to and taste for the real is equally the basis on which "the new historicism" of Michel Foucault founders. Here, however, we are closer to Nietzsche, who did *not* shrink from endorsing his contempt for sanity by plunging into madness. Foucault is similarly quit of the charge of promoting madness but preferring sanity. Within the limits of the possible he was a paradigm of consistency—recklessly coherent in his plunge into a Nietzschean hero role. Sartre in art and life had focused on "totalizing." Here it is operative in a boundlessly destructive extremism. James Miller feared with some justification that his recent study of Foucault might have the counterproductive effect of supplying ammunition to Foucault's critics. But what can a critic add to Foucault's own radically self-reversing options?

Foucault emerged, still young, from a synthesis bearing the hallmark of post-World War II avant-garde Paris. Juvenile heroes: de Sade and Goya. Enemy (read rival): Sartre. That leaves, as key figures of the post-War Parisian stage, five stars from the German-language heaven: Hegel, Marx, Nietzsche, Freud, Heidegger. Add Becket ("Waiting for Godot" had a Paris premier in winter, 1953) and Ludwig Binswanger, who sought to synthesize Freud and Heidegger. (In 1954 Foucault published a commentary on a 1930 essay of Binswanger's.) This kind of "synthesis" could and did strike such notes as social "solidarity" and "humanist" anthropology. For Foucault, however, this compound began to dissolve in the late 1950s and, by the 1960s, had given way to newstyle philosophic research and reflection.

The idea was to reconstruct in meticulous fashion the changing beliefs and practices that defined both the knower and the world to-be-known. It is easy to make Foucault a cult hero, not so easy to follow in this path. Research, for Foucault, was rooted in a welter of personal dilemmas and expressed a determined exploration of personal experience. A key supposition of this program was that no structures are native either to the knower or to the known. All are contrived and conventional (Nietzsche, Heidegger, Sartre).

In *Folie et déraison* (1961) (ET: *Madness and Civilization*) Foucault traced the changes rung on true and false, sane and mad, right and wrong, normal and pathological, as they defined and redefined knower and known. It will not serve our purposes to deal with particulars of new-historicist research. For one thing, the major themes collapse under critique, even when their weaknesses are cunningly disguised and countervailing evidence is ever so lightly acknowledged. To be sure, minor theses and minor aspects of major theses may survive, and have sometimes proven to be immensely suggestive to others.

So far as Foucault himself was concerned, erudite archival research—in outward form imposingly impersonal—was always an expression of the personal, especially personal dedication to the Nietzschean quest of becoming "other"; more exactly, of "getting rid of oneself" through limit-experiences. Nietzschean and Heideggerian oracles were important to Foucault, who cherished them as clues and stimuli to this life-project; to the outside observer they appear to lead nowhere. Are there grounds for waiving the demand for rationale and verification? Foucault does not present them, and they are not self-evident. Such limit-experiences as madness, anonymous sado-masochist games, or drugs have no verifiable role in human self-transcendence.

Foucault's appeal to a Nietzschean quest of "higher necessity" or to a Heideggerian invasion of the sphere of "the unthought" is undermined by the canon of parsimony: stay within the verifiable. In actual practice Foucault acknowledged requisites for research. Thus, he abandoned hundreds of manuscript pages of his history of sexuality because they failed to meet the insight gained (by LSD experiment) into the roots of his own sexuality. But "rationale," though it existed, remains uncommunicated or incommunicable. It is not ideology that is at work here, but a struggle with alienation. Foucault was moved by—in a phrase from Rilke—"those unembodied presences that make us act" *(ces absences qui nous font agir).*

Foucault chose Nietzschean terms to interpret his life. But the quest that in his last years, and last work, he summed up in a phrase charged with pathos—the quest "to get rid of oneself" *(se déprendre de soi-même)*—recalls, rather, Kierkegaard's analysis of the despairing alternative to faith, the sickness unto death that entails the sick man's dilemma: "despair at not willing to be himself." He finds that "he cannot get rid of himself." Despair is a fire that enters what cannot burn. For "every man is primitively planned to be a self, appointed to become himself," and here is "refusal to see one's task in the self given him." Which hypothesis better and more persuasively accounts for experience, the Nietzschean or the Kierkegaardian? Foucault found a cue in Nietzsche's strategy of heroically risky experiment—the discovery of "positive truth" in its "downward fall." What is this but empty, mystifying rhetoric?

There is no denial here of Foucault's seriousness. He was serious. His seriousness does not say why anyone should find wisdom, or point, in the leads he took from Nietzsche and Heidegger. As for the "higher necessity" to be found "deep down" within us, Nietzsche himself never claimed to have found it. And Heidegger on the unthought? *In thought* it was the unprecedented, "hurling the human being through a breach" in which "suddenly the unbound powers of being come forth and are accomplished as history." *In fact,* it was the dreadful nightmare from which the world was delivered in 1945 at exorbitant cost.

The radical irrationality of the Nietzschean-Heideggerian way lay in flouting not some bourgeois code, but the norms inscribed in human intentionality prior to all codes. Foucault's readiness to take his chances with the way of "negativity" was pathological, free in the sense of superfluous.

A human world and a humanity without intelligibility, essence, or structure is the perfect context for postmodern pluralism. This context, however, is not the least bit new. Idealists like G.R.G. Mure, Thomists like Josef Pieper, critical realists like Bernard Lonergan began soon after mid-century to voice penetrating, well-articulated complaints about this illusory line of thought, which had been established at the opening of the century. Reject this line as illusory, and the basis for a supposedly new pluralism is gone. Its specific difference, the refusal to believe in any meta-narrative, is not new and substantial but old and threadbare: gratuitous unbelief and denial mistaking itself for insight.

The new pluralism is modernist and postmodernist cant. To adopt this view, to be sure, one should meet the condition that a case be made for (1) belief in general and (2) the positive value of particular beliefs. Gadamer's analysis is en route to becoming classic. "The Enlightenment" had as its specific difference from other historic enlightenments the rejection of religious tradition—the Church and the Bible. Luther had not succeeded in mounting an altogether coherent critique of the Church in the name of the Bible, for he still held to the canon, patristic-Church-tradition. Dilthey had no trouble showing that Reformation hermeneutics had failed to emancipate itself from tradition and "dogmatic bias." The *philosophes* would finish the job.

Their attack on Christian prejudice labored, however, under an element of overkill, becoming a super-prejudice: the prejudice-against-all-prejudice. Hence the emasculation not only of Christian, but of all, tradition. For the first time *Vorurteil/préjugé/prejudice* signified not early or (legally) premature judgment, but "unfounded judgment." Belief became a boo-word. Kant rendered the Horatian tag, *Sapere aude* by "Have the courage to use your own intelligence!"

Some forgetfulness of being, a scotosis generating blind spots, in particular an obliviousness to conditions of knowledge as group endeavor, and of culture as collectively generated meanings and values, settled in the European psyche in the wake of the Enlightenment campaign. Human growth, be it in knowledge or any other enterprise, is a group enterprise, the product of many working at functionally diverse tasks. The condition of the possibility of their working together is that they can believe one another.

Most of what any of us knows depends on belief. Even what we find out for ourselves—by our observation, curiosity, questions, and answers—is not held apart in isolation, but is enmeshed in a network of things we know owing to the observations, curiosity, questions, and answers of others. Even the most basic knowledge of geography is a matter of belief. True, this is kind of supposition under remote control; but that simply means that it is reasonable to believe and that we have no alternative. Remove belief and we revert to the stone age. This holds not only for ordinary citizens, but equally for the scientific community in every known discipline, natural and human. The slide rule, the calculator, the map, the concordance are as truly instruments of belief as the television set, the radio, the newspaper.

This detracts not one whit from the primacy of immanently generated knowledge and it cannot substitute for the immanently generated knowledge, in a particular instance, that says: this particular call to belief and prospective act of belief is fully worthy of my belief. This is a judgment of value. It is immanently generated only if I grasp the virtually unconditioned: the realized credibility and credentity (= reasonable believability and belief-worthiness) of the prospective belief. The act of belief calls for a decision, but this immanently generated positive value-judgment is what makes *responsible* both the decision to believe and the actual assent that is belief.

It is worth accenting against the backdrop of the Enlightenment campaign against belief in general and religious belief in particular that the *philosophes* were blind to the reality and indispensability of belief in the whole of human life. Once that scotosis is cured and the blind spots removed, it becomes possible to see some point in the laborious effort of biblical scholarship to recover the massive particulars relevant to the believability of both the narrative and the meta-narrative presented to us by the gospels.

A recent hermeneutical effort, a conference on New Testament studies held not long ago in England, offers sporadic efforts to commend postmodern pluralism. We mentioned above that "ideology" has many meanings. Among them is the postmodernist meaning. One way of treating New Testament texts, for example, the privileging as true of the soteriology that Paul commended to his young missionary churches, or of the story told in the gospel of Mark, becomes "ideological" in a negative sense if it is "too exclusive or too uncritical." At first, a reader might think this view of ideology to be viable—or at least salvageable—in token of its conditional element. In fact it is neither, for it supposes from the start that any treatment is "too exclusive or too uncritical" which takes these texts on their own terms to be believed as true, for they thus acquire a form of "normative status."

Until dialectic is brought to bear on it, "ideology" seems to be in the eye of the ideology-critic. Dialectic, however, sets the scene for a confrontation of conflicting horizons. It is a little like the shake-out in times of severe economic competition, which not all enterprises survive. Some positions, like some companies, will stand and some fall. The criterion in dialectic will be the facts of conscious human intentionality.

The postmodernist view of ideology has the virtue of being straightforward. To take Paul or Mark or any other exponent of the gospel as to be believed at face value is to fall into the trap of ideology. Unbelief is insight. No need to show this to be the case; it is "blindingly obvious." Without any full-blown effort of dialectic and subsequent shake-out, we might simply put the question of whether the postmodernist view is self-reversing and illusory.

Pluralism, then, is an end in itself. An interpretation becomes "ideological" in a pejorative sense when it raises itself above the plurality and claims some form of normative status for itself.

But this postmodernist pluralism reduces all competing views to ideology; in short, it raises itself above the plurality and claims some form of normative status. Did we just hear the sounds of sawing, then of a branch breaking?

Unbelief may be insight, as postmodernists suppose. Lonergan offers a complementary truth: insights are a dime a dozen. What really counts is finding out which insights can make their implicit claim to truth stick.

Conclusion

The hallmark of critical realism is its insistence on the empirical (data), the intelligent (questioning and answering), the rational (the grasp of evidence as sufficient or insufficient, the personal act of commitment) as—all of them together—entering into true judgment. For present purposes, the value of critical realism is its inbuilt antibodies against ideology. The result is to let the New Testament be what it was meant to be and do what it was meant to do. But critical realism could not be of service to the New Testament in this way unless it were able to be of service to any text whatsoever. It is universally applicable, a general theory relevant to all interpretation.

Here we have been concerned with alienation, rationalization, illusion. Among these failed efforts there is a view of knowledge so fundamental and so fundamentally mistaken as to merit the status of "cognitional myth." The myth is that fully human knowing is like sense-knowing and, in particular, like ocular vision: passive and of itself infallible. When for whatever reason its pretentions are unmasked, there is a risk that the reaction will be extreme and the dullness of modelling fully human knowing on sense-knowing will be replaced by the extravagance of converting mere knowledge into a new creation.

Respecting "reading" we raised the issue of whether texts mediate meaning to us, or we merely ascribe meaning to texts. The issue here is analogous: whether we discover our worlds of meaning or merely project them. The middle position is like the middle position on reading: the meaning of the text is retrieved by the experience, understanding, and judgment of the reader. Objects generally are similarly grasped: Euclidian geometry did not preexist in quantity, just waiting to register itself on the mind of Euclid; nor was Galileo's thinking preexistent in free-falling bodies, nor Dante's poetry in the strife of Guelph and Ghibelline.

Finally, ideology is not the last word. The sad, shabby historical tale of Western "intellectuals" since Nietzsche has often had the effect on sane, informed, intelligent people (an example is Paul Johnson and his trenchant study, *Intellectuals*) of undermining all hope of a rational cosmopolis, a cultural superstructure of sane people. More positive and hopeful, critical realism renews the affirmation of truth and goodness as human possibilities.

PART III

THEOLOGICAL HERMENEUTICS

Twenty years ago Peter Stuhlmacher published an essay on the theological interpretation of scripture and especially of the New Testament. The essay responded to the worsening condition of New Testament scholarship. It was not exactly a crisis, but it was an unsatisfactory state of affairs, which might be formulated as a dilemma. One of its horns was the mass of ill-grounded, extravagant "experimental results" presenting themselves as fruits of "historical-critical interpretation." The other horn was recoil from the methods of philologically exact historical method. This was due in some measure to disgust with the selfsame experimental results. The dilemma, then, was hermeneutical. Did the interpreter have to choose between philology and theology? Between exact philological method and theologically responsible interpretation of the text?

Stuhlmacher's task was twofold: first, to dissolve the dilemma by showing that the "experimental results" were not necessary nor in some instances even authentic products of historical-critical methods. They did not, then, supply good grounds for abandoning hard-won gains such as the resources—philological, literary, and historical—that made possible a precise recovery of meaning; second, to show that what practitioners of historical-critical methods needed in order to achieve a theological interpretation of scripture lay on the side not of the text nor of method, but of the interpreter. Two factors emerged. The first was a positive, if provisional, stance vis-à-vis the text. This was not "faith" (faith is more than provisional) but an antecedent readiness to take in, to agree, to consent. The second was the cultivation of non-trivial questions, questions that in some way responded to the text at the level of the text.

The so-called experimental results, when they were brought together in a few pages, did create the impression of a discipline in trouble. Superficiality, lack of exigence respecting evidence, habitual oversight of countervailing evidence, telltale indications of the inroads of ideology (a priori rejection of transcendence, for example, or a theology demanding political demythologizing) contributed to a dismal catalogue of aberrations. One aspect of Stuhlmacher's strategic response in the years that followed lay in tracing a historically enlightening view of hermeneutics across the ages. Another lay in simply continuing to work on the project of a philologically grounded, solidly theological interpretation of biblical texts.

Many on the international scene shared Stuhlmacher's views of the discipline of New Testament studies and began to gather their forces in the early 1980s, conducting regular seminars and making the results of their work available in monographs and articles, for example, in the journal *Ex Auditu*. The effort was to substitute lighting a candle for cursing the darkness.

Probably the most important single accent in the 1980s fell on the role of faith in the interpretation of the word of God and on the more and more clearly unsatisfactory work competing from a neutral history-of-religions standpoint with an explicitly theological interpretation of the texts. Increasingly, the work of Stuhlmacher and his allies has become explicitly religious, theological.

Part III follows in this track. We should, however, spell out the limits and qualifications under which we are proceeding. In Lonergan's account of method in theology, the functional specialty "doctrines" presupposes the functional specialty "foundations." We cannot undertake work in the speciality "foundations"; neither then shall we take up doctrinal questions such as "inspiration," which accounts for scripture as "the word of God" and for the canon of scriptures. Without requiring prior explanation, we approach the text as word of God and in the spirit of faith, but neither offering doctrinal refinements on "faith," "word of God," "canon," etc., nor denying that such doctrinal positions are ultimately called for.

In chapter seven we shall attempt an approach to the kind and level of questioning to which New Testament texts are answers.

In chapter eight we shall concentrate on the way in which "faith" is called on to qualify the work of interpreting these texts.

In Lonergan's framework of theological collaboration, the crucial categories derive neither from divisions of "the data" (field specialization) nor from divisions of "results" (subject specialization); the first yields fields such as "the Law," "the prophets," "the writings," the second yields subjects such as "semitic languages," "ancient near eastern history," "pre-literary and literary forms." Our key category, by contrast, is "functional specialization" having to do with stages in the process of moving from data to results. These include "research," "interpretation," "history," "dialectic," "foundations," "doctrines," "systematics," and "communications." In the limits we have set ourselves there is, perhaps, the implicit suggestion—stronger language would be out of place—of a possibility and an ecumenical opportunity. To put the matter in provisional terms: it would seem that, in order to practice an appropriate *(sachgemäss)*, connatural interpretation of the scriptures, there is no antecedent need of methodically confessional hermeneutics. Rather than representing a limit, this may offer an opportunity, making it possible for ecumenically collaborating interpreters (those like-minded on hermeneutical issues) one day to approach *together* the tasks of dialectic, foundations, and doctrines.

Finally, before directly engaging the issue of the horizons of the New Testament, we should freely acknowledge that there are altogether legitimate reasons for individual persons to turn away from the theological interpretation of scripture in favor of other forms of biblical scholarship. Among them is the interpreter's self-understanding. Like the tower-builder, he/she might take stock of personal resources before deciding to build. Many are more disposed to and better equipped for analytic tasks in which interpretation is not the main element. Though graduate schools might often overlook it, the issue of personal preferences and resources is by no means trivial.

Apropos of the issue of resources, Collingwood pondered the question of what it takes to write the kind of history that would deal seriously with "progress." He offered a set of utterly realistic perspectives, in which self-knowledge regarding resources played a major role. The historian must know himself, for he has to know whether or not he is in a position to grasp at least two periods, two ways of life, and to grasp them both with enough sympathy and insight to reconstruct their experience for himself. He must satisfy himself and his readers that no blind spot in his own mind, and no defect in his equipment of learning, keeps him from entering into the experience of one less fully than into that of the other. Having fulfilled that condition, he is entitled to ask whether the change from the first to the second was a progress. The answer will hinge on his hold on the problems that the first way of life met, as well as those that it failed to meet, and which led it to subside into routine or to perish; and it will hinge finally on his settling whether the second way of life, without losing its grip on the solutions of the first, also solved the problems that eluded and defeated the first.

Collingwood's concluding reflections on this kind of inquiry are equally realistic. It could not ambition comprehensiveness, he observed, for it could not take up every aspect of the first and the second ways of the life. For many tracts of experience we have insufficient data, or we have data, but we lack the kind of experience that might allow us to interpret them in penetrating fashion. His example of the latter was Roman religion. The lack of widespread resources for interpreting Roman religious experience which he took to obtain in the 1930s may in the 1990s begin also to apply to interpreting Christian religious experience.

Apropos of the issue of preferences, it belongs to happy human variety that some prefer analytic puzzle-solving to interpretation. Still, it is somehow incumbent on the community of New Testament scholars to make sure that interpretation, as the primary and main enterprise of New Testament studies, is successfully cultivated. The scholarly community, while fully open to literary, historical, social-scientific, and other modes of analysis, should not be taken in by the proposal that such analyses *replace* interpretation, that they be accepted as functional *surrogates* of interpretation; or that ideological analyses (Marxist, Freudian, Nietzschean, etc.) be accorded the dogmatic status that ideologues (Marxist, Freudian, Nietzschean, etc.) regularly claim for them. Such resources may be drawn on productively, but ideological use is not productive.

Despite a certain convergence in "openness in principle" to the variety of kinds and styles of analyses, we have no reason to agree, and good reason to disagree, with views urging that the two, "interpretation" and "analysis," be put on a par; that the ground of openness is an undiscriminating general principle of thereby doing justice to the texts' "semantic potential"; that religious content too might thus be taken account of, should one "wish" for a "fuller" hold on the text. Here rather we suppose what we said above: texts have a *prima facie* claim on the reader, namely, to be interpreted in accord with their intended sense. This is not an exclusivist claim, but it is a claim to priority. In principle, interpretation is prior to analysis, which serves or supposes it. Religious literature calls for interpretation alert to religious meanings and values. The issue is the utterly basic one of catching on, or not. Catching on is not automatic. We are not, then, dealing with the mere option of "fuller" understanding.

In North America there has been a marked move away from the treatment of religious texts as religious, often with a covering explanation such as that "religion" in the reality of the ancient Near East touched every aspect of the culture; hence, the objects of social-scientific and religious inquiry were inadequately distinct at best. This may be followed by, say, an interpretation of Jesus as primarily a political peace-advocate or a manager of cultural conflict—signs of some, possibly basic, confusion.

Whatever the explanation, a recent decline in the importance of theological purpose and perspective in New Testament studies in North America is a given. Its acknowledgement should be accompanied by the cool admission that this is not necessarily disadvantageous. Not everyone is equipped for the primary task. There are many mansions in humanistic and religious studies. The purpose of Part III of this primer, however, is to be of service to those who do wish to undertake the primary and principal task of New Testament studies as this is specified in advance by the nature and purpose of the literature. We should face the issue of finding an entrée to the horizons of New Testament literature. We should know what the conditions of the possibility of a theological study of the texts are. We should satisfy ourselves on whether dialectically opposed horizons exist in the New Testament. We should deal with the qualities that favor excellence in theological interpretation.

7

Access to the Understanding of the New Testament on Its Own Terms

The fusion of horizons that Hans-Georg Gadamer made famous as a description of what happens in successful interpetation can no longer be simply assumed as the typical experience of New Testament interpreters.

We shall bracket the way a Barthian fideist might conceive "a fusion of horizons" as a condition of the possibility of successfully interpreting the word of God. If Barth's critique of efforts contemporary with him is indicative, fideists today might, but need not, find fault with the kind of philosophic option represented by critical realism. This is an effort to meet the obstacles blocking arrival at the meaning of the text. Similarly, Bultmann's call for a "life-relation" to the things that the text is about was wholly justified. In any case, even a fideist theologian will grant the relevance to our issue (the effort to find a vantage point from which to grasp the New Testament on its own terms) of the history we are about to review very briefly: the way Europeans, especially since the 1830s, have directly or obliquely treated this issue of vantage point.

The original contexts of this great effort have been numerous. Among the most significant has been the de-Christianization of the West from the Enlightenment to the present. The question has long been, was there a divine revelation at the root of Christianity? Those answering in the affirmative had a second question: in what terms should we understand it? These questions have often been treated, but since they are rooted in constantly evolving cultural processes, the questions are subject to subtle changes in sense, tone, reference, angle of vision. Even the best past treatments may no longer be serviceable to us today.

Theological and biblical studies from the eighteenth and nineteenth centuries have acknowledged this radical questioning in a variety of ways. Yet, when we ask what out of the era from Hegel to World War II might offer guidance to us today, not many lines of thought impose themselves. Who in the nineteenth century (apart from John Henry Newman on the theme of development and Søren Kierkegaard on authenticity and faith) offers words still indispensable to this radical questioning? What line of thought, apart from the centrality of the kerygma, calls for ongoing further development?

In continental Europe, Germany especially, religious thought relevant to the interpretation of the New Testament ran in channels partly determined by the university situation. In the early nineteenth century the Church was charged with the question of "faith," the university with that of "knowledge." Assumptions of harmonious relations of faith *(Glaube)* and knowledge/science *(Wissenschaft)* lasted from the latter eighteenth century till the 1830s. Such harmony had often enough been achieved by pietists at the expense of reason and the natural order and by rationalists at the expense of the integrity of faith.

Among Catholics harmony between faith and knowledge was taken as an issue settled in principle throughout most of this period. The settlement was reaffirmed in the First Vatican Council (1870); it became acute only with the advent of Modernism (early twentieth century) when for the first time the full force of the historical consciousness registered on the internal affairs of Catholics, and bold spirits adopted historical-critical modes of interpretation. After the decades-long badgering of Richard Simon by self-appointed guardians of orthodoxy, this style of biblical study had not been honored among Catholics. Again attacked by Church authorities in the early twentieth century, it was fully accepted only after the Encyclical Letter of Pius XII, "Divino Afflante Spiritu" (1943).

Among Protestants the first decades of the nineteenth century witnessed German idealist and romantic efforts to harmonize faith and knowledge. Hegel and Schleiermacher offered distinctively shaped rationales of harmony. After the appearance of Strauss' *Leben Jesu* (1835–1836) this harmony could no longer be taken for granted. Strauss' brilliantly simple procedure as a biblical critic—systematically to review the entire gospel record, playing rationalists off against supernaturalists to the disadvantage of both and to the advantage of "the mythological interpretation"— dissipated an ambiguity in Hegel: whether the historicity of the gospels belonged to the content (*Begriff*/concept) of Christianity, or might be relegated to its husk (*Vorstellung*/representation). Strauss chose the latter and built a massive case for this choice.

Protestant theology has never entirely recovered from this trashing of the historicity of the gospels. Strauss, to be sure, had not intended an attack on Christianity itself. He thought of his work as an enlightened effort to clarify and salvage it. In the concluding dissertation of his *Leben Jesu* he offered his own view of how faith and knowledge were kept in harmony, namely, through a pedestrian humanist variation on Hegel's christology.

He carried on this program in his *christliche Glaubenslehre* (1841–1842), but now stating cautiously why harmony could no longer hold, at least not among those willing to acknowledge the claims of knowledge. The war between faith and knowledge, he argued, was partly due to the limits of faith as (in its native form) primitive, mythical, inconceivable; partly it was due to the requisites of knowledge, that is, of light from the Enlightenment and the demands attendant on mankind's taking history into its own hands. In the end Strauss repudiated Christianity (except as an ethical ideal).

Feuerbach was in many respects a kindred soul, whose career exhibited a dozen similarities to that of Strauss. Both started in theology and, eventually breaking with Christianity, ended in materialism, Hegelianism having served as intermediate phase. In their own time their early efforts had a powerful impact but lacked staying power not only because of their own shortcomings, but because the Hegelian vision that sustained their early, influential thinking itself lacked staying power. Why? It was a tower of insight. As we have seen, however, insight is hypothetical. So a tower of insight can also be a house of cards, riven from top to bottom with structural faults—the absence of grounded *judgment*.

Hegel's range of vision is enormous; indeed, it is unrestricted in extent. But it is always restricted in content, for it views everything as it would be if there were no facts. It is a restricted viewpoint that can topple outwards into the factualness of Marx or inwards into the factualness of Kierkegaard. It is a viewpoint that is transcended automatically by anyone that, in any instance, grasps the virtually unconditioned and affirms it.

Here critique lies in transcending "vision" by making contact through judgment with the real order of things. Elements of that order of things might be found in Marxist social criticism or in Kierkegaardian interiority, which relegated the ethical concerns whether of Marx or of Liberal Christianity to a form of life explicitly inferior to the form that was faith and that Kierkegaard himself represented and commended.

Kierkegaard, even in his pseudonymous works (for example, in his *Philosophical Fragments,* a response to Leibniz and Lessing, whose views came to him through, among other channels, a Danish version of Strauss' *Glaubenslehre*) proved to be right about Hegel and faith. He was equally right about the Liberal theology taking shape in his own time. Franz Schnabel's detailed account of the career of this school of thought leaves the impression that, though liable to censure, it was more to be pitied than censured. So far as staying power is concerned, Liberal theology lacked it on several grounds. First, Christianity is not reducible to religious ethics. Second, it is not enough simply to decide for oneself what Christianity is; if in the sight of God its claims belong to the real order, it is bound to have a history independent of its critics' conceptions, and authentic contact with authentic Christianity includes finding out how the historical Church has understood itself.

Idealist and romantic speculation is a poor substitute for this sort of historical realism. Christianity must have a defining identity forged in fact and in time, independent of the thinker. From this standpoint, the Hegelian sound and fury of Strauss' *Leben Jesu* and of Feuerbach's *Wesen des Christentums* ran the risk of finally signifying nothing. If God meant Christianity for the world, he must have equipped it with the possibility of being culturally and historically incarnated. This specifies not an ideological task (so not a Hegelian, Straussian, or Feuerbachian task, which viewed the world from the peaks of ungrounded insight), but a historical task: to discover in history the independent reality of Christianity.

This is what Newman did. If the main line of development in Germany was radical secularization, in England the Oxford movement sought a vitalized sense of tradition in the *via media* between Protestantism and Rome. Newman criticized efforts to define the essence of Christianity as both presumptuous and reductionist. (This did not keep him from contributing to the task in his own way: the essence, in the sense of the thematic matrix from which Christianity's essential dimensions—the sacramental, hierarchical, and ascetic—were derivable, was the Incarnation.)

In 1840–1845 Newman instituted and sustained an inquiry on this basis, which ended with his entry into the Roman Catholic Church and the publication of his *Essay on the Development of Christian Doctrine.* The inquiry had obviously met his chief problem as an Anglican with respect to the self-understanding of Catholicism: the failure of Catholic doctrines and practices to meet the norm of Vicentius (Vincent of Lerins, d. 450). Vincentius had urged that we accept *quod ubique, quod semper, quod ab omnibus creditum est,* "that which has been believed everywhere, always, by all." Newman's inquiry was into the conditions of the specifically historic existence of any belief, any "idea" or movement. That condition was change. More specifically and positively, it was "development," which adds to change a lasting accord with the original selfhood of what undergoes it. "Development" thus makes a defective selfhood worse, in accord with its defects. When, however, selfhood is integral and authentic, development, that is, change in faithful accord with selfhood, becomes a revelation of what the movement is. This was the solution that the principle of Vincentius had not sufficed to provide to the modern world.

Newman's thinking was not designed to solve the problems of Protestants. (Protestantism he considered to be historically rootless in the sense of not finding its vindication in the historical reality of Christianity in any period.) Liberal theologians and historians, notably, Adolf von Harnack, mounted efforts to meet the issues that engaged Protestants respecting foundations, authority, faith, and reason (studies in the creeds, definition of the essence of Christianity). Members of the nascent History-of-Religions School helped define new problems and to accentuate others (Weiss on the Kingdom of God, Gunkel on early Christianity as syncretism). The dearth in the late nineteenth century of common Christian horizons and Christian community at any level—common field of experience, common ways of understanding, common judgments, common commitments—dogged every effort to find a center for early Christianity, until the quest changed form, becoming an exegetical issue. Here finally was a common focus: scriptural texts held in common reverence. The debates on creeds in the last decade of the nineteenth century and the discovery of creedal "fragments" in the New Testament in the first decade of the twentieth century created a new and more promising state of the question.

This line of research reached a certain maturity in the wake of the first World War. Between the wars it came to lapidary expression in the kerygma-theology of Rudolf Bultmann and followers and in C. H. Dodd's work on kerygma and didache. Finally, the post-War period produced a harvest of international and ecumenical studies of early faith-formulations, as well as related work on unity/division and uniformity/diversity in early Christianity. This ended in a certain consensus ("the gospel/the kerygma" was the literary matrix of the Christian movement and literature); the consensus, however, turns out to be shared by parties differing in religious, philosophic, and theological horizon, so that agreement has proven apt to fail when called on to meet any serious test, for example, the task we are concerned with: identifying New Testament horizons and making them accessible to prospective interpreters.

Our sketch ends, then, not in futility, yet in insufficiency. This slowly evolving achievement, for all its positive consequences for the study of the New Testament, does not yet effectively meet our issue. We do have here a conclusion to cling to: earliest Christianity was a mode of common life and had a common message. The community harbored the claim to be "Israel restored," and was bound together not by blood, but by a common confession, a defining gospel. All the relevant terms and referents connected with this gospel have been studied diachronically and synchronically in great detail. We have works on Paul's gospel and its importance for his theology; on apostolic preaching and its possible relations to the gospels, on every kind of faith-formula: proclamation and confession, liturgical texts, hymns, and other formulaic materials scattered throughout the New Testament. All this intrinsically worthwhile work nevertheless fails to meet our own issue or other comparably foundational issues. We not only lack common ground for a common understanding of the New Testament; we lack a common grip on why common ground is missing.

Finding out how to lock onto the wavelength of these writings can be a baffling project, for it will not yield to the standard devices of philological, literary, and historical scholarship. Like every other fundamental issue in New Testament studies, this *belongs to foundational hermeneutics, in which cognitional theory and epistemology play basic roles.* This crucial ascertainment prepares the way for our inquiry: how to make our way to the city on the mountain.

Important components of the problem of locking onto the New Testament wavelength are at hand in critical realism. Three may be specified. First, by appeal to a comprehensive or universal viewpoint, critical realism makes possible a precise identification of every kind/area of thematic meaning occupied by New Testament literature. (No other technique presents itself as an alternative route to the accomplishment of this task.) This in turn provides heuristic guidelines to grasping the intended sense of the texts. A recovery of the intended sense of the key texts on the kerygma would promote a far more realistic estimate than we have had in general of what the early Christians understood of the Christ event, its dimensions, and the human destiny it portends.

Second, through the application of dialectic, critical realism can contribute to discernment among competing and contradictory lines of recent and current scholarship. So far as foundational issues are concerned (e.g., whether there was a revelation at the root of Christianity, whether the story of Jesus is credible, whether his "absolute eschatology" makes any sense, etc.), nonphilosophic resources alone do not measure up to the task. Still more dedicated philological, literary, historical, sociological, or anthropological research will for the most part be irrelevant. The key issues are simply of another kind.

Third, within the context of identifying and attempting to appropriate New Testament horizons, I see two main possibilities and anticipate that many others may well be found. The first way is by application of dialectic to competing views of the kerygma.

The German existentialists who made kerygma theology important were not equipped (as we have already noted above) to meet
and make sense of the kerygma on its own terms (including, e.g.,
the insistently recurrent motifs of expiatory death and of resurrection insofar as it entails what Paul calls the *sōma pneumatikon,*
the "transformed body of the risen"). Their cognitional-theoretical resources were derived from late nineteenth-century Neo-
Kantianism. (To be of any real help today, dialectic would have
to deal with the whole range of cognitional-theoretical options.)

The second possibility (the one I have chosen to explore in
this chapter) is through treatment of the problem that arises for
a theist from the massive phenomenon or fact of evil. The theist
(or the classical theist) knows, from the sheer incompatibility of
God and evil, that there is a solution to the problem of evil. His
question is, what might it concretely consist in? His thinking runs
as follows: given the irreducible incompatibility of God and evil,
the one thing that is clear in advance is that *the solution squarely
meets the problem.* We can therefore trace the outlines of the solution by first of all finding the core of the problem, then bringing insight to bear on it, and exigent judgment to bear on the
insight.

History as Problem and Solution

To the theist, history is an experiment that puts the human
race to the test. *Tu autem in te manes,* prayed Augustine, *nos
in experimentis volvimur* ("You abide in yourself whereas we are
ever turned about in trials"). History becomes a dramatic issue
for any theist (in the classical sense of wholly intelligible theism:
the affirmation of God is an affirmation of God as all-knowing,
all-powerful, and all-good). For the theist cannot take the panorama of physical and moral evil that history presents as a merely
and deeply baffling fact and leave it at that. The problem lies in
the impossibility that creation should fail, that the human race
should fail, that the historic panorama of evil could coexist with
the reality of God. Precisely the same considerations that exclude
evil as a merely dispiriting fact to be borne in stoic fashion or
revolted against in gnostic fashion and that ground its necessarily *problematic* nature (in view of God's wisdom, goodness, and
power) tell in favor of the problem's *necessarily* having a solu-

tion. No way exists in which to escape the incompatibility of God, source of being, with the condition that transparently holds in present and historic human reality: the fact of gross, widespread illusion, sophisticated counterpositions, savage self-assertion, murderous injustice; the malicious, irrational, barbarous egoism of the historic human race.

If evil is a problem, and if the problem must have a solution, the question arises: what is the solution? What has God done and what is God doing about human evil?

This is a very different question from the related questions we raised in chapter four on the notion of being (= drive to being) in its existential phase, the quest of the good. There we took up the structure of the moral issue, which touched on the difficulty of the moral life; offered a schematic outline of how society and the individual person interact in the quest of the good; sketched the social groups intermediate between the individual and society at large; proposed the indispensability of values (vital, social and cultural, personal and religious) and the role of virtues such as practical wisdom/*phronēsis,* justice, courage, and self-control. We considered the slow and complex process by which the child moves toward responsible self-determination, but we hardly glanced at the actual history of human folly. When we asked how human beings function in fact, the issue was not history; it bore on the facts of proper, effective, self-assembling, normative human functioning. Now, however, we are concerned with actual human functioning in the historical sense.

We might begin by reference to our inheritances from classical and biblical antiquity. By nature the human race (said classical antiquity) is good and oriented to the good. *Polla te deina* ("Many things are wonderful") *k'ouden anthrōpou deinoteron pellei* ("but none so wonderful as man"). Some common notes are struck in the many "visions" of the human being and the human race that reach us from the poetry of antiquity, Greek and (in Arnold Toynbee's term) Syriac, in other words, ancient Near-Eastern and biblical. Among them is one dimension of the view of man: high, confident, awestruck (a view congenial to the Greek context of cosmic order and even more congenial to the biblical context of creation). The Greeks and the Bible both yield finally dialectical views, which play off high (or positive) and low (or negative) factors against one another. The *polla te deina* chorus of Sophocles presents man as the crown of cosmic order; in one perspective, at least, the Syriac view exalts man as "a little lower" than the gods of the divine court (Ps 8) or "the angels" (LXX Ps 8).

It is noteworthy how well the high view or vision of the human being and the human race has worn, despite the long history of human self-destructiveness (the vision of ruin and debris seen at his feet by Walter Benjamin's "angel of history," blown backwards into the future by the storm of progress) and despite the energetic cultivation in the modern age of radically reductionist theories of the make-up of man. The ancient visions and celebrations of man may be taken to have worn well in virtue of human vanity and the consolations of illusion. Still, this is not the only explanation. They may have worn well because they reflect significant facets of human reality. The question is open.

One way of dealing with it is to trace, with Bruno Snell, the elements of human intentionality as the Greeks assembled them, starting with Homer; or, by way of biblical counterpart to Snell's history, to trace the development of religious sensibility in the Bible, starting from the theophanies of the Exodus and the appropriation of themes from Canaanite myth and ritual, moving through Elijah on Horeb to Ezekiel's vision of restoration. Gradually elaborated, these visions of the human subject among the Greeks and the Hebrews, whether (as among the Greeks) intensely curious about and observant of human subjects, or (as among the Hebrews) bent on rightly conceiving Israel's relations to God, were products not of naïve optimism but, in the first case, of a finally tragic vision of man and, in the second, of a consciously dark history of sin.

What we learn from the Greek and Hebrew models is the need to bring into some equilibrium great human potentialities against dark times, dark deeds, a history of evil. Actual history is what led Hebrews and Greeks alike to posit a native condition of the human race unimaginably superior to the empirical and familiar. The empirically familiar is understandable in terms of human shortfall, defects that resist correction: a blindness and perversity without reference to which we cannot make sense of ourselves to ourselves.

The problem is catastrophe, suffering, and death; but it is far less these things than moral collapse under pressure of these things or the prospect of these things. The problem, in a word, is less challenges than the ruthless act of running roughshod over challenges, the dismissal of dilemmas in favor of power. The core of the problem is moral, not physical, evil: collapse under the pressures and enticements of the "deadly sins." It is what we are taught to pray to escape: *mē eisenegkēs hēmas eis peirasmon,* "keep us from failing when tested," or "do not let us crack under pressure."

To specify the human problem still further: it in some way includes death and the ever-present shadow of death, early death, infant death, unjust death, just as it somehow includes pain and especially unmerited or unjust or disproportionate pain. It most of all consists in a generalized failure to mount and even more to sustain a life of wisdom, justice, courage, and self-mastery. It is clear that we are dealing with a "problem" or "dilemma" that is by no means peculiar to the Hebrews and the Greeks. Both biblical and Greek wisdom specify it as a human problem. It does not change its character from generation to generation; it exhibits a mulishly recurrent and melancholy sameness.

Elsewhere I have offered a far fuller survey leading up to Lonergan's analysis of the problem. The survey evoked various lines of current culture criticism, the phenomenon of able, successful, fortunate, yet deeply unhappy men, the extraordinary testimony of Tolstoy's *Confession,* analysis of the contrary causes of social and cultural progress and decline, William Barrett's penetrating reconsideration of the theme of the human subject and soul from Descartes to the computer *(Death of the Soul),* Leszek Kolakowski's analysis of human deficiency and its soteriological remedies in the tradition that runs from Plotinus to Hegel and Marx, Josef Pieper's dark evocation of a dreadful penultimate state of human affairs in *Über das Ende der Zeit.* . . . All this made up an almost casual, random choice out of a boundless sea of data on concrete conditions with which a theist's affirmation of God as all-knowing, all-powerful, and all-good is ultimately incompatible.

Lonergan's response consists not in an irrational abandonment of theism, but in assembling the heuristic specifications of "the solution" that must exist if, in conformity and consistency with himself, God has squarely met and continues to meet "the problem." Since there is one God, one world order, and one individual and social problem of evil, the solution will be one. Since the problem is not restricted to human subjects of a particular class or a particular time, the solution will be universally accessible and permanent. Since the problem is human, the solution will be adapted to human beings as they are. Since the problem lies in powers by which the human person functions, the solution will bear on some transformation of those powers.

This last sentence should be more fully spelled out. The root of the human problem may be variously conceptualized, for example, as the power over human beings of the seven deadly sins. Lonergan's analysis took the form of uncovering biases and blind spots—dramatic bias that generates scotosis: unconscious aberrations deriving from censorship of psychic process, exclusion of unwanted insights, the blockage of further relevant questions when the insights occur, dread of and recoil from correction; inhibition, repression, and the rationalizing of the blinding process and its resultant blind spots. There is further the bias of individual egoism; group bias (that of classes, professions, "interest groups," etc.); the bias of common sense (e.g., the businessman's common sense, which may reject not only economic theorizing, such as abstract macroeconomics, but any theorizing that fails to correlate with business interests); such bias tends to pay small attention to long-term consequences. All the kinds of common sense have their virtue within their proper ambit, but similarly betray the tendency to claim an omnicompetence that is painfully mistaken. The psychological side of intentionality analysis largely replaces the sketchy, pre-technical psychology that moral philosophy has relied on. (The theologically charged myth material of the Bible, on the other hand, may be quite helpful here.) The human problem lies in the conditions affecting the exercise of precisely these human powers.

Since nature generates the problem, the solution must in some sense be supernatural. The solution must meet all the problems that arise from the natural condition of man. Above, we have just evoked the spontaneous interference of sense-life with reasonable decision (dramatic bias); individual and group egoism; commonsense practicality extended beyond its range. The solution must offer resources that counteract the natural tendency to adopt clear, easy, "blindingly obvious," but dead wrong principles of theory or speculation (the counterpositions).

The solution, then, is conceived as irreducible to nature, and yet as a harmonious continuation of the order of the universe. Now, the order of the universe is a process: emergent probability, an operative mix of classical scientific law and of statistical law in accord with schedules of probability. This process exhibits "vertical finality": systems of development and adaptation move toward higher integrations. "The solution" that we are attempting to specify will accordingly itself constitute a higher integration, capable of development and adaptation. This evolutionary/developmental conception anticipates an entry-in-stages of the solution into history, in other words, an emergent trend is to be anticipated in which the solution in its full form first becomes effectively probable.

If the central element of the solution is a transformation of human powers, we should note that it ought not to be conceived in line with Platonist and gnostic thought as a change in the makeup of the species, a sloughing off of material being. It accords, by contrast, with the prophets' hope, for it calls on the one hand for a renewal of the one human race that actually exists, on the other, for a genuinely creative act. The problem, the prophets thought, lay in "the heart . . . most crooked . . . beyond remedy" (Jer 17:9), the heart of stone that God would remove (Ezek 36:26). The new creation, which Isaian tradition celebrated (Isa 42:9; 43:19; 48:6; 65:17), and the realization of which Paul would identify with "being in Christ," and so with faith/baptism (2 Cor 5:17) lay in transforming the human subject by new powers: faith, hope, love.

These supernatural powers constituted the bond with Being that Platonist dialectic called for, though many in the ages-long post-Plotinian tradition of Platonism (e.g., from Eckhart to Fénélon) would interpret the change as self-annihilating fusion with Being. On the contrary, Paul, the later Augustine, and Thomas Aquinas would take it to be the transforming realization of the self intended in creation. The tendency of Christian tradition from Paul through Augustine and the Middle Ages to the present has been to epitomize this new creation in terms of faith, hope, and love.

Love, because nothing less—not justice, for example—can repair the ravages of injustice and truly restore the good that evil has violated. Justice alone might bring back the good of order, but what of the antagonisms that absurdity has left in its wake? Hope, because what is needed is to admit (against presumption) that life without God is unmanageable and (against despair) that the individual sinner is not utterly worthless. Faith, because the solution is for all, whereas knowing (the alternative to believing) is beyond their reach.

The solution must (under "transformation of human powers") include a cognitive aspect bearing on the pursuit of truth. In the analogue of the scientific community, the pursuit of truth is a collaboration in which "science" in the concrete is a compound of belief and immanently generated knowledge. But among scientists this collaboration is an entirely human affair. Brought to bear on human living, a purely human collaboration would be flatly implausible. Hence, the new and higher collaboration belonging to the solution could hardly be the work of human beings alone. It must be mainly the work of God. Indeed, if a human role is to be functional at all, the solution must provide an enabling form qualifying the intelligence of human subjects for a share in this cognitive quest. We may call this form "faith"; and since belief and only belief is universally accessible and fits harmoniously within a continuation of the actual order of the world, this faith will be a transcendent belief, its motive the omniscience, goodness, and omnipotence of God, originator and preserver of this divine-human collaboration.

The act of faith will include affirmations on man and on God: affirmations of man's spiritual nature, freedom, responsibility, and sinfulness, of the existence and nature of God, and of "the solution," that transcendent solution that God provides for man's problem. It will include an announcement and an account of the solution.

How is the human subject to acknowledge the solution? By responding to the announcement intelligently, reasonably, and responsibly: this implies having grasped the existence of the problem of evil and of human inability to cope with it; inferring that divine wisdom must know many possible solutions, that divine omnipotence can effect any of them, and that divine goodness must have effected some one of them; recognizing that there has been in human history first, an emergent trend and, later, the full realization of a solution that possesses all the traits determined or to be determined in a heuristic structure like this one.

Whereas the Enlightenment *philosophes* and their spiritual progeny, ideologists of the nineteenth century, imagined solutions every one of which would sweep evil out of the world in swift and irresistible fashion, this solution offers no magic cures for the blind spots of the dramatic subject, no proof against disaster, nor emancipation from bias, nor antibodies against error, folly, and sin. Even given the solution, blind spots will continue to betray themselves in ordinary human failure, in the extremes of angelism and animalism, in the working of bias. Group bias will urge replacing a single universally accessible solution by a multiplicity of solutions for different nations, cultures, and classes. General bias will continue to introduce and promote counterpositions. Counterfeit and truncated versions of the solution will by no means be excluded.

The solution will nevertheless be effective. It will generate its heroes, mostly saints. Should it turn out that the solution is absolutely supernatural, in other words, equipping and destining humanity for absolute beatitude in the vision of God, there will result a heightening of the tension that arises whenever the limitations of lower levels are transcended. Mere humanism would then be out of the question. To measure up to their own destiny, human beings would have to sublate (i.e., to affirm and transcend) natural fulfillment.

There should be no confusing of the solution with the present argument or search-technique or effort of transcendental retrieval. The solution itself is one, permanent, universally accessible; the argument is an effort of reflection. It belongs in a general way to wisdom; it sets up its own requisites for the fusion of horizons that allows the argument to be cogent. It is important to notice that alternatives to the solution envisaged here, like this or any argument, are not identical with the solution, nor plausible candidates to be the solution, precisely because they are not universally accessible. Postmodernist superpluralism, for example, if defined as the incapacity to legitimate claims to knowledge by accepting meta-narratives, cannot be the solution unless it is shown that "belief in meta-narratives" is invariably a root of illusion and evil. In itself incredulity is no solution to human problems of any kind. If, on the other hand, this pluralism is defined as a kind of beckoning wisdom, able and willing to draw on all the meta-narratives for whatever limited contribution they might make to human well-being, we again have—for the umpteenth time in history—an offer that cannot be taken for the solution to the human problem, because like all efforts toward wisdom it is far from being universally accessible. "The solution" we have been on the track of cannot be limited to the *aristoi,* the privileged few; it must be available to the many, the *mikroi/elachistoi/nēpioi,* the little ones, the least, the simple.

In *Insight* Lonergan left it to the reader to identify the solution that actually obtains. The specifications of the solution, however, leave little doubt as to their concrete goal: *The divine solution known to us from Bible and Church—especially as focusing on the death and resurrection of Christ, the salient traits of the Church, and the transformative role of faith, hope, and love—is the divine solution to the problem of evil.* In a later essay, Lonergan remarks:

> This analysis fits in with scriptural doctrine, which understands suffering and death as the result of sin, yet inculcates the transforming power of Christ, who in himself and in us changes suffering and death into the means for attaining resurrection and glory.

If intelligently grasped and reasonably affirmed, this line of reflection yields access to the horizons of earliest Christianity. That is, it terminates in the capacity to understand what the New Testament is about. By way of samples illustrating the easy and natural entrée it offers to New Testament texts, consider first those that present the solution as God's gift:

> Happy the poor, for the reign of God is for them!
> Happy those in mourning! Happy the lowly! Happy the hungry!

The terms of our argument also facilitate entrée to texts on the availability of the solution to all:

> I thank you, Father, Lord of heaven and earth,
> that, hiding these things from the wise and intelligent,
> you have revealed them to the simple!

The "all" alluded to above include "the wise and intelligent," who nevertheless remain capable of refusing the offer of salvation. Our identification of the solution makes for a comprehending entrée to texts on the paradox of the rejected and glorified Messiah:

> Whoever is set on saving his life / will lose it
> and whoever loses his life for my sake / will save it.

The divine solution to the problem of human evil, we said, is a new creation. This corresponds to the gnomic Pauline cry:

> To be in Christ / is new creation!

Or again:

> The God who said, "Let light stream out of the darkness," has flooded our hearts with light, the light of the knowledge of God's glory streaming from the face of Christ.

Ezra Pound accented the importance not only of what one holds, but of "the level at which one holds it." The reflection on the kind of solution that is called for to meet the problem of evil squarely is not the equivalent of the gospel story, but *it prepares one to take in the gospel story at the proper level.* This level is not the mild interest of the *bien pensant* (conventionally or politically correct). It is much closer to the missionary passion of men who frequently faced death for the mission:

> As God keeps his word, I tell you, our word to you has not been Yes and No. For the Son of God, Christ Jesus, whom we preached to you—Silvanus, Timothy, and I—was not Yes and No. He has been pure Yes. For, whatever promises God has made, their Yes is in him.

The gospel, then, will be no praiseworthy paradigm of transcendence alongside a dozen others. Rather, it will be God's solution for the world: unique, universally accessible, permanent, adapted to human beings, offering a transformation of human powers, meeting the problem of sin by the efficaciously expiatory death of one for all, meeting the problem of death by a paradigmatic, already realized eschatological event of resurrection from the dead, and meeting the problem of a dark or dicey future by the promise of the Day of the Son of Man and advent of the reign of God.

The effort to retrieve the divine solution anticipated by a theist on the basis of the incompatibility of God and evil or, more precisely, the incompatibility of God on the one hand, the triumph of evil over his creation on the other, may function as a heuristic index to the horizons of the New Testament even for one who does not share the convictions of the theist and does not affirm the gospel as the solution of the problem of evil. For this searching inquiry into the problem of evil presents to the non-theist, or to the non-classical theist, an approximation to the early Church's engagement of mind and heart, and to the level of that engagement. It allows an outsider to form some idea of what the insiders are saying to one another, why they are saying it in the tones and with the gestures that they do, and why, in a word, they take it all so hard. The outsider may lack a *Lebensverhältnis* (or "life-relation") to *die Sache* (the thing or referent signified by "gospel"), but he has been provided with the clues and indices, at least, to why across the centuries the New Testament has packed the wallop that it has. It will also allow him to form some preliminary estimate of works purporting to reveal the figure of Jesus as a magician, or founder of a peace-movement, and so forth.

We have been pondering a movement of heuristic retrieval, seeking to limn in advance the contours of "the solution" on the basis of the contours of "the problem." This search-structure, or movement of heuristic reflection, can be variously pressed into the service of ulterior functions, as we have done here, in our effort to find a way to a fusion of horizons with the earliest Christian literature.

It may be appropriate to observe how limited this function is. It should not be thought to have settled in advance any exegetical or historical question whatever. It has not, for example, settled such questions as whether the New Testament celebrates a Christ and Christ event that far transcends the category of "solution." This transcendence of "solution" has itself been a theme variously entertained all through Christian history, and a classic theological question since the High Middle Ages. Charles Fox Burney proposed that the Christology of Colossians (esp. Col 1:15-18), exploiting Genesis 1:1 and Proverbs 7:22, "The Lord begat me . . . of old," or more exactly:

> The Lord begat me,
>> the beginning of his way,
>> the antecedent of his works,
> of old.

Christ is the *archē* of creation, conceived prior to creation. And regardless of whether Burney's exegesis is accurate, several texts converge to assure us that we have here a solid datum explicit in deutero-Pauline texts and plausibly implicit elsewhere in the New Testament. Our effort to find an orientation to New Testament horizons is just that, an orientation. It is not a limit on the assessment of these further concrete data on Christ.

"The solution" is a climactic, definitive happening, an event, not a text. But the texts that have registered that event have as their matrix "the gospel" or news of the event. There is then this proportionately reasonable apriority: texts reflecting a movement whose self-expression is one and the same "gospel" will ultimately cohere among themselves. This expectation does not include the least surprise at variety and diversity in outlook, lifestyle, or expression.

Nevertheless, in the light of the several cultures that the texts reflect and in the light of the extraordinarily swift and substantial development of the Christian movement, one might wonder whether the diachronic line especially might not have generated tensions and occasioned breaks. Gregory Dix defined this—the issue of whether "identity" had been maintained from the first Church of Jerusalem to post-Pauline Catholicism—as the principal question agitating New Testament historians from the Ferdinand Christian Baur (fl. 1830–1860) era to Dix's own time (d. 1952). We conclude this chapter with an orientation to this question.

Unity and Division, Uniformity and Diversity

The question has by now entered into its fourth half-century. It remains the central historical question that Dix in the early 1950s defined it to be. This is not the place to deal directly with the historical question. (Nevertheless, something can said here about the first significant conflict, in the 40s of the first century, apropos of the Mediterranean mission sponsored by the Christian community of Antioch, a conflict rooted in earlier diversities on the part of the speech-communities, Aramaic and Greek, among Jerusalem Christians.) But, though leaving aside the concrete historical issues, it can hardly be amiss in a primer on hermeneutics to offer some reflection on clues to the issue of Christian identity and development. There is hardly another question, apart perhaps from the historical-Jesus question, as religiously and theologically charged.

We have posed the question in diachronic terms; but in view of the simultaneity of the *hebraioi* and *hellēnistai* in Jerusalem of the 30s, it is also a question for the earliest period taken by itself. The two language-groups were inevitably bonded to one another by the messianic Lord who had bequeathed them the "Spirit" and the spiritual *naos*/sanctuary, or Church. The *hellēnistai*, resident in Jerusalem either temporarily or permanently from the Greek-speaking Jewish diaspora, had in all probability been won over to the new movement no earlier than the post-Easter preaching of the Aramaic-speaking *hebraioi*. The Acts of the Apostles offers a stylized account of this earliest missionary move. The question of whether the *hebraioi* took the initiative of preaching in Greek-speaking synagogues is left in abeyance. The *hellēnistai*, first-fruits of the Pentecost event, learned from their Aramaic-speaking brethren whatever they knew of the story of Jesus, but they interpreted the story in their own independent way. This implies confident theological leadership among them, and trains a focus of attention on Stephen. The *hellēnistai* did not share the buoyantly optimistic way in which those gathered around Cephas and the twelve deployed the interpretative rubrics that they had inherited from Jesus. They worked out their own way of interpreting the meaning of Christ's resurrection for the world.

To judge from these earliest beginnings, there was no fear of diversity among the first Christians. The dynamic and aggressive Greek-speaking wing of the movement was driven from the city, and settled, among other places, in Antioch on the Orontes, whence in the middle and latter forties of the first century they launched the first Christian mission. Their missionary appeal reflected their own way of life. It was a breaking of news of salvation through Christ's death and resurrection. In Jerusalem this bypassing of the Torah brought to a boil a subsurface issue: whether Judaism and the Torah were part and parcel of messianic salvation.

It is astonishing how frequently the contributors to the Kittel-Friedrich theological dictionary imaginatively posited unattested breaks and divisions in the earliest Church. Where the texts say "conflict," the scholars said "division." Thus, Aramaic-speaking and Greek-speaking Christians, Jerusalem and Antioch, Peter and Paul, James and Paul, Paul and his young missionary churches supposedly betrayed divisions at every turn, despite a total lack of direct, concrete evidence of *division*. In discussing the issue of ecclesial unity it would be unwise to overlook this extraordinary disregard of the need for data to work on and the need for rigor in working on the data. Our main hermeneutical point, nevertheless, is an observation on categories. *Einheit* and *Vielfalt,* unity and diversity, fall triplingly from the tongue, but like "Italians and lawyers," they represent a cross-classification. The contrary of unity is not diversity, but division; the contrary of diversity is not unity, but uniformity. There is no reason in the world why the earliest Church should not have simultaneously cultivated unity and diversity. There is not the slightest possibility, in fact, that the Church could have maintained unity without simultaneously cultivating or acknowledging diversity.

The critical issue for the Church of the world mission was to find a way of accommodating cultural diversity without sacrificing ecclesial unity. The forces for diversity were at bottom cultural. Cultural diversities doubtless generate theological diversities, and in the Corinthian literature (we shall draw here only on 1 Cor) we meet topic after topic illustrating points at which the culture of Hellenistic paganism posed at least a remote threat to Christian identity. Paul repeatedly found himself having to function as a *ḥākām,* "man-of-practical-discernment," specifying the points at which intervention was called for: the "divisions" *(schismata)* rooted in Greek social mores respecting teachers of "wisdom" (1 Cor 1-4); irregular marriages (1 Cor 5); food offered to idols (1 Cor 8); reduction of the Lord's Supper to a memorial meal on the standard Hellenistic model (1 Cor 11); the impact of popular philosophy on "some," at least in the community, who could not see their way clear to break with the commonplace wisdom of "dead men are not raised" (1 Cor 15).

Greek culture, then, was a constant source of problems to Christian missionaries, but Paul had no cultural axe to grind. He was not at all concerned to promote or enforce Jewish cultural values as such. All in all, his impact on Christianity was selectively to de-Judaize (not thereby to hellenize, but, as Gregory Dix put it, "to allow Christianity to be itself—Christianity"). Paul did not, for example, find fault in principle with eating meat that had been sacrificed to idols; his basis for urging against the practice was simply that one's example might inadvertently lead fellow-Christians to act against their own (mistaken) consciences. It was the primacy of the law of love for one's fellows in the Christian community that counted.

The question of dialectically opposed horizons should be posed, but evidence of dialectically opposed horizons among the Christians of the first century is very scanty. The clearest available example is that attested by Luke, who represents the far right-wing of the Jerusalem community of Christians as maintaining "that those who were not circumcised in accordance with Mosaic practice could not be saved" (Acts 15:1). This is not a mere difference of view, it is rather a difference of horizon, from both sides of the Jerusalem leadership (the centrist, James, and the left-wing of Cephas and John). It is not a trivial difference of horizon, but a maximally significant one. It is, then, an instance of authentic dialectical opposition.

We also learn of ecclesial secession in the Johannine letters. Careful discussion shows both the strength and weakness of the uncompromising treatment of the problem by the author, with the themes of predestination, satanology, and the like playing a role of no little importance. In this kind of experience—a religious community committed above all to the law of love finds its very identity under pressure of attack and in danger of dissolution—can truth be sacrificed to love? Must love be sacrificed to truth? Is there a third possibility? Hypothetical reconstruction of events is possible, and various reconstructions are available, but despite the passion of the writer, we have too few secure data on this community conflict to know whether or not it measures up to our definition of dialectically opposed horizons.

Other candidates for dialectical opposition might be offered: the "some" of 1 Corinthians (15:12, 34) who say that "there is no raising of dead men" (1 Cor 15:12, 13) or "dead men are not raised" (1 Cor 15:15, 16, 29, 32). Regardless of how the dispute over the logic of the Pauline argument is resolved, it seems that the "some" do not deny the kerygma of Christ's own resurrection. This means that Paul is dealing with confusion, not with dialectical opposition. (It is assuredly not one whit less true that Paul apodictically repudiates the view of the "some" as destructive of the kerygma, but the "some" need not undergo a radical conversion; they need simply to recognize that they have perhaps unwittingly involved themselves in a piece of unacceptable incoherence.)

The great majority of putative "contradictions" among the early Christians are actually incompatible conceptualities. There are many ways of conceiving salvation in Christ. If the propositions in question are true, they cannot be mutually contradictory. But this is no guarantee that the conceptualities involved are interchangeable; that the true propositions can be fitted into one another's systems or styles of thought. Jesus conceptualized the impact of his teaching on the Torah as a radicalizing completion thereof; Paul offers no account of Jesus' own way of thinking on this; he not only affirms (with Jesus) the provisional nature of the Mosaic dispensation, but also the end or abolition of the Torah with the advent of salvation in Christ. On concrete matters of the messianic code of conduct, Matthew, representing the Jesus of tradition, and Paul cohere. But the two conceptualities are simply incompatible. Neither fits into or with the other. The fact that they differ in conceptual plane only means that, whether or not we ourselves can work out a higher viewpoint in which their differences are reconciled, we can still anticipate a resolution of this kind. The real order, to which we have access by truth, is not concretely contradictory. It is hermeneutically inept to brush all such reflection aside in impatience, simply insisting on "contradictions" and "divisions." This kind of commonplace ineptness attests the ecclesial and theological culture of division that is current in our world. Whether it is Cephas and Paul at Antioch or James and Paul on "faith," the same set of factors is recurrent.

In attempting to find satisfactory heuristic categories for dealing with both the data of unity and division and the data of uniformity and diversity, the present writer has discovered that the great mass of data could be treated under the headings of "identity" (correlative to "the gospel," and offering the key to unity) and "self-definition," having to do with how "identity" is culturally incarnated. The latter term breaks down into three subheadings, all important sources of cultural diversity: horizons, self-understanding, and self-shaping, or behavior. The only matter on which I would insist, however, is that one distinguish between two issues: "unity vs. division" and "uniformity vs. diversity." If others can find better resources for dealing with the data of diversity than "self-definition" (comprising three culturally significant subheadings), more power to them.

8

Subjectivity Correlative to the Word of God

In the preceding chapter we took it that entry into the New Testament world of meaning required an enabling insight into the kind and level of questioning to which New Testament texts are answers. Such a point of entry we found in the intolerability (in the light of the goodness, wisdom, and power of God) of the defeat of mankind by the cumulative surd that is evil.

Now we go beyond the issue of approach to that of transactions with New Testament literature. From the perspective of general hermeneutics, enabling dispositions on the part of the prospective interpreter include freedom from the dogma of the secular as ultimate horizon and inner distance from the research-games affected by ideologues, games never more beguiling than when, with stunning clarity, they tell the investigators just what they wanted to hear.

Here we shall briefly recall themes of general hermeneutics; once they are stated, we shall specify the perspective in which they are now to operate. Interpretation, as we have seen, has conditions of possibility, all of them touching the resources of the interpreter: a hold on what the text is about; philological resources for the understanding of the text itself; adequate self-understanding; the capacity and will to reflect on evidence of how probable one's understanding of the text is, and to express what one takes to be a probable understanding of the text. Add to these fundamentals such dispositions as connaturality with text and referent and (to make our thinking measure up to its object) whatever measure of human authenticity one can attain: religious, moral, intellectual. On the negative side there are counterparts of these dispositions. They are the traps and hindrances tending to undermine interpretation. They include alienation, ideological commitment, skepticism, inattention to bias, excessive reliance on peer-group thinking, inner distance from topic and text, theory of interpretation or of history that is mistaken or misleading.

Now, however, we confront a datum not previously considered: the status of the biblical and specifically New Testament text as *word of God*. If the text to be interpreted is the word of God, and if one hopes to measure up to the text precisely as the word of God, more is required of the interpreter. For the general theorem still holds: interpretation to be true must be objective, and the way to objectivity is through authentic subjectivity. This is the key to the history of art and thought. Who grasped, who even glimpsed, the shifting beauty of pools of water lilies before Claude Monet caught it on canvas? Had anyone got past scissors-and-paste method in economic history before Marx? The record of discovery is a history of developing subjectivity. What on the part of the interpreter's subjectivity is requisite to move toward an objective hold on the text as word of God?

Subjectivity and "Word of God"

The short answer is "faith," understood in New Testament terms as energized by love (Gal 5:6; Jas 2:18-26; Heb 10:22-24; 2 Pet 1:5-7). Faith is "yes" to the gospel; "the gospel" is that divinely begotten (2 Cor 5:19c) word of the apostles/the Church, the news of the death and resurrection, for the sake of every human being, of Jesus made Christ and Lord (1 Cor 15:1-11). When the person or household or village responds with the "yes" of faith, the gospel is the saving power of God (Rom 1:16). Faith, then, far outstrips that provisional disposition of goodwill, or antecedent disposition to attend, listen, consent, which general hermeneutics commends. Faith, rather, is a firm, habitual, divinely graced act of self-surrender to the saving act of God in Christ.

Two points on faith must be made straightway, for though self-evident in the apostolic age, they are no longer so today. First, the sphere of faith is the community of faith, the Church. The correlation of faith and baptism is frequently supposed in Pauline texts. It is entailed by 1 Corinthians 6:11 (the theme of righteousness):

> you have had yourselves washed *(apelousasthe),*
> you have been consecrated *(hēgiasthēte),*
> you have been made righteous *(edikaiōthēte).* . . .

The implication of this formulation, probably a fragment from the baptismal liturgy of Antioch, is that the faith by which justification—the act of being made over, made righteous, made new in the sight of God—takes place is precisely the faith ordered to and expressed by baptism. The sphere of faith is the Body of Christ, one body born of baptism (1 Cor 12:13) and the Eucharist (1 Cor 10:17), the Church.

The second point about faith is the radical coherence that it derives from the absolute coherence of God. "The word of God" is the word of one self-revealing God, who, "in times past spoke to our forefathers in ways numerous and various through the prophets but in this, the final age, has spoken to us in his Son . . ." (Heb 1:1-2). In the oldest literary work in the New Testament Paul congratulated his converts in Thessalonica that they had accepted the missionary message "not as the word of men but as what it truly is, the very word of God" (1 Thess 2:13). It has been possible in the past and remains possible in the present to settle on a wooden estimation of what "word of God" means, stripping it of the concreteness by which it is also the word of human writers. (From this concreteness arises, as we shall see, the possibility of fruitful dialectic: the tension of metaphorical Antioch with metaphorical Alexandria.) Inquiry into whether there are true dialectical oppositions in the New Testament supports the expectation that the word of God "spoken to us in his Son" has a radical coherence for all the conceptual, hermeneutical diversities of this richly various literature.

There are many ways of reading the New Testament as if, first, it were not the word of God; as if, second, "faith" were not a factor; as if, third, even if it were a factor, it would still be separable from "Church," incoherent, unpredictable, intrinsically free of any *kanōn* (Gal 6:16) governing religious judgment. Early Christian and especially Pauline sanity stands in opposition to free-wheeling suppositions of this kind. An example: bracketing the theological-hermeneutical realism of ecclesial context, we may suppose, musing on Matthew 25, that at the last judgment what will count according to Jesus himself is a lived compassion for the poor and naked, the hungry, those ill or in prison—not some confession of faith. An interpreter operating whether on the basis of general hermeneutical suppositions of coherence or on that of the coherence of faith, or both, will immediately reflect on how the selfsame gospel of Matthew highlights the great judgment precisely as the sanction of Jesus' proclamation (e.g., Matt 7:22-23, 24-27; 10:4, 32-33; 12:41-42; 16:27). Consider the text of Matthew 10:33, where the issue of "acknowledging" and "disowning" Jesus is explicit in the promise that, at the judgment, he will acknowledge whoever has acknowledged him, and the threat that he will disown those who have disowned him—a text heavily paralleled (Mark 8:38; Luke 9:26; 12:8-9), which moreover entered into Christian faith-formulation: "if we endure, we shall reign with him / if we disown him, he will disown us . . ." (2 Tim 2:12). Such is the coherence of faith. As we intimated above, however, even apart from the relevance of faith, any idea of the norm of righteousness/unrighteousness in Matthew 25 that goes out of its way to *separate* it from faith and Church alike, as if the Matthean text had been meant to say that "salvation is simply independent of confession"—be this of itself true or false, liberating or otherwise—is defective interpretation reflecting defective hermeneutics.

Our focus is not only on coherence, though we shall offer one or two further examples, but on other aspects of the subjectivity of the interpreter vis-à-vis the "word of God," as well. The fundamental fact of the Christian situation is the boundlessly blessed destiny of all who have taken hold of "the solution" in faith, thanksgiving, "fundamental hope," festivity, and celebration. Nietzsche looked not hard, but in vain, for this festivity, which existed in his generation as it does in ours and always has since the coming into being of the new song that was the first Christian celebration. Church Fathers east and west insisted on the unending holiday of salvation. Nietzsche, concentrating as always on the Königsbergian grey that hovered over and bounded his field of vision, was himself blind to the realities of Christian celebration, as are his fans and followers today.

In the light of connaturality with the inner life—horizons, perspectives, core-convictions, self-understandings, guiding principles, tastes, and preferences—of early Christianity as it comes to expression in New Testament literature, celebration and festivity are part of Christian history even, perhaps especially, under conditions of persecution. By the same token, all the sour antipathies, flights, recoils—from revelation and celebration, from truth, orthodoxy, and "Church"—are indices to alienation.

Unlike linguistics, we said above, interpretation cannot do without the referent; that here there is a circle of "things and words" *(Sache und Sprache);* that the interpreter must have a vital relation to the things in order to draw the sense from the words. This is why we cannot drop the issue of the interpreter's personal religious authenticity any more than we can those of moral and intellectual authenticity. "Faith" empowered by love is the heart of the subjectivity correlative to the word of God. This disposition, intrinsically transcendent respecting natural human acts, does not transcend in the sense of leaving these same natural human acts untouched but pervades, heals, heightens, confirms, sublates them. Faith—*pistis di' agapēs energoumenē,* "faith made operative by love" (Gal 5:6)—informs the principles of general hermeneutics.

We turn to the history of interpretation in search of nurture and themes of reflection. We may begin not with what has long been known and acknowledged, but with what baffles, pulls up short, forces reflection, for instance, the forms of obscurantism that so often have accompanied the assertion of truth. We assume from the start that whatever crossed the grain of classicist cultural ideals (more on this presently) begot hostility, suspicion, rejection or, at best, meager and grudging expression. We are likewise ready from the start for a clean break with the obscurantism often tolerated, sometimes cultivated, by the biases of classicist culture. There is a long list of items that the classicist found hard-to-take.

Consider interpretative limits: the fact that there are texts we are unable to interpret; the fact that our interpretations are probable and revisable. The ancient school of Alexandria from Clement and Origen through Athenasius to Cyril, though well aware of limits, operated on the basis that these limits could all be managed and their force blunted. In principle the school looked to comprehensive understanding. We, on the other hand, must be ready (1) to abandon the illusion of complete understanding of the scriptural text and (2) to accept, fully, the critical stance.

Paul urged that in the last days the scriptures had become newly intelligible (e.g., 1 Cor 10:6, 11) but this is understood on the supposition (1 Cor 2) that the interpreter has set heart and soul under the ascendancy of the Holy Spirit. The text is not simple letter (*gramma,* 2 Cor 3:6-7), but Spirit. "There is no question of our having sufficient power in ourselves," says Paul.

> We cannot claim anything as our own. The power we have comes from God; it is he who has empowered us as ministers of a new covenant, not written but spiritual; for the written code kills, but the Spirit gives life (2 Cor 3:4-6).

As we pass into post-Pauline history we find this set of ideas (on letter and Spirit, on Spirit and understanding) endorsed and qualified and pressed into the service of the illusory view that the Christian interpreter should expect to be able to attain the ideal of comprehensive understanding of the text. When grasp of the intended sense of the text leaves something to be desired, turn (for example) to allegory. . . . But today this view is no longer credited. We may anticipate the clarity of scripture, all of it, but only as *Grenzbegriff,* "limiting-concept," for we can expect this clarity to come to expression in critical work only laboriously, sporadically, gradually, in piecemeal fashion, never perfectly.

There is neither need nor excuse for keeping this realistic assessment as the professional secret of the few, meantime working out a kind of nonscientific, "ecclesial interpretation" for the many in the Church. This policy which would merely reinstate the essentially illusory ideal of comprehensive (but factitious) understanding cultivated by ancient Alexandria. What we need today is a new synthesis of Antioch and Alexandria, stripped of the vices of both, strong in the virtues of both.

An example of the inhibiting power of the Alexandrian ideal in Church tradition: the incapability of churchmen/the Church to acknowledge the critical insight of Porphyry, the third-century Neoplatonist philosopher. This is an example worth pausing over.

> We are informed by Jerome that: "Porphyry wrote his twelfth book against the prophecy of Daniel, denying that it was composed by the person to whom it is ascribed in its title, but rather by some individual living in Judea at the time of that Antiochus who was surnamed Epiphanes; he further alleged that 'Daniel' did not fore-

tell the future so much as he related the past, and lastly that whatever he spoke of until the time of Antiochus contained authentic
history, whereas anything he may have conjectured beyond that
point was false, inasmuch as he would not have foreknown the
future.''

Today it is commonplace to differentiate the ideological and the
critical. Applied to Porphyry, this means considering his critical
position (which was extraordinarily acute) independent of his advance rejection of prophecy (standard rationalism). It seems that
this differentiation was long beyond the resources of Christians.

What explains the rejection of Porphyry's insight for well over
a millennium? A fully satisfactory answer is perhaps not yet available. In general terms we might anticipate that the answer will
lie somehow in the limits and errors of classicist Christian hermeneutics. This has been a long and powerful tradition. Its last
gasp may have been the series of decisions (e.g., the view,
presented as flatly unacceptable, that the book of Isaiah was not
in its entirety the product of the eighth-century prophet, Isaiah
of Jerusalem) by the Pontifical Biblical Commission as it operated early in this century on modernist propositions. Few are the
defenders today of this uncritical conservatism. And yet, among
Catholics, the *general readiness* to acknowledge this kind of literary and historical critique is barely fifty years old. Classicist conceptions and classicist hermeneutics, which refused to entertain
such views, lasted well over a millennium and a half.

The proposed "new synthesis" of Antioch and Alexandria
would depend on acknowledging the opposed hermeneutic faults
of the two schools. "Antiochene" means not only the interpreter's
commitment to the literal sense (good!), but also the rationalist's
recoil from mystery (not good!). The latter disposition accounts
for Newman's passionate repudiation of Antioch as "the foun-
tain of primitive rationalism" and "the very metropolis of heresy," in accord with the Antiochene principle that "there is no
mystery in theology." The Alexandrine fault, on the other hand,
was factitious exegesis operating as a cloak covering ignorance.

Given the resources of critical realism, the ideals of the
schools—respectively, sober commitment to the literal sense (Antioch) and affirmation of the intelligibility and cohesiveness of
salvation and of the scriptures that attest it in celebration and
hope (Alexandria)—can be served simultaneously. There is no

room here for either rationalism or the pretense of comprehensive knowledge; there is plenty of room for the claims of the biblical text, the claims of the integrity of faith, and the claims of human authenticity. The capacity and the will to meet all three claims is what the proposed new synthesis of Antioch and Alexandria means.

The great majority of New Testament interpreters are already enlisted in the Antiochene cause; it may be worth our while, then, to spell out what is involved in the Alexandrine cause. Some years ago, having traced the exegetical vagaries in the treatment (in Germany and the British Isles from 1870 to the present) of the main Pauline texts on the coming resurrection of the dead, I found a root of exegetical error in "estrangement from particularities of the text and, above all, of the referent. . . ."

> This controlling estrangement—the chronic vice of one great wing of biblical scholarship since Spinoza—converted the observer viewpoint into an alienated viewpoint and the historical task into the construction of chimerical trajectories, from supernatural Judaic fantasies to a reasonable Hellenistic wisdom (Teichmann), from harsh and fanatic dualism to maturity of experience (Dodd), from fumbling efforts to fairly effective efforts of accommodation to the Gentile mind (Knox).

As the hope of resurrection lost its credibility among many modern Christians and little by little disappeared from their horizons, so did every prospect of a firm hold on the texts. So Ernst Teichmann, C. H. Dodd, and Wilfred Knox (and these were merely examples picked from a larger history) had recourse to "development" in explaining Paul's strange mentality. Something similar happened, with appropriate variations, to the interpretation of 1 Corinthians 15 by Rudolf Bultmann.

Enlistment in the Alexandrine style or mode is countercultural commitment to the faith and hope of the earliest Church. There is thus no room for *Sachkritik* of the word of God. The demythologizing that emerged out of *Sachkritik* was itself liable to *Sachkritik* on the basis of faith. To put it positively, the fundamental hope expressed in 1 Thessalonians 4, 1 Corinthians 15, and 2 Corinthians 5 belongs among those "things of God" that, according to Paul, no one understands except by the Spirit of God (1 Cor 2:11; cf. Mark 4:11 = Matt 13:11 = Luke 8:10; Matt 11:25-27 = Luke 10:21-22; Matt 16:17; John 6:44; 15:5).

Subjectivity and the History of Interpretation

The history of interpretation can be astonishing. From the era of the Fathers to the latter nineteenth century the topic of Romans, chapter nine, was taken to be the predestination of the individual to glory. This view is no longer entertained today. The long rich history of interpretation is, of course, a matter of the keenest interest to doctrinal theology. We learn how the Greek Fathers dealt with the not easily correlated data of divine initiative and human freedom; the influences under which Augustine worked out his own various treatments of the same issues; how the schoolmen, who throughout the thirteenth century were working out systematically coherent views of "grace," took in the Pauline text; the views of God developed by the Reformers as they wrestled *ab ovo* with the predestination theme; and so on until in the latter part of the last century the cumulative resources of philology made possible a breakthrough to Paul's actual topic, namely: how are we to make sense of Israel's non-entry into messianic salvation?

How can it have happened that, by and large, the community of interpreters across the ages *mistook the topic dealt with in the text?* Surely one relevant answer is that the gentile Church, Greek, Latin, medieval, of the Renaissance, the neo-classical and romantic eras had long since found itself alienated from Judaism and had lost all vital theological interest in "Israel" of the present day. The long dark history of the gentile Church's bonds with Jewish Christianity and with Judaism condemned the interpreter of New Testament texts to find some meaning other than the intended meaning in the biblical text. What was Paul excited about? Was it the conflict between the respective claims of the priority of God's grace and the reality of human freedom? Not for a minute. Not the drive to resolve a speculative conundrum, but existential anguish over a missed rendezvous, the climactic divine visitation by which Jesus met the People of God. It was the dark irresolvable conundrum of the destiny of God's, and Paul's, own people. The speculative puzzle—granted, it had its compelling side, a question that bore on all of us, the person of the interpreter included—is what the interpreters were excited about. But how could the thrust of the text have been missed, over and over and over again, one generation after another, epoch after epoch?

Is there a satisfying answer? Was this a blindness born of love grown cold? The matter is baffling in the way that the irrational is always baffling. There is something missing, namely positive intelligibility, in the object-to-be-understood. So much for Romans 9–11.

We are dealing with interpretation of the word of God. We should make clear to ourselves that this interpretation does not bear merely on some one layer or fraction of the text. We are not dealing only with "biblical theology," nor exclusively with texts having an explicitly religious and theological content. We have to do with the whole of the literature. We are indeed offering an unambiguous yes to the question of whether there was a revelation at the springs of Christianity. There was prophecy and revelation in the kerygma and career of John the Baptist, in the kerygma and career of Jesus, in the testimony to resurrection-appearances and the like. As the kerygmatic school at mid-century often insisted, the gospels yielded no evidence of non-kerygmatic narrative. Something similar may be said of the whole of New Testament literature.

As the tone-deaf cannot interpret music and poetry, so (wrote Josef Pieper in his 1979 essay on "interpretation") "there can be no such thing as an unbelieving theologian, provided we understand theology as the effort to interpret revelation validly." If what is at stake in our efforts to interpret the New Testament is God's word, the truth-issue gets a few upward ratchets. Can there be any room at all in the interpreter for offhandedness toward the issue of truth? For casual carelessness or pococurantism, given what is at stake in "word of God"? This is to say nothing of allergies to orthodoxy. A depreciatory view of truth, its attainability and worthwhileness, ill accords with scripture, or word of God, bearing on the gift God has made to us of himself in his Son (de Lubac).

On this general topic, we might offer an instance or two from recent history of interpretation. A debate among some Catholic exegetes in Germany in the 1970s focused on whether, historically, it is plausible that Jesus should have added to the offer of forgiveness inherent in his proclamation of the reign of God a further condition involving his expiatory death and the acceptance thereof in faith. The question, as put by Anton Vögtle and his student, Peter Fiedler, elicited serious discussion. Though the question, "is it plausible . . . ?" had a partly rhetorical ring. Rudolf Pesch offered a suddenly illuminating answer. The motif "expiatory death" arose from the nation's gradually crystallizing refusal of Jesus. There was a factor intrinsic to Jesus' historic career that Vögtle and others had not sufficiently attended to: the mission was an offer of restoration, fulfillment, life. Precisely as election-historical, however, the offer was not optional. A "yes" response was not only called for, but requisite; a "no" from Israel as a whole would mean that the nation ran a risk of condemnation, frustration, death. Hence the question that faced Jesus: "what could be done for the refuser in the situation of refusal?" His response was to convert the crisis into the expiatory offering of his own life—for Israel and the nations.

In retrospect, what we have here is more than the grasp of a historical detail, more even than an insight into the heart of the historical situation. Correlatively, failure to grasp the function and intention of "expiatory offering" was more than mere historical oversight. Since there is no need to lay claim to comprehensive understanding of the biblical text, there is no need to have a hold on the evidence for every element of the faith of the Church that happens to be subject to historical inquiry. One may confess one's bewilderment in the face of historically bewildering texts, as many have done with respect to those sayings of Jesus in the Synoptic tradition that seem to predict an early end of the world. One might likewise acknowledge a nearly total bafflement respecting the historical intelligibility of the will of Jesus to go to his death as expiatory offering for the life of Israel and the world. The confession of bafflement is entirely unobjectionable. On the other hand, putting in doubt an element of the faith of the earliest Church as richly attested as the expiatory death of Christ (Mark 14:24; Luke 22:20; Matt 26:28; John 6:51; Gal 1:4; 2:20; Rom 3:25; 4:25; 5:6-8, 12; 6:23; 8:3; 1 Cor 15:3; 2 Cor 5:14-15, 21; Eph 5: 2, 25; 1 Tim 2:6; Titus 2:14; 1 Pet 2:21; 3:18 . . .) is liable to objection. From any standpoint (be it theological intelligibility or simple historical intelligibility) an expiatory death cannot be conceived as an unwilled act. This kind of debate accordingly reflects more than a diversity of historical views; it betrays a radical diversity of hermeneutic and theological mentalities.

Among contemporary research projects, some mention should be made of another significant disagreement, in part reported on, in part argued, by John P. Meier, touching research on New Testament apocrypha. The elements of this research that have some claim to theological significance include various efforts to posit an early date for materials from the New Testament apocrypha. Of these efforts Meier found John Dominic Crossan's treatment of the *Gospel of Peter* "perhaps the most impressive."

Crossan had proposed that prior to this second-century text and incorporated into it had been what might be called a *Cross Gospel,* the unique source, in Crossan's view, of the Passion story in all the canonical gospels. It dated from the middle of the first century. Meier's treatment of the question left aside such general considerations as the extremely tenuous probability that the canonical narratives on the suffering of Jesus should have derived from a single written source. He focused mainly on the issues that Crossan himself had chosen and refined in the course of working out his hypothesis.

The details may be found in Meier's book, *A Marginal Jew: Rethinking the Historical Jesus.* They include reference to an earlier and equally devastating treatment of Crossan's theorizing on the *Gospel of Peter* by Raymond E. Brown in his presidential address to the SNTS (Studiorum Novi Testamenti Societas), published in *New Testament Studies* in 1987, and they consist of a detailed account of the conditions of possibility that must be met if the hypothesis is to hold. Vis-à-vis these conditions the state of the data yields a cumulative final impression of utter improbability. That is, there seems to be little if any chance that Crossan's hypothesis might be verified to the point of any credible claim to probability. Here our interest in this debate lies in its larger context, which is ideological. What is the point of the mind-numbing argument that Crossan has elaborated to favor so meager a possibility?

Meier, summarizing and supporting the views of Raymond E. Brown, reasonably implies that it is allied with a programmatic research effort to lend legitimacy to the claim of second-century gnosticism (an expression of late antique alienation from and rebellion against world, body, and matter) to have grown out of and to be a legitimate expression of primitive Christianity.

In hardly more than a generation following the startling appearance of Jesus in Israel, that is, from the 30s to the 60s of the first century, Christianity crystallized a unique set of conceptions: "the savior God and his savior-Son," "salvation" conceived in terms that originated in Israel but transcended the conceptual resources of the Old Testament. Paul himself betrayed an all but irresistible tendency to conceive of Father, Son, and Spirit as authoring and effecting the salvation of the world (Gal 4:6; 1 Cor 2:10-16; 6:11, 19; 12:4-6; 2 Cor 1:21-22; 13:13; Rom 1:1-4; 15:16, 30). The total phenomenon of Jesus and his new people, new sanctuary, new cult led Arthur Darby Nock and Eric Voegelin to a striking conviction. The meteoric, mind-boggling phenomenon of Jesus and his movement occasioned, in its wake, not indeed the origin, but the *explosion* of gnostic speculation; and it was the selfsame meteoric phenomenon of Jesus and the Church that, from Paul to Irenaeus, equipped Christianity to challenge and vanquish the gnostic movement.

Making room for gnosticism as an heir, sharing at least equal legitimacy with orthodox Christianity of the second century, has been the apparent aim of the research effort mentioned above. It has been a major interest of a group of scholars in the United States over the past two decades. This is history-of-religions research, not theology. Still, interpreters and historians who have made it their business to listen to the New Testament text precisely as word of God cannot afford to let pass without critique the eccentric style of research that supports this program. This includes the research represented by Crossan's *Cross That Spoke*.

Ideological interests are, not always, but sometimes at stake and to be observed in the research effort mounted on "Q" and "the Q community." Our interest here is not the technical side, which would call for a lengthy discussion, but the tie of research with ideological interests.

By Q is meant the current of tradition common to Matthew and Luke. That there is a body of material common to the two is clear and certain; that it represents a special "current of tradition" seems to me probable, though this is certainly not the only way of explaining material common to Matthew and Luke. My own supposition in any case is minimal: this material once constituted a distinct current of oral tradition. Leaving further theorizing aside, we simply note (Jacques Dupont among others has offered a detailed study, but one limited to the materials of the Sermon on the Mount) that the form of the tradition as it came to Matthew was not identical with the form of the tradition as it came to Luke. We note further, in accord with Hans-Theo Wrege, that this tradition betrays diverse histories of specifically oral transmission. Wrege followed Jeremias in pointing out that in *Stichwort*-passages, the concrete *Stichwörter,* or mnemonic devices, differed in Matthew and Luke respectively. (Like Jeremias, Wrege was unconvinced that there had ever existed a written redaction of Q independent of the canonical gospels; but he did not *demonstrate* that there had never been a written redaction of Q.)

Wrege's dissertation might then be said to have left the door ajar for what would soon become a major research project: to show that Q had originated in a written redaction expressing the quite distinctive faith of an otherwise unattested "Q community." When could such a redaction have taken place? *After* an independent origin and transmission of some of the materials in two streams of tradition (how much? perhaps most?) but *before* the written gospels (i.e., canonical gospels). The ideological dimension appears in a series of carefully contrived suppositions: that the Q current of tradition was the plenary expression of the faith of some community; that this tradition took shape as a distinct written redaction; that the Q-redactors were a group different from those we know of in early Christian history: whether they were Jews or gentiles, their non-eschatological conception of Jesus bore the marks of gnosis and possibly of Cynic social reform.

Once again, then, the gnostic connection turns up, like King Charles' head. Scholars may spend years on the technical aspects of Q research, but it is increasingly clear that they will be lone voices in a Q wilderness (no longer on the cutting edge) if they wander outside the limits requisite to the gnostic connection. Just as there are academic groups among whom any politically incorrect opinion would be astounding, so there are now groups among whom a non-ideological treatment of Q is simply not expected.

Conclusions on Critical Realism

We begin with practical considerations on authentic subjectivity and move to the more theoretical issue of critical realism in relation to cultural change.

Exercises in conscious pursuit of authentic subjectivity include the effort to align cognitional acts with the intention of being—

the capacity and pure drive to know—and they include the effort to align existential choice with the drive to the truly good.

Of these efforts, corresponding as they do with the cognitive and existential phases of fully human intentionality, the second is the more crucial. But the two phases are reciprocally conditioning and determining, for fully human knowing and desiring works both from above downward (from the controlling role of love to the wonder made thematic by one's questions) and from below upward (from one's questions, insights, and judgments to one's values, decisions, and all-commanding loves).

Exercises toward authentic subjectivity include above all the effort to project and sustain horizons congruous with religious, moral, and intellectual conversion. Religious horizons condition and are conditioned by a responding love of God; here there is room and readiness for worship, prayer, self-sacrifice. Religious conversion, however, is usually more than generic. As Jewish religious horizons, for example, have distinguishing religious traits that reflect the biblical and post-biblical traditions of Judaism, so Indian, Christian, or Islamic religious horizons are rooted in their respective histories.

The horizons of the morally converted include the critique of the egoism that reduces intelligence to merely instrumental status as well as the unending effort to withdraw from all such egoism in one's own life. They further include the effort to keep some control over the stream of mere satisfactions; to attend to and grasp the sense of the truly good and to cultivate it in advance of the incidence of moral crisis, which forces choices sometimes dramatic and often long-term in effect and far from perfect.

This book, however, is mainly focused on intellectual conversion, which we have defined by the antithesis of picture-thinking, modelled on sense and imagination, and of thinking conceived in terms of intelligence itself, that is, derived from the intention of being and fulfilled in intelligent grasp and reasonable affirmation.

The traits of this consciously constituted stance include attention to the descriptive account of cognitional acts as a dynamic unity, and to the theory of objectivity and truth that tries to say why this unified, self-assembling dynamism can and does terminate in knowledge of the true and the real. More specific traits consequently include cultivation of the pure desire to know; affirmation of the grasp of reality exclusively in the act of true judgment (*ens per verum innotescit:* reality becomes known through the true); refusal in theory and practice to shunt aside the exigences of a triple-corded objectivity (empirical, normative, terminal). To put the last named trait in simple, positive terms, it is insistence on sufficient evidence (technically expressed by the grasp of the virtually unconditioned).

Finally, we might bring these traits down to the level of hermeneutical competition and conflict. Critical realists are, first of all, not taken in by the fear of and flight from subjectivity. Intentionality analysis has given them some hold on the difference between authentic and inauthentic subjectivity: respect for and demand for evidence; readiness to find the truth in the heresy; disinclination to give mere novelty a free ride; an eye for the principle of the empty head in its sundry guises (e.g., one is not a better historian for being a religious, theological, and philosophic *naïf;* one is not a better interpreter for having clung to the birthright of philological ignorance or ineptness). As the examples suggest, bias applies the principle of the empty head selectively; for instance, best is the head empty of religion and philosophy but brimful of literary theory or some social science, with variations that say the exact opposite. But no such recipes hold the key to success. There *is* nevertheless a way to success: that natural appetite, disinterested, intelligent, rational, which is a pure desire to know, its effectiveness maximized by a mind as well-stocked as possible. Bias yields to sanity.

It is fundamental to critical realists that they differentiate between elementary knowing and its correlative world of immediacy, on the one hand, and fully human knowing and its correlative world mediated by meaning and motivated by value, on the other. This practically excludes being taken in by the fallacy of insight as pure projection. Hence, while acknowledging that worthy, if marginal, gains may emerge from the vogue of deconstruction or the new historicism, critical realists base their rejection of the pure form of these ideologies on appeal to epistemological insights empirically grounded and reasonably affirmed.

The quest and cultivation of authentic subjectivity is far more important than opposition to this or that current theory. Again, the "rock" of not-yet-objectified human intentionality is by far the most basic and effective resource for all theory. It invites the theorist to make his/her approach to intentionality honest, attentive, persistent, and exigent. All accounts of this "rock" exhibit a recurrent difficulty, which

> arises from a failure to distinguish our actual performance and our abbreviated objectification of that performance. Both the world of immediacy and the world mediated by meaning are abbreviated objectifications. They are not full accounts of what actually occurs.

This gives an accent of sober realism to the discussion of the kind of knowledge that is involved here. It also leaves room for and invites ever greater precision in the ongoing task of objectifying human intentionality.

This primer proposes an entry into philosophic principle as the basis for a style of doing interpretation, history, and theology in the field of New Testament studies. "Philosophic principle" refers to what we have just been discussing: human intentionality itself as well as the intentionality analysis and epistemological analysis that converts as-yet-unobjectified transcendental method into a usable philosophic tool. No hermeneutics that ducks the tasks signified by intentionality analysis and epistemological analysis can measure up to the situation of today. Investigation of the New Testament and participation in the discussion of New Testament theology (in the present writer's considered opinion) recurrently demand recourse to what Lonergan called "that recondite department of hermeneutics that involves one in cognitional theory, epistemology, and metaphysics."

The word "hermeneutics" has been used in so many ways over the past generation as to lose its definiteness. Like every fundamental or radical theory, critical realism in some sense defines it afresh. In this primer (especially chapter four) theory includes reflection on the human good; this, I hope, adds a distinct accent to the present text. "Technique" has become a telling feature of the sophistry that everywhere in the West offers to meet the human dilemma in all its dimensions. Dr. Joyce Brothers has offered to show her readers *How to Get Whatever You Want Out of Life*. That hope that we all have of truly meeting questions of meaning and value calls for something far better than simply "whatever you want out of life"; and it calls for far more than "techniques" designed to get it for you.

In the light of the total contemporary situation, including that of the historical dialectic of progress and decline, it is no longer enough to offer the literate world a scholarship outfitted with this or that scholarly apparatus (social-scientific theses, history-of-religions theses, etc.). The biblical exegesis of Latin-American liberationists, despite its often severe shortcomings in several significant contexts (philology, philosophy, theology), has exhibited clear, telling, undeniable elements of a radical seriousness that favorably compares with North American work of putatively great relevance to the present. The search today is for a mode of interpretation invested with cognitive and existential concerns, philologically solid, alive to the threat of cultural decline. If this is true, it would seem that critical realism is markedly relevant to our situation. How does it relate to the history of modern Western culture?

At least three factors were crucial to the rise of modernity: sciences of nature no longer bound to a metaphysical framework and fully exploiting mathematics; emergence of a historical consciousness; human studies, late-blooming in the nineteenth century, torn between orientation to the natural sciences (e.g., behaviorist psychology) or to philosophy *(Geisteswissenschaften).*

These concluding reflections suppose that modernity—all but defining itself by its resistance to final definition—still dominates the cultural state of the question. We begin with a question about the misunderstandings, suspicions, and hesitations that have burdened Christian and especially Catholic tradition through much of the modern period.

Bernard Lonergan has asked: what exactly was the root of the negative relation of Catholics to modernity? His fully articulated answer is worth pondering. It is founded on an analysis of cultural change; it explains the misunderstandings, suspicions, and hesitations, and also explains why it is true, and has been true for some time, that they no longer need to be sustained. Finally, it illuminates the ongoing task of managing cultural change.

Lonergan presented the basis of his analysis, namely, the distinction between classicist and empirical culture, in a lecture, "Dimensions of Meaning" (Marquette University, Milwaukee, May 1965). Classical/classicist culture, which had characterized the life of Europe from medieval times till the late seventeenth century and which hung on, in the life of the Catholic Church, until the present century, broke down first in science. Aristotle in the Prior Analytics had defined "science" as true, certain knowledge of causal necessity.

> But modern science is not true; it is only on the way towards truth. It is not certain; for its positive affirmations it claims no more than probability. It is not knowledge but hypothesis, theory, system, the best available scientific opinion of the day. Its object is not necessity but verified possibility: bodies fall with a constant acceleration, but they could fall at a different rate; and similarly other natural laws aim at stating, not what cannot possibly be otherwise, but what in fact is so.

A new notion of science led, naturally, to a new science of man. The classicist orientation to the essential, the universal, the necessary, the normative gave way to a historically conscious attention to the historical, the particular, the contingent—not to the finite project of a treatise on abstract man, but to an ongoing, never-ending treatment of all human phenomena, a study that,

> by its complete openness, by its exclusion of every obscurantism . . . can achieve ever so much more than the conventional limitations of classically orientated human studies permitted. From the modern standpoint classical culture appears as a somewhat arbitrary standardization of man.

Theory and practice alike are altered by this massive cultural change. Since it had been a trait of Catholic tradition from the second century onward through the Middle Ages to the Renaissance to penetrate, pervade, and transform the social fabric, entering the Hellenistic world of the Church Fathers to adopt and adapt its structures, shaping, as principal architect, the social fact and cultural forms of the Middle Ages, plunging almost recklessly into the ambitions and ideals of the Renaissance, it was inevitable that Catholic thought and practice should have been deeply involved in classicist cultural forms.

These forms have now passed and are gone; their passing was slow but final. The new forms, meantime, that bade to take or succeeded in taking their place have been profoundly ambiguous, involved in various biases, philosophic compass-errors, wholesale repudiations of the past, and in antipathy (that varied in quality and degree across the spectrum from mild to implacable) toward Christian, and especially Catholic, tradition. In Western Christendom—and in its secularized successor "the West"—society and culture (respectively, diverse Western peoples' ways of life, and the meanings and values that underpinned and vitalized those ways of life) have still not settled into any final configuration.

The Catholic Church was among the last great social forces in the West to accept the legitimacy of many of these new political, social, intellectual, and cultural forms. Rearguard action ran from Pius IX in the mid-nineteenth century to Pius XII in the mid-twentieth. But, though the process of accommodation started slowly in the 1920s, it has now accelerated in every sphere. Predictably, the acceleration has yielded trial runs and errors, some instances of indifferent adaptation, some striking successes. The will to accommodate has been qualified by a consciousness of the unremitting need of discernment, since so much of what is being accommodated to is in many respects suspect.

Lonergan has offered a comment on this long history. He took note of a convergence on the date 1680. This was the point at which Herbert Butterfield on modern science, Paul Hazard on the Enlightenment, and Yves Congar on dogmatic theology posited a new beginning. When science became modern and the Enlightenment began to impose itself, theologians, having lost their taste for the understanding of the mysteries of faith, began to reassure each other about their doctrinal certainties.

Catholicism today and most markedly since Vatican II (1962–1966) is locked in an encounter with the age. As for theology, models from the past offer opposite options. Thirteenth-century theology followed its age by assimilating Aristotle; seventeenth-century theology resisted its age "by retiring into a dogmatic corner." If today Catholic theology has some inclination toward both, Lonergan's own achievement has lain in the shaping of a centrist position: one that refuses to join the "solid right" that insists on living in a world that no longer exists; that equally refuses to join the "scattered left" in its paradigm-shifts and swings from one fascination to another. This centrist position insists on "working out one by one the transitions to be made"—a slow business, entailing a refusal of half-measures and insistence (in the area of foundations especially) on "complete solutions."

If we do not advert to history, we have little chance of distinguishing successfully between competing ways of defining what is "Catholic." From 1680 to Vatican II the word "Catholic" carried classicist connotations that Lonergan has referred to as no more than the "shabby shell" of Catholicism. Now they are gone—not entirely, to be sure, but much "period trash" (to adopt Austin Farrer's irresistible phrase) has yielded to new meanings and values. Those most alert to this state of affairs have no wish to revive the vices of classicist Catholic culture—the obscurantism that it tolerated, the truculent apologetics that it affected, the triumphalism, juridicism, and clericalism disparaged at Vatican II. Even less do they wish to join the contemporary "scattered left" that reels from fad to fad, now settling on an unprincipled ecumenism, now absorbed in a covertly nihilistic postmodernism.

The great mass and substance of the Catholic heritage is far from period trash. "Catholic" is concretely defined by traits reflecting the Church's self-defining historic decisions. Many decisions were essential to the maintenance of identity: the repudiation of docetism in favor of realism; the repudiation of gnosticism in favor of tradition and reason; the repudiation, on the basis of this lived tradition and tradition of reason, of Marcionitism and Montanism. These acts of repudiation had positive aspects and positive consequences. The decision against Marcion secured the legacy of the scriptures. Hilary Armstrong observed that the decision against gnosticism meant openness to philosophy. But, as the decision against Arias showed, this would not be rationalist philosophy. The scriptures (affirmed against Marcion) and reason (affirmed against gnosticism) were crucial to the later emergence of such Catholic phenomena as the great monuments of medieval scholasticism. Again, the decision against Donatism meant that the Church was for the masses; that against Pelagius meant that it lived only by God's grace.

It seems that the Catholic Church was not so much intent on figuring out its own nature as on protecting itself from movements that, if allowed to run rampant, would have wrecked it. A trait recurrent in Catholic history was not so much intelligence as a kind of stolid solidarity with tradition, a theme prominent in Peter Brown's *Augustine of Hippo* and explicit in the chapter "Fundatissima Fides" (on Augustine vs. Pelagius). In Augustine's view heretics and heretical thinkers clarified matters over and over by their obsessive and resolute explorations. Even when the effort to define "Catholic" is out of sympathy with the to-be-defined (as in the debates in German Church-history-writing on *Frühkatholizismus*), much of permanent value has come to light. Adolf von Harnack was wrong about the hellenization of the gospel, but he was certainly right about the conditions of the possibility of the success of the mission. Those conditions—for instance, the search among Christian resources for "the correlates of the Graeco-Roman soul" and the inclusion of "Church" *(gens tertia)* in the mystery of redemption—were distinctive elements of Catholicism.

Most of the substantial and permanent traits that Newman found himself looking for in the early 1840s doubtless enter relevantly into the historically-conditioned definition of "Catholic" today. It should be remembered that Newman considered it a marked trait of Catholicism that its interpreters understood the scriptures deeply and truly. One exegetical and theological theme carried over by the Reformation into *altprotestantische Dogmatik* and shared by Catholic and Anglican tradition was the focus on the threefold office of Christ as king, priest, and prophet—likewise a theme of ecclesial participation in Christ. It was among the fertile themes of Newman's thinking both as Anglican and as Catholic. Christ, he argued, combined in his person and work the main conditions of mankind. Nicholas Lash evokes Newman on this in an Oxford sermon:

> As one who "performed the priest's service . . . on the Cross" he represents "one large class of men, or aspect of mankind . . . that of sufferers—such as slaves, the oppressed, the poor, the sick, the bereaved, the troubled in mind" (p. 54) [cf John Henry Newman, *Sermons Bearing on Subjects of the Day* (London, 1869)]. As king, as the embodiment of God's rule, he represents "those who work and toil, who are full of business and engagements, whether for themselves or for others. . . ." As prophet, he represents "the studious, learned, and wise" (p. 54).

The *prophetic* office is exercised in such activities as the exposition of the scriptures. In Catholic participation in this task as it is carried out today, be it in universities and the context of the history of religions, or in an explicitly ecclesial and theological context, this office may be cultivated in a manner explicitly open to the spirit of prophecy. The prophetic ideal in fact corresponds well with the ideal sketched here: to accord with science, but to prefer the bread of truth to the stone of research.

Whether the current community of Catholic New Testament scholars will prove as a group to have measured up to this task cannot be clear in advance. But the *ideal,* it does seem clear, has to do with cultivating a set of ideals which include many of those hermeneutic ideals that have been discussed in this primer.

Appendix

Rational Affirmation of the Existence and Attributes of God

Reflection on the growth of knowledge in the modern world and in particular of mathematics and the natural sciences since the seventeenth century has changed the state of the question for the rational affirmation of the existence of God. Empirical science has become for Western civilization the supremely obvious instance of valid knowledge. It is empirical, for it proceeds from data and returns to data to verify all its affirmations in them. "Verification" in the strict sense is a cumulative convergence of direct and indirect empirical confirmations.

There are no data—no empirical givens—on God. Accordingly, God cannot be an object of scientific knowledge. Science calls for limitation to the verifiable. There is no verifiable principle by which to conclude from the world to God, for a principle is verifiable only if there are data on both the terms that the principle relates. Since there are no data on God, there can be no principle verifying a relation of the world to God. Thus, the scientifically educated, if informed of the prospect of a rational proof of the existence of God, may ask, "By what unverifiable principle do you propose to infer the existence of God from our world?"

The fact is that the rational affirmation of God's existence does not fall within the ambit of empirical science. Verification, on the other hand, crucial as it is to empirical science, is not relevant to every kind of knowledge. Thus, there is no basis on which to insist on verification (in the strict sense) of common sense, or of mathematics or logic. Not of common sense, for empirical data cannot be expected to reveal whether a possibly relevant unity or relationship (insight/construal) is actually relevant to this, or this kind of, concrete case. Not of logic or mathematics, for in neither case are empirical data the relevant fulfilling conditions sought by reflection on hypotheses. In logic the fulfilling conditions are what satisfies criteria of clarity, coherence, and rigor; in mathematics they are what reduces, in virtue of conclusions rigorously drawn, to any freely chosen set of suitable postulates.

As for "general transcendent knowledge," in other words, the rational affirmation of God, the only "principle" apropos of which the issue of "verification" might arise is the human mind itself—a principle more fundamental than any process of verification, since every such process supposes it. And since any process of verification of any kind supposes it, there is no point in talking about verifying it.

A final preliminary: the invalidity, in all its forms, of the ontological argument for the existence of God. The principal acts constituting fully human knowing respond respectively to two questions. The first asks of X what it is (*quid sit?*); the second asks of X whether it is (*an sit?*). In all forms the ontological argument violates this structure. To make existence a necessary part of the answer to the question "What is God?"—that is, to understand God as a necessarily existent being—is to answer a *quid sit?* question and to leave still unanswered the *an sit?* question whether there is in reality anything corresponding to this conception of "a necessarily existent being." The structure of intelligence does not vary with variation in its objects. So, regardless of the particularity of the idea, the rule still holds: what is an "idea" in the premises remains an "idea" in the conclusion. Real existence does not become affirmable on the basis of reflection on the content of an idea.

Another way of putting this: when we grasp the idea of God, we do not grasp God, that is, an unrestricted act of understanding. We grasp an extrapolation that consists in removing the restriction from a restricted act of understanding (our own).

Another way of putting it: the ontological argument requires that we make the transition from analytic proposition (a necessary and universal judgment relevant to possibility, i.e., leaving concrete existence bracketed) to an analytic principle (analytic judgment whose terms and relations are existential, that is, occur in judgments of fact). But we cannot make this transition except by affirming the fact of God's existence. Thus, the affirmation of the existence of God is *requisite to* the ontological argument; it is not its result.

There are numerous valid demonstrations of the existence of God. Here we shall be content to summarize Lonergan's offer, in *Insight,* of the most comprehensive form of the demonstration. We present it in the format of a conditional syllogism. Its point of departure is intelligibility.

There are two uses of the term "intelligible." First, the ordinary sense: what is and can be understood; second, the primary component in an idea, the ground or root of intelligibility in the ordinary sense. As the demonstration arrives at "the idea of God," we shall appeal to the second sense.

The demonstration: if the real is completely intelligible, God exists. But the real is completely intelligible. Therefore, God exists.

(1) Argument for the second (or minor) proposition. Being is completely intelligible; but the real is being; therefore, the real is completely intelligible. In support of the proposition that being is completely intelligible: insight intends being, and true judgment attains it. But insight occurs and true judgment occurs in function not of some limited desire to intend and attain being, but in function of a pure, disinterested, and unrestricted drive to know. The object of such desire is intelligible not in part only, but completely intelligible.

Question: whether here, in asserting that being is completely intelligible, we are going beyond our experience. We do have the experience of knowing, of ascertaining concrete matters of fact. But we have no experience of knowing the *completely* intelligible.

Response: true, we do not *know* the completely intelligible; but we do *intend* it, and we can know that we intend it. For, if what we intended in the ordinary experience of human knowing were no more than an incomplete intelligibility, at some point in our inquiry we would find ourselves quite at ease in brushing problems, hesitations, doubts aside, in suppressing objections, in settling on conclusions whether commended by sufficient evidence or not, and in arbitrarily refusing to allow new questions to arise. We would reach

> a point where the half-answer appeared not a half-answer but as much an answer as human intelligence could dream of seeking. If the dynamism of human intellect intended no more than incomplete intelligibility, the horizon not merely of human knowledge but also of possible human inquiry would be bounded. Whether or not there were anything beyond that horizon, would be a question that could not even arise (*Second Collection,* 41).

But the question does arise and it keeps arising—a transcultural experience that will not be denied. This follows: though we have no immediate knowledge of complete intelligibility (i.e., we do not see God in this life), we do have the immediate experience of wonder, its boundlessness or utter unrestrictedness. So far from being meaningless to us, complete intelligibility is at the root of all our efforts to mean anything at all. We move from the experience of wonder to its understanding and affirmation. When affirmation is preceded by grasp of the virtually unconditioned, to affirm (so assenting reasonably) is to know the existence of. We thus come *to know* wonder as intending complete intelligibility. We accordingly infer that complete intelligibility is at the root of our every effort to grasp meaning, to focus on evidence, to judge, to evaluate, to choose, to live meaningfully, to love.

The real and being are identical. For "the real" is what is meant by the name "real"; but what is meant by "real" is either a mere object of thought or it is both an object of thought and an object of affirmation. The first is excluded, for we not only intend, but also attain the real, for instance, in ascertainments of empirical fact (like that of the man who, finding his house a smoking ruin, observes that "something has happened"). Moreover, the second (the real is an object of both thought and affirmation) is all-inclusive. The real = being is identical with *all* that is to be known by intelligent grasp and reasonable affirmation.

(2) We return to the major proposition of the demonstration: if the real is completely intelligible, God exists. For, if the real is completely intelligible, complete intelligibility exists. If complete intelligibility exists, the idea of being exists. If the idea of being exists, God exists.

Just as the real could not be intelligible if intelligibility were non-existent, so the real could not be completely intelligible if complete intelligibility were non-existent.

Moreover, if complete intelligibility exists, the idea of being exists. Intelligibility is either material or spiritual or abstract: material in the objects of physics, chemistry, biology, and sensitive psychology; spiritual, when it is identical with understanding; abstract, in concepts. Abstract intelligibility is necessarily incomplete, for it arises only in the self-expression of spiritual intelligibility. Spiritual intelligibility is incomplete as long as it can inquire. Material intelligibility is necessarily incomplete, for it is contingent in its existence and occurrences. The only possibility of complete intelligibility lies in a spiritual intelligibility that cannot inquire, for it understands everything about everything. Unrestricted understanding is the idea of being.

If the idea of being exists, God exists. For if the idea of being exists, there exists the content of an act of understanding that is unrestricted, that is in no way still-to-be-understood, in no way obscure or vague; that is one, but of many, immaterial but of the material, non-temporal but of time, non-spatial but of space.

There must be a primary component, which is the unrestricted act of understanding itself, and a secondary component in the unrestricted act's understanding of everything else inasmuch as it understands itself.

Inasmuch as knowing is not looking, but is rather a cognitive identity, there is no duality of act and content in the idea of being. Knower and known are one: subsistent self-understanding.

The act and content of this unrestricted understanding of everything is spiritual and personal; he is self-explanatory, and so necessary rather than contingent. He is without any principle of limitation and so is infinite; but he would not be infinite if he were not all-knowing and all-loving, all-wise, all-good, and all-powerful. He is therefore all of these.

One may ask, where is the flaw in this argument? Is there a flaw in the logic of the major proposition (if the real is completely intelligible, God exists)? No. Complete intelligibility guarantees "the idea of being": subsistent self-understanding. Is there a flaw in the minor proposition ("But the real is completely intelligible")? No. Our own participation in intelligence is in function of a pure disinterested drive to know, an intending that is unrestricted. This is not the experience of knowing the completely intelligible; but all human beings have the experience of unrestricted intending, and to this experience some human beings add the understanding of this unrestricted intending, the grasp of the conditions of this unrestricted intending—its transcending of the intending that is sense-knowledge, its free exercise on any unknown, its susceptibility to being shaped as questions—the fulfillment of these conditions and, finally, the affirming-in-judgment of this unrestricted intending.

There would be some flaw in the argument if in its logic and resources it had not already represented a clean break with naïve realism and its variants ("materialism, empiricism, positivism, sensism, phenomenalism, behaviorism, pragmatism"), with relativism, essentialism, and idealism, whether pre-critical, critical, or absolute. But once it is granted that the real is being, that being is known by intelligent grasp and reasonable affirmation, then God is a reality if he is a being and he is a being if intelligent grasp conceives him and reasonableness affirms what intelligence conceives.

By way of conclusion to this appendix: we do not accept any argument for the goodness of God (in the sense of God as moral agent caring for the world) from an independent premise of the goodness of the world. The world is good and life is good on condition that God, the author of world and life, is good. If the creative *fiat* is good, then the world and world process, the origin and destiny of the world are good, and it is good to be in tune with the world. The philosopher who attends heart and soul to the philosophic reasons for the goodness of God will find nourishment there to sustain his sense of the world and world process as good. For most of the world, it will be from other sources, perhaps unsearchable, inaccessible sources that, as in Anna Franck, give rise to this conviction of the goodness of the world, despite all appearances. It may well be that the horizon requisite to the rational affirmation of the existence and attributes of God is not open to many. Of the numerous blocks to that horizon, some may prove to be relatively irremovable. Others, however, may yield to the cultivation of specifically religious experience.

Glossary

Accommodation/Actualization: application of a text to a new situation, one not foreseen or intended by the author. The terms "accommodation" and "actualization" are especially used of biblical texts. (The term "ascription" refers to the ascribing of new meaning to an old text; it has a wider than biblical application.) This rejuvenation of older, well-known texts may be inventive or hackneyed. It may deepen or diminish the original meaning of the text, and so may represent on balance a gain or a loss. But it is not misinterpretation (*see* Misinterpretation). Literary tradition lends itself naturally to all such processes. Already at work powerfully in Old Testament literary production, the same processes are found in the gospels and epistles. In the New Testament an allegorical account of the parable of the Sower actualizes the parable of Jesus. Allegorical reading of "the Good Samaritan" (by Origen, Augustine) is an early Christian example of accommodation.

Alienation: the state of being out of kilter with some aspect or dimension of human reality or proper human functioning. Since alienation may be rationalized by ideology, every aspect of meaning and value is subject to conflicting judgments. Conflicts of this kind may be resolved if (1) the way in which human beings actually function (the way human intentionality actually works) can be established, and (2) of the conflicting views of meaning and value some can be shown to be coherent, and others incoherent, with human intentionality. *See* Ideology, Dialectic, and Positions and Counterpositions.

Analysis: examination of a complex, its elements, and their relations. Analysis differs from interpretation in that its object is not limited to meaning intended and expressed; any aspect of the text is open to examination. Structuralists, psychologists, social scientists, critics of ideology, and others may fasten on what is significantly but unintentionally objectified in the text. Since it is unintended, it may even be hidden from the writer. Thus, Ernest Jones in *Hamlet and Oedipus* (Garden City: Doubleday, 1954) offers a Freudian analysis of "Hamlet"; Paul Ricoeur in *Freud and Philosophy* (New Haven: Yale University Press, 1970) offers a construal of Freud in the light of philosophic analysis. Analysis may prepare for or follow upon interpretation but is not an adequate substitute for interpretation.

Apologetic: designed to affirm doctrinal or moral convictions that have come under attack. Apologetic motifs are found throughout the New Testament, an indication that earliest Christianity had a decent respect for the opinions of mankind, was committed to the reasonable and especially to the reasonableness of belief.

Approfondissement: a plumbing of thematic depths, or a treatment that penetrates to the depths of a theme.

Center of Gravity: that factor or element that is the main carrier of the writer's intention and affirmation. In what form criticism defines as "the pronouncement story," the center of gravity normally lies in the pronouncement. One way to misinterpret is to locate mistakenly the text's center of gravity.

Circles of Interpretation: paradoxical formulas describing how an interpreter actually comes to understand. Let the circle of whole and parts serve to illustrate: "I understand the whole only in function of understanding the parts; I understand the parts only in function of understanding the whole." Other circles: "things and words," "reader and text." Literary analysis is reducible, in general, to the truth of the circles of interpretation. Thus, genre-criticism and redaction criticism are grounded in the fact that "I understand the parts only in function of understanding the whole."

Cognitional Theory: that branch of philosophy concerned with describing exactly what one is doing when one knows. Cognitional theory is thus the foundation of hermeneutics or interpretation theory, for "interpreting" is a particular instance of knowing.

Common Sense: a technical term in the cognitional theory of critical realism.

> The realm of common sense is the realm of persons and things in their relation to us. . . . We come to know it, not by applying some scientific method, but by a self-correcting process of learning, in which insights gradually accumulate, coalesce, qualify and correct one another, until a point is reached where we are able to meet situations as they arise, size them up by adding a few more insights to the acquired store, and so deal with them in an appropriate fashion. Of the objects in this realm we speak in everyday language (*Method*, 81).

How does common sense knowledge relate to interpretation? Interpretation requires that we bring ourselves "to an understanding of the common sense of another place, time, culture, cast of mind" (*Method*, 160). Common sense is not for all that the measure of wisdom:

> Common sense commonly feels itself omnicompetent in practical affairs, commonly is blind to long-term consequences of policies and courses of action, commonly is unaware of the admixture of common nonsense in its more cherished convictions and slogans (*Method,* 53).

Comprehensive (or Universal) Viewpoint: a heuristic structure assembled with a view to locating a civilization, culture, a brand of common sense, a particular consciousness, a literature, or a text on an explanatory map of human intentionality. The expression at first seems oxymoronic; this is because we are dealing with the conditions of the move from description (with its relativity to a limited viewpoint) to explanation (in which elements of meaning are related not to some particular audience, but to each other). The only audience that can fully profit from this exercise, however, is one that, like the intentionality analyst, is in firm possession of the same comprehensive viewpoint: a heuristic structure that draws on every major resource of intentionality analysis. It draws, then, on (1) generalized empirical method, or the way human beings function in fact, and the objectification of this way, its levels and chief "operator," the notion of, or conscious drive to, being as knowable and lovable; (2) diverse ways of retrieving the facts of conscious intentionality and diverse appreciations of objectivity: naïve realism and empiricism; pre-critical, critical, and absolute idealism; and critical realism; (3) the understanding of the subject to whom common sense relates everything (basic to this subject are the patterns of experience: biological, aesthetic, dramatic, intellectual, etc.); (4) the understanding of the common-sense subject who habitually relates everything in his field of vision to himself, as well as on the biases to which common sense is subject; (5) the basic differentiations of consciousness (responses to exigences). Science responds to the explanatory exigence; philosophy, to the critical exigence, etc. Established in the realm of interiority/subjectivity, philosophic arrival at a comprehensive viewpoint allows one to grasp the procedures of common sense, mathematicized science, religion, philosophy, and theology. All possible vantage points and all possible relations among them are potentially included in this heuristic structure of the elements of meaning. At present, the best example of this explanatory interpretation and appeal to the explanatory ideal in history has been provided by Lonergan's tracing of the development of Trinitarian thought in *The Way to Nicea*.

Conceptualism: tendency to overlook the pivotal role of insight/construal in favor of accenting the importance of concepts, abstractions, universal ideas. Rather than focus on the critical relation of the intelligible to the sensible (the unity or pattern grasped by insight), the conceptualist focuses on the relation of the universal to the particular. The result is removal from the concrete, immobilism, the classicist fixation on the essential, the necessary, the immutable. *See* Lonergan "The Subject" *(Second Collection)*.

Consciousness: that in function of which a subject is so present to himself as to make himself a psychological subject. Certain operations (sensing, imagining, wondering, construing, reflecting, etc.) generate "awareness," which has two dimensions: one makes an object present to the operator, the other makes the operator present to himself. As cognitively present to himself, he is in a special (psychological) sense a "subject." We call the object-oriented dimension "intentionality," and the subject-constituting and subject-revealing dimension "consciousness." *See* Meaning.

Correspondence Theory of Truth: the view that in human knowers truth consists in the conscious correspondence or conformity of intelligence to its object (or of the mind to reality). The fact of correspondence is explicable in Aristotelian terms: intellect is capable in its own distinctive way of becoming all things *(potens omnia fieri)*. This is the view of truth operative in critical realism. The correspondence theory of truth should not be confused with the copy theory of knowledge, which is proper to naïve realism. To deny the correspondence theory of truth is to deny that when the meaning is true, the meant is what is so.

Critique: the effort to evaluate a work. It may include a report on personal encounter with the work, an effort to determine how skillfully a text has been composed or to show how it compares to other works or to determine the measure in which what a writer means and affirms corresponds to reality.

Demythologizing: the interpretation of myth-elements (the representation of the this-worldly in other-worldly terms) such as eschatology in strictly existentialist terms.

Diachronic: See Synchronic/Diachronic.

Dialectic, Dialectical: relating to irreducible oppositions. An index to such oppositions: "Each considers repudiation of its opposites the one and only intelligent, reasonable, and responsible stand . . ." *(Method,* 247). Dialectical oppositions are horizonal. What in one horizon is found to be intelligible and true in another is found to be unintelligible and false. What for one is good, for another is evil. The crucial question at this point becomes: which horizon corresponds to the facts of conscious human intentionality, and which does not?

Differentiation of Consciousness: phases and modes of the development of one's horizons and perspectives. An infant first distinguishes itself from its surrounding world. Eventually, the child moves beyond the world accessible to the senses (the world of immediacy) to the larger world mediated by meaning. Lonergan *(Method,* 303–305) proposes ten instances of the differentiation of consciousness: (1) the development from immediacy to meaning; (2) skill in mastering the procedures of common sense; (3) grasp or discovery of the transcendent: God's gift of his love; (4) grasp and use of symbol; (5) emergence of systematic meaning through hold on an explanatory view of some sphere of experience; (6) adoption and adaptation of elements of explanatory views into the fund of common sense; (7) the thematization of method; (8) elaboration of scholarship; (9) development of post-scientific and post-scholarly literature; (10) exploration of interiority or subjectivity.

Encounter: personal contact with and response to the meaning of the text. As "all real living is meeting" (Buber, *I and Thou* [New York: Scribner, 1958] 11), so is all real reading and interpreting. The point of working out an understanding of the text is that the encounter be with its true sense. This contact with and response to text and implied author is the nexus between interpretation and critique; and critique is first of all a report on encounter, a revelation of text and interpreter/critic alike.

Exegesis: interpretation. *See* Interpretation.

Existentialism: a movement centering attention on concrete human existence. Pioneered by Søren Kierkegaard (1813–1855), this movement, which came to maturity in the work of Jaspers, Heidegger, and Sartre, focused on crucial moments of human experience. (The term is also used of discovery of the role of *esse*-existence in metaphysics, e.g., by Jacques Maritain and Etienne Gilson.) Some individual thinkers (e.g., Gabriel Marcel, José Ortega y Gasset) are often named existentialists (Marcel rejecting, Ortega accepting it). Themes associated with existentialism: risk, decision, fate, commitment, destiny.

Form Criticism: investigation of pre-literary formation of sayings and narratives. Applied to the gospels, the narratives are: pronouncement stories, miracle stories, biographical and cultic legends, and "stories about Jesus." Sayings: discussions, wisdom sayings (exhortations, proverbs, macarisms), prophetic sayings (proclamations, warnings), legal sayings, first-person sayings, parables.

Fundamentalism: term used in a specific and a general sense. First (and specifically), it designates a movement from the early twentieth century which defined itself by five points fundamental to authentic Christianity: (1) the inerrancy and infallibility of the letter of the Bible; (2) the virgin birth and full divinity of Christ; (3) his physical resurrection from the dead; (4) his death as a sacrifice atoning for the sins of the world; and (5) his second coming in bodily form to preside at the last judgment. Second (and more generally), it signifies a systematically "conservative" mode of interpreting, with the accent on literalness. Unless the Bible specifies otherwise, the biblical text should be understood according to the proper (not figurative, symbolic, etc.) sense of the words.

Genre, Genus litterarium; Genre Criticism: the first two terms refer to "a specific literary type," the third to analysis aimed at determining what specific literary type a given text belongs to. Type becomes specific insofar as structure and style mediate a distinctive handling of content. The two most basic genres of the New Testament are "gospel" and "letter." But the differences between Matthew and John and between Romans and Hebrews suggest an unknown to be known: how should the two basic genres be more precisely defined? Furthermore, the Acts of the Apostles, the two-part work of Luke (gospel and Acts), and the Apocalypse of John call for precise definition. Genre criticism asks not only what makes a gospel a gospel, but also under what literary influences did the gospel genre take on definitive contour?

Gospel: term used in two senses. First, "gospel" is a proclamation of news of salvation. Early Christians adopted the term from the book of Isaiah 40:9; 41:27; 52:7; 61:1. In Paul's use, it is the good news of salvation for every human being through the death and resurrection of Jesus, made Christ and Lord. Second, "gospel" became the name of a literary genre (Matthew, Mark, Luke, John). The "Gospel of Thomas," a non-canonical, gnostic work, is a Coptic translation (probably from Greek) of a collection of sayings from the second or third century, now lost.

Hermeneutic: noun and adjective referring to interpretation theory or principles of interpretation. *See* Interpretation, Interpretation Theory.

Heuristic: what, in a context of inquiry, sets limits and, within those limits, invites a determinate answer. Definitions answer a "what?" question. Some definitions answer the question incompletely: they leave an element of "what" still in the answer. These are heuristic definitions.

> Q: What is righteousness?
> A: Righteousness is what makes one pleasing to God.
> Q: What makes one pleasing to God?
> A: New creation in Christ.

Here the last answer answers the first question. But this answer has a precision that, unthematic in the original question, was thematized by an intermediate step consisting of a question and answer raising a further question. The intermediate step is heuristic: open to, calling for, and guiding further concrete determination.

Historicity: two senses. As used by historians, it refers to the factuality of past action. As used by philosophers (especially existentialists) it refers to man's historicness, his being subject to time, uncertainty, and a destiny over which he feels he has little control.

History: past actions or knowledge of past actions. R. G. Collingwood defined history in the latter sense as:

> (a) a science, or an answering of questions; (b) concerned with human actions in the past; (c) pursued by interpretation of evidence; and (d) for the sake of human self-knowledge (*The Idea of History,* 10–11).

He thereby defined the nature, object, method, and value of history.

Horizon: literally, the limit of one's field of vision; metaphorically, the limit of one's knowledge and interests. The metaphorical use became a technical term in Husserl, Heidegger, Gadamer, Merleau-Ponty, Ricoeur, Coreth, Rahner, Lonergan, and others. In Lonergan's use the raising and answering of questions grounds a threefold division: the known (questions I can raise and answer), the known unknown (questions I can raise but cannot as yet answer), and the unknown unknown (questions I cannot raise, for they are without meaning for me). "Horizon" is the boundary between the second and the third.

Hypothesis: a more or less fully worked out answer to a question, but an answer conceived as only possibly true. To be affirmed as actually true requires a grasp of sufficient evidence or, more technically, grasp of the virtually unconditioned. That is virtually unconditioned whose conditions are known and known to be fulfilled.

Ideology: rationalization of alienation. Since any view of knowledge, meaning, truth, and reality may be accused of being the mere rationalization of alienation, the matter ought to be somehow open to intelligent and reasonable adjudication. "Dialectic" is the critical realist proposal as at least setting the stage for an intelligent, reasonable, and responsible decision on views that are significantly and radically opposed, inasmuch as their horizons are irreducibly opposed.

Immanent: Lonergan uses the term chiefly to signify views of knowledge as failing to intend and attain the real. (In such accounts knowledge is merely subjective.) "Immanent" is also used to signify the presence of God to creation (God is both transcendent, infinitely beyond creation, and immanent, i.e., variously present to creation). "Immanent" is also used to differentiate operations of living beings that are initiated from within from those of inanimate beings, which derive from extrinsic causes.

Implied Author/Reader: not the flesh-and-blood author and reader without qualification, but the author exclusively as the principle of this work (the voice, the presence, that inhabits the work) and the reader implicitly called for by it. Unwittingly, those critics who discovered the implied author by that very fact discovered the correspondence of meaning *(intentio intendens)* and meant *(intentio intenta)*. See Meaning.

Inspiration: the name of the charism in virtue of which the biblical text is considered by Jews and Christians to be "the word of God." Inspiration is distinguished from revelation, for a text may be "the word of God" without containing any divine disclosure to man. Contemporary theological discussion of inspiration has yet to work out a satisfactory clarification of the charism, its nature, and impact.

Intentio intendens, Intentio intenta: to intend something is to make it present to oneself as an object. The intending subject, conversely, is conscious, in other words, present to himself as subject. *Intentio intendens* signifies intending as the conscious act of the subject; *intentio intenta* signifies the product of this intending, some intelligible content. The *intentio intendens* is the act of meaning; the *intentio intenta* is "what is meant. " The two exactly correspond; so "how" the implied author means something is part and parcel of "what is meant," or "the intended sense."

Intentionality: that in function of which an object is present to the consciousness of a subject. For details, *see* Meaning.

Interpretation, Interpretation Theory: (first term): the act of working out an understanding of the text, judging how accurate this understanding is, and stating what one judges to be an accurate understanding of the text. (Second term): the theory that works out the conditions of the possibility of interpreting, the conditions of excellent interpretation, and like questions. "Cognitional theory" says just exactly what we are doing when we are knowing, and "epistemology" explains why the doing of those things constitutes "knowing." These philosophic disciplines deal with the understanding of understanding in general; "interpretation theory" (= hermeneutics) is a subquestion: understanding the understanding of texts.

Langue/Parole: Langue designates speech resources shared by some speech community and implies the competence to use them; *parole* designates an actual utterance, a use of *langue*. The distinction comes from Ferdinand de Saussure, who, wishing to define the object, method, etc., of linguistics, accented *langue*. Interpretation and interpretation-theory, on the other hand, focus on use of language in discourse and are thus (unlike Saussure) obliged to consider referents, authors, readers, human functioning, and the like.

Lebensverhältnis: term from Bultmannian era of interpretation. Independent access and attentiveness to and understanding (*Vorverständnis*) of the referent or thing (*die Sache*) that the text deals with are supposed by the understanding of the text; and an appreciative understanding of the text presupposes a vital interest in, or "life-relationship" to, the referent. The term implies a clean break with positivist conceptions of "objectivity."

Linguistics: study of the units, nature, structures, and modifications of a language or languages.

Literary Criticism: a catch-all for study of literature: genre, structure, style, sources, forms, and so on. Wysten High Auden reduced literary criticism to two main questions. (1) This is a literary contraption. How does it work? (2) What is the writer's idea of "the great good place"? Structure and style dominate in the first question; vision and value dominate the second. T. S. Eliot's proposal on the point of literary criticism is comparable: the illumination of works of art and the correction of taste.

Meaning: intending = functioning as a psychological subject. Intending is seeing, hearing, touching, smelling, tasting, perceiving, feeling, imagining, wondering, inquiring, construing, conceiving, formulating, reflecting, marshalling and weighing evidence, grasping the virtually unconditioned, judging, deliberating, evaluating, deciding insofar as by these operations the operating subject is made aware of an object. The object is what is intended; the operation as object-oriented is intentional; that in virtue of which an object becomes present to the consciousness of the subject is intentionality. As operations by being intentional make objects present to the subject, so also by being conscious they make the subject present to himself. Both intending and what is intended are communicated by language, body language, habitual action, art, and symbol. Meaning is thus linguistic, intersubjective, incarnate, artistic, symbolic. But acts of meaning are not only cognitive and communicative; they are also effective/productive:

> Men work. But their work is not mindless. What we make we first intend. We imagine, we plan, we investigate possibilities, we weigh pro's and con's, we enter into contracts, we have countless orders given and executed. From the beginning to the end of the process we are engaged in acts of meaning; and without them the process would not occur or the end be achieved (*Method,* 77–78).

Furthermore, meaning may be constitutive:

> Just as language is constituted by articulate sound and meaning, so social institutions and human cultures have meanings as intrinsic components. . . . The family, the state, the law, the economy are not fixed and immutable entities. They adapt to changing circumstances; they can be reconceived in the light of new ideas; they can be subjected to revolutionary change. But all such change involves change of meaning . . . (*Method,* 78).

Two final observations. First, in interpretation theory meaning is equivalent to "what is meant," which is inclusive of "how" it is meant and the kind and degree of affirmation of what is meant. For meaning in the sense of what is meant may be present to human intentional consciousness in diverse ways: as question, hypothesis, probability, ideal, etc. Interpretation grasps and expresses what others have meant; critique, among other things, says how much of what is meant is so.

Misinterpretation: interpretation that is formally erroneous. To be formally erroneous two conditions must be fulfilled: (1) the sense construed and expressed by the interpreter does not correspond to the intended sense of the text; (2) the conscious object of the interpreter is precisely to grasp and express the intended sense of the text. If the second factor is inoperative, the interpretation is only materially erroneous. In much of the literature of interpretation this second factor is by no means thematic, or thematic at all. The gospels' allegorizing of the parables or actualization of sayings are thus not misinterpretations.

Object, Objectivity: terms used in intentionality analysis. Intentional object adds something to grammatical object: it makes the object present to the awareness of the subject sensing or imagining or understanding or loving. We distinguish "object" in the world of immediacy (the relation between seeing and what is seen is immediate) and "object" in the world mediated by meaning (what is intended in questions and known through satisfactory answers). The object of the first is already-out-there-now:

> It is *already:* it is given prior to any questions about it. It is *out:* for it is the object of extraverted consciousness. It is *there:* as sense organs, so too sensed objects are spatial. It is *now:* for the time of the sensing runs along with the time of what is sensed (*Method,* 263).

The object of the second lacks these traits. Hence "objectivity" differs in the two cases.

> In the world of immediacy the necessary and sufficient condition of objectivity is to be a successfully functioning animal. But in the world mediated by meaning objectivity has three components. There is the experiential objectivity constituted by the data of sense and the data of consciousness. There is the normative objectivity constituted by the exigences of intelligence and reasonableness. There is the absolute objectivity that results from combining the results of experiential and normative objectivity so that through experiential objectivity conditions are fulfilled while through normative objectivity conditions are linked to what they condition. The combination, then, yields a conditioned with its conditions fulfilled . . . (ibid.).

Objectify: by intending something, to make it present to oneself as an object of wondering or thinking or desiring, etc. In the expression "the intention of the author as objectified in the text," the words "objectified in the text" mean "embodied in words." The point of this whole qualifying phrase is to limit consideration of intended sense to actually operative determinants (excluding considerations such as the psychology of the author at the time of composition, etc.).

Positions and Counterpositions: basic stances in conformity with or in difformity from the facts of conscious human intentionality. For example, intentionality analysis reveals that "wonder" is an unrestricted act of intending the real. Systematic attention to this act, the affirmation of its existence and functional role in fully human knowing (as in critical realism) are "positions"; the systematic exclusion of any such act (as in critical idealism) is a "counterposition."

Principle of the Empty Head: a simplistic conception of objectivity which, on the supposition that knowledge is modeled on ocular sight, affirms that the less one has in one's head as one knows, the more objective knowledge of the object is likely to be. The Principle of the Empty Head thus prolongs the Enlightenment ideal of presuppositionless interpretation and history, according to which interpreters take texts to be self-interpreting and historians allow facts to speak for themselves.

Sache, die: the thing the writer is writing about or that the text refers to. *Die Sache* is not, then, the sense of the text, but its referent. (Sometimes "subject-matter" translates *die Sache,* but that term is perhaps too specific.) *Sachfrage* is a "content-question" or "referent-question"; *Sachkritik* is a criticism of what is said, not merely of how it is said.

Sache und Sprache: interdependence of actual use of language and referents. F. de Saussure dealt primarily with language and linguistics, not with utterances; hence he made no reference to referents; other analysts did and do, as the following table shows:

Frege:	Expression	Sense	Reference
Carnap:	Expression	Intention	Extension
Ogden & Richards:	Symbol	Thought	Referent
Pierce:	Sign	Interpretant	Object
Saussure:	Signifier	Signified	

Self-understanding: to be distinguished from spontaneous self-awareness. Self-awareness is the subject's consciousness of being an intending, self-orienting center. Self-understanding, on the other hand, is the product of reflexive intentionality, the acquired fruit of reflection on the self.

Significance: technical term for the unintended meanings that in time accrue to a text by reason of its being set and seen in new contexts and compared or contrasted with them. Johann Gottfried Herder neither envisaged nor sympathized with the Nazi movement; but owing to ambiguities in his philosophy of history, Herder's philosophy could hardly fail to acquire a sinister significance from the Nazis' appeal to some of its categories. The work of Roman poets took on a significance in medieval culture in some respects alien to their original meanings. "Sense" is what the writer meant; "significance" is the superadded meanings (some close to and revelant of the virtualities of the sense, others far from and perhaps subversive of original intentions) attached in time to the texts by the interpretations that they generate.

Story-line: the action of a narrative, sequence of events, working out of the plot. We "stay within the story-line" when we consider the story not as a story (i.e., as told to an audience), but purely as a sequence of events, and when accordingly we treat the figures in the story in relation not to ourselves as readers/hearers, but simply to one another within the sequence of events.

Structuralism: adaptation of linguistic system to literary purposes, first among French literary figures (e.g., Roland Barthes) who, applying analytic categories to biblical texts, set in relief some striking traits of biblical thinking. Unintended "structures" can yield interesting results to structuralist literary analysis, which are unreachable in any other way. This form of analysis, however, does not generate enough, quantitatively or qualitatively, to establish itself as a major resource of biblical scholarship.

Structure: the arrangement of and relationships among the parts that all together constitute the whole of the work. Structure is a major element of form in literary works. Unintended structures of various kinds, on the other hand, are objects not of interpretation, but of analysis (e.g., structuralist analysis; form-critical analysis, psychological analysis).

Style: choice and arrangement of words. The definition supposes the competent use of language and evokes qualities that contribute to excellence, for example, lucidity, distinctiveness, power, elegance in the choice and arrangement of words.

Sublation: a technical term devised by German idealists *(Aufhebung)* but adopted in a modified sense by Lonergan, who would use this notion

> to mean that what sublates goes beyond what is sublated, introduces something new and distinct, puts everything on a new basis, yet so far from interfering with the sublated or destroying it, on the contrary needs it, includes it, preserves all its proper features and properties, and carries them forward to a fuller realization within a richer context (*Method,* 241).

Symbol: an affect-laden image. From the standpoint of rhetorical analysis, a symbol is a metaphor from which the subject of the metaphor is omitted; in other words, it is the red rose that is left if "my sweetheart" is omitted from "My sweetheart is a red, red rose." Symbols evoke feelings and are evoked by feelings. The appropriate resources and manner of symbol decipherment, analytic or interpretative, is settled by the inquirer's purpose: literary or therapeutic or whatever.

Synchronic/Diachronic: terms devised by Ferdinand de Saussure circa 1913 and relating to modes of organizing linguistics. The more basic mode is synchronic: structural and systemic. Diachronic modes of organization are genetic, having to do with successive change over time. Anthropologists, sociologists, literary critics, philosophers, and others have usefully borrowed the terms. Compare the distinction between the situation of the chess-board at any given moment in the match (synchronic) with the move-by-move account of how the game went (diachronic).

Thematic, Thematize: explicit, make explicit. We are conscious of more than we explicitly intend, fasten on, objectify. There is accordingly a twilight of consciousness (which depth-psychologists and psychiatrists call "the unconscious"). To bring something out of the twilight of consciousness by objectifying it is to thematize it or to make it thematic. By analogy, to highlight a phenomenon or aspect thereof by making it a "theme" is to thematize it.

Truth of Interpretation: the interpretation's correspondence to the intended sense of the work interpreted. This "truth" is accordingly a matter of interpretative correctness. Although the truth-claim of the work itself is included in "the intended sense," the *truth* of the work is the object not of interpretation, but of encounter and critique.

Voluntarism: tendency to depreciate intelligence in favor of sheer will, whether in human or divine activity. Notorious examples in philosophy and politics mark the past two hundred years. A brilliant study of the absolutization of the will: J. P. Stern, *Hitler: The Führer and the People* (London: Flamingo, 1984) 56–77.

Vorverständnis: "pre-understanding," or the understanding of "the thing" or referent that is prerequisite to understanding the words that refer to the thing. (Hans-Georg Gadamer prefers the expression *Vorurteil,* "prejudgment/prejudice," since it is stronger and implies some measure of commitment to the referent.) The term signifies a break with an Enlightenment ideal: presuppositionless interpretation.

Wirkungsgeschichte: technical term for the impact of texts in time and especially their capacity to generate tradition. In the view of Gadamer it is important for the interpreter to cultivate a *wirkungsgschichtliches Bewusstsein,* a consciousness informed by the impact of the work, or the tradition that it has generated.

Writer-Reader Relation: that aspect of the writer's intention which bears on the responses he wishes his work to evoke in his readers. Does Mark wish his readers to respond unsympathetically or sympathetically to the disciples in his story? Are they invited to identify with the disciples? If so, with what limits? The interpreter may not understand relations within the story-line until he has settled the matter of the writer-reader relationship.

Notes

Preface
viii **As Heinrich Schlier put it** Schlier, 1975, 6.
ix **"has opened the way."** de la Potterie, 1988.
xi **Third Reich** Arendt, 1968, ix.

Part I, Introduction
2 **". . . works without exception."** Frye, 1947, 427–428.
2 **"curious marks on paper."** Collingwood, 1946, 244.

Chapter One
8 *Die Worte Jesu* Dalman, ET: 1902.
10 **A text in Tertullian** Tertullian, *De baptismo* 20.2.
10 **anything shameful** Text may be found in Jeremias, 1967, 105; or 1971, 202.
11 **"and make us stand firm . . ."** suggested by Alan Mendelson 2.19.93 (oral communication).
11 **"and do not let us fall victim . . ."** Jeremias, 1971, 199.
12 **Jerome** Commentary on Matthew, cf. Jeremias, 1971, 199.
12 **adversary."** Joüon, 1930, 31.
13 **process.)** ibid., 42.
14 **father. . . ."** Dalman, 1902, 283.
14 **In 1922 Georg Bertram** Bertram, 1922, 13.
15 **In Albert Schweitzer's view** Schweitzer, 1954, 393, 396.
15 **Ernest Lohmeyer must be credited** Lohmeyer, 1928, 28.
16 **(a stylistic trait** Weiss, 1897, 28–30.
16 **half a century later** Bultmann, 1947, 6, n. 10.
16 **appeared two new efforts** Cerfaux, 1946, 117–130.
17 **rightly argued** Jeremias, 1966a, 308–310.
18 **humiliation** Meyer, 1979, 64–65.

18   **the Father."** Meyer, 1986, 80–82.
18   **readership)** Pound, 1934.
19   **(Dieter Georgi** Georgi, 1964.
19   **(Otfried Hofius** Hofius, 1976.
19   **Joseph A. Fitzmyer** Fitzmyer, 1988.
19   **Charles Harold Dodd** Dodd, 1935/1961.
19   **by Wilhelm Weiffenbach)** Weiffenbach, 1873.
20   **The critique** Sullivan, 1988.
20   **1941** Jeremias 1941.

Chapter Two
22   **dime a dozen** Method, 13.
22   **Distinctive:** *Insight,* 354–356. (CW: 378–380.)
22   **Puzzling:** ibid., 359–360. (CW: 383–384.)
23   **orientation** ibid., 359–374. (CW: 383–398.)
24   **"No."** ibid., 271–272. (CW: 296–297.)
24   **"probable"** ibid., 275. (CW: 300–301.)
24   **sitting on** Collection (b) 207–208. (CW: 193.)
25   **or not** *Second Collection* (d), 70.
25   **"virtually unconditioned."** *Insight,* 280–281. (CW: 305–306.)
28   **In 1932 Olaf Linton** Linton, 1932.
29   **Peter Strawson** Strawson, 1949. Ezorsky, 1967.
31   **mind."** Feuerbach, 1957, "Preface."
31   **John Henry Newman** Newman, 1960, 59.
31   **Adolf Harnack)** Harnack, 1901.
32   **schools).** Bultmann, 1956, 59–93, 135–174.
32   **Later** See below, 151–156.
33   **to be developed.** Meyer, 1979, 61.
34   **Isaiah 53** Jeremias, 1965, 89. Meyer, 1993, 18–20.
35   **restored to life."** Schlatter, 1962.
36   **(Johannes Weiss** Weiss, 1892.
36   **(Herman Gunkel** Gunkel, 1903.
37   **God "founded"** Schlier, 1972. Hofius, 1989.
38   **John Dominic Crossan** Crossan, 1992. Borg, 1984, 1989.
      Horsley, 1987, 1989.
38   **Eugene E. Lemcio** Lemcio, 1988, 1990. Dunn, 1990.

Chapter Three
40   **'You are not true.' "** Wilbur, 1988, 288.
40   **Heidegger** Gadamer, October, 1972 (oral communication).
41   **"slick."** Copleston, 1976, 180.
41   **condemns** Abrams, 1989, 277.
41   **movement** ibid., 277–280.

41 **John Searle** Searle, 1990, 40.
42 **truth.** ibid.
42 **J. P. Stern** Stern, 1978, 13-15.
42 **vice-versa?** Kermode, 1967, 133-148, esp. 139-140.
42 **oppression?** Bergonzi, 1990, 111.
43 **philosophic argument** Rorty, 1979. On this classic mode of self-reversal see Meyer, 1991a, 2.
43 **against it** Nietzsche, *Assorted Opinions and Maxims* (1879) no. 26; *Beyond Good and Evil* (1886) nos. 4, 14.
43- **no one of his judgment** Rochefoucauld cited from *Insight,*
44 272. (CW: 297.)
44 **of cognitional theory** *Collection* (b), 228-230. (CW: 211-214.)
44 **human mind to be."** *Method,* 21.
45 **into his knowledge.** *Second Collection* (b), 31.
45 **relic of substantialism** Collingwood, 1946, 82.
46 **himself."** *Second Collection* (d), 83.
46 **revision** *Method,* 19.
46 **a passage in Lonergan** *Verbum,* 13-14.
47 **consciousness.** Collection (a), 175-176. (CW: 164.)
48 **responsibly** ibid., 176. (CW: 165.)
49 **beyond the self** *Method,* 7-8.
49 **and the third** "Existentialism," 20.
50 **viewpoints** *Insight,* 558. (CW: 582.)
50 **judgments.** *Nicea,* 7.
50 **past achievement"** *Method,* 237.
51 **what the truth is."** Brown, Peter, 1967, 198.
52 **what is transcended** *Method,* 241.
52 **otherworldly love."** ibid., 242.
53 **conversion** ibid., 243.
55 **concept.** Mackinnon, 1968; cited in *Method,* 254.
56 **spontaneously. . . .** ibid., 255.
57 **public.** ibid., 17.

Part II: Introduction
60 **horizon-analysis** *see* Meyer, 1994.

Chapter Four
61 **fully human knowing** *Second Collection* (b), 30.
61 **objectivity.** *Collection* (c), 232. (CW: 215.)
62 **dogmatic realism** Gilson, 1986, 154-155 and passim.
62 **alone.** *Collection* (c), 233-234. (CW: 216-217.)
63 **data."** ibid., 235. (CW:218.)
64 **being. . . .** ibid., 236. (CW: 218-219.)

65 **otherwise merely supposed.)** Gilson, 1986, 205-206.
66 **satisfactions of the first** *Insight,* 251. (CW: 276.)
67 **appearance.** ibid., 252. (CW: 277.)
67 **affirmed."**) ibid., 371 (CW: 395) and often elsewhere. The formula is paraphrased as *relevant understanding* and accurate formulation of *correct judgment* or *prudent belief.*
68 **picture-thinker** Rorty, 1979; objects of knowledge: 40-41, 44-46; clear: 45.
69 **sufficient.** Meyer, 1989, 86.
69 **one will be.** *Method,* 157.
70 **interpretation.** Bultmann, 1984a.
71 *grounded Method,* 101.
71 **decline?** ibid., 102.
72 **Ernest Becker** Becker, 1973, 1975.
72 **nature,"** *Second Collection* (d), 86.
73 **consistent atheism** Sartre, 1946, 94.
73 **know them creatively** ibid., 22.
74 **what it is** *Insight,* 694, 696, 702. (CW: 716, 718, 724.)
75 **drive, power.** *Method,* 30.
75 **agreeable/disagreeable and values** ibid., 31-32.
77 **sins.** ibid., 252.
77 **meeting"** Buber, 1958, 11.
77 **argued Lonergan** *Second Collection* (g), 154-155.
78 **authenticity.** ibid.
78 **after death** Pieper, 1965a, 12ff.; also in Pieper, 1954.
78 **a social order** MacIntyre, 1984, 111-145 passim, 265-278.
79 **Yves Simon's** Simon, 1993.
79 **the quest of goods).** *Method,* 47-52.
79 **Hans-Georg Gadamer** Gadamer, 1989, 21-22, 312, 322.
79 **of order."** *Method,* 49.
79 **terminal value** ibid., 48-50.
81 **handmaid.** Aquinas, *Summa Theologiae* I-II Q. 66, a. 5, ad 1.
81 **excellence** ibid., I-II Q. 56, a. 2, ad 2.
82 **theology** *Collection* (d), 255-266. (CW: 235-244.)
82 **or experiment** *Third Collection* (d), 135-137.
83 **Paul Hazard** Hazard, 1953.
83 **results** *Second Collection* (f), 103-104.
83 **categories** ibid. (g), 161.
84 **empirical, culture** Collingwood, 1946, 328-330.
85 **but** *reasonable Insight,* 325. (CW: 349-350.)
85 **from modern culture** *Second Collection* (f).
86 **moral attainment** ibid., 115-116.
86 **Marxists.** ibid., 115.

Chapter Five

88   **understand."** Aquinas, *Summa Theologiae* I Q. 84, a. 7, corpus.
90   **medium of thought)** Steiner, 1975, 74.
90   **said Alfred Whitehead** Whitehead, 1933/1942, 263.
91   **sense of the text** *Method,* 155.
91   *Sprache).* Coreth, 1969, 64–65.
91   **(Luther).** Gadamer, 1989, 171.
91   **means of his words** *Method,* 160.
91   **interpretation** Culler, 1985.
92   **one Hamlet** *Method,* 209.
92   *(Lebensverhältnis)* Bultmann, 1950; Meyer, 1989, 50, n. 13.
92   **"the dialectic"** Coreth, 1969, 64–65, 116–117, 123–127.
92   **play of referents** Cunningham, 1984.
92   **master of the disgusting."** Landor cited by Moore, 1899, 3.
93   **tradition."** *Method,* 161.
94   **incredulity. . . .** ibid., 161–162.
94   **(contrary to** Hirsch, 1967, chapter one.
95   **in the meaning."** *Second Collection* (b), 16.
95   **common memory)** Pound, 1934.
95   **it is true."** Lewis, 1966, 121.
96   **Point of View."** Gadamer, 1989, 180.
97   **system).** Culler, 1985, 30, 80–84.
97   **E. D. Hirsch** Hirsch, 1967, 210–211.
97   **Gottlob Frege** Frege, 1952.
97   **two New Critics** Wimsatt and Beardsley, 1955.
98   **Meir Sternberg** Sternberg, 1985, 8–57, 69–70.
98   **storm-god)** Emerton, 1958.
98   **champion of Israel)** Collins, 1977, 141–147.
99   **Many years ago** Brooks and Warren, 1958.
99   **old texts** Meyer, 1990.
100 **meanings** *Insight,* 564–568, 738–739. (CW: 587–591, 760–761.)
101 **analysis** Held, in Bornkamm, Barth, Held, 1963, 165–299.
101 **Lukan text?** Gerhardsson, 1986, esp. 28–30.
101 **exaggerated** Meyer, 1989, 129–145.
102 **thinking** Collingwood, 1946, 266–274.
103 **important** Riesner, 1988, 2–96.
104 **for Jesus."** Jeremias, 1958, 57.
104 **cross).** Bultmann, 1964, 24.
104 **as Marjorie Chambers** Chambers, 1970.
105 **historically probable** Gadamer, 1989, 215–218.
105 **advance in method!** cf. Crossan, 1991.

105 **acts of meaning.** *Method,* 239.
106 **specifically human action** Meyer, 1979, 76–81.
106 **resulted** *Method,* 198–199.
106 **orientations.** Meyer, 1979, 77–78.
107 **values** *Method,* 250.
107 **future.** . . . ibid., 185.
108 **arrives.** ibid., 216.
108 **Hitler's "diaries,"** cf. Hugh Trevor-Roper: Lord Dacre.
108 **Stalin.)** Gould, 1990.
108 **four informed and honest historians** Meier, 1991, 1–2.
110 **handling of these questions** *Method,* 224–233.
111 **itself.** ibid., 227.
112 **Be responsible** ibid., 231.
112 **matters of fact.** ibid., 232.
112 **of our lives"** ibid., 233.
113 **"the past"** Plumb, 1969, 19–61.
113 **or self-transcendence** *Method,* 233; cf. 338.

Chapter Six
114 **poetry** Aquinas on *mirandum:* Commentary in Metaph. 1, 3, no. 55.
115 **left intact** *Insight,* xiii. (CW: 7.)
115 **higher lunacy."** Kierkegaard, 1967, 4.
116 **Scotist reason** *Verbum,* 24.
116 *realissimum* Nietzsche, 1988. " 'Reason' in Philosophy" no. 4 in *Twilight of the Idols.*
117 **old woman."** Nietzsche, 1988. " 'Reason' in Philosophy" no. 5 in *Twilight of the Idols.*
117 *(Heiterkeit).* Nietzsche, 1988. "How the 'Real World' at last Became a Myth," no. 5 in *Twilight of the Idols.*
117 *different"*? Nietzsche, 1988. "Morality as Anti-Nature," no. 6 in *Twilight of the Idols.*
117 **second enlightenment,"** *Third Collection* (a), 63–64. Cf. Lawrence, 1981b.
118 **existence.** *Collection* (b), 238. (CW: 220.)
118 *whatever."* Nietzsche, 1967, 149. Also, 1988, "The 'Improvers' of Mankind" in *Twilight of the Idols.*
119 **ancestry.)** Stern, 1978, 15.
119 **Says who?)** Johnson, 1993, 21–22.
120 **shining planet** Becker, 1973, 1975.
121 **modernity** Johnson, 1993.
121 **God help us.** Leff, 1979, 1249.
122 **faulty premise."** Johnson, 1993, 22.

122 **meta-narratives** Lyotard, 1979, 7.
123 **handy example** Langlois & Seignobos, 1898.
123 **themselves?** *Method,* 201.
124 **and inhibit** Meyer, 1989, 138-142.
125 **science."** Robinson, 1984, 150.
126 **textual interpretation** Meyer, 1991b.
126 **"community of vision"** Frye, 1982, 230.
127 **scholasticism** Sartre, 1956, e.g., in the "Introduction."
127 **contingent** Sartre, 1938, 180-192; ET, 170-182.
128 **that the existentialists posed** Heidegger, 1976, 13-14.
128 *intentio intendens Insight,* xxv. (CW: 19-20); *Collection* (c), 228. (CW: 211-212.)
128 **1932 study** Heussi, 1932.
129 **1813).** *Method,* 214-220.
130 **"interesting,"** *see* Abrams, 1989, 280-287 on Stanley Fish.
131 **human being.** Barrett, 1986, 130.
131 **sensibility.)** ibid., 158.
132 **nature.)** Meyer, 1990, 753-755.
132 **fall of Paul de Man** Lehman, 1991.
132 **M. H. Abrams** Abrams, 1989.
133 **psychology."** Donoghue, 1980.
133 **skepticism.** Abrams, 1989, 265.
135 **unforgettably detailed** de Lubac, 1948.
136 **"the Phaedrus"** Pieper, 1965a.
136 **of being there."** Larkin, 1988, 196.
137 **James Miller** Miller, 1993, 8.
137 *Civilization)* Foucault, 1965.
138 **make us act"** Rilke, 1957.
138 *soi-même)* Foucault, 1985, 8.
138 **to be himself."** Kierkegaard, 1968, 186, 188-189, 196.
138 **rid of himself."** ibid., 152.
138 **to become himself,"** ibid., 166.
138 **given him."** ibid., 202.
139 **found it** Nietzsche cited in Miller, 1993, 406, n. 20.
139 **Lonergan** Contingent empirical being is structured by potency, form, and act. *Insight,* 431-434. (CW: 456-460.)
140 **judgment."** Gadamer, 1989, 270-277.
140 **believe one another** *Insight,* 291-293. (CW: 316-318.)
140 **that is belief** ibid., 703-713. (CW: 725-735.)
141 **in England** Watson, 1993a.
141 **uncritical."** ibid., 10.
141 **obvious."** ibid., 2.
142 **itself.** ibid., 10.

142 **a dime a dozen** *Method,* 13.
142 **true judgment** *Insight,* 325. (CW: 349–350.)
142 **myth."** *Method,* 238–239.
143 **(an example is Paul Johnson** Johnson, 1988.

Part III, Introduction
145 **Testament** Stuhlmacher, 1977.
146 **the ages** Stuhlmacher, 1986.
146 *Ex Auditu* (Allison Park, Penn.: Pickwick Publications).
147 **"communications."** *Method,* 125–132.
148 **first** Collingwood, 1946, 328–329.
149 **hold on the text** Jeanrond, 1993, 88.

Chapter Seven
151 **New Testament interpreters** Gadamer, 1989, 306–307, 374–375.
153 **ethical ideal).** Frei, 1984.
154 **affirms it.** *Insight,* 373–374. (CW: 396–398.)
154 **Franz Schnabel's** Schnabel, 1955.
155 **Incarnation.)** Newman, 1960, 59.
155 **Adolf von Harnack** Harnack, 1901.
156 **state of the question** Seeberg, 1903.
156 **C. H. Dodd's work** Dodd, 1936.
157 *basic roles Third Collection* (b), 87.
158 **insight** *Insight,* 687–730. (CW: 709–751.)
159 **Syriac** the name is discussed in Toynbee, 1962, 72–84.
160 **"angel of history,"** Benjamin, Theses on the Philosophy of History (9).
160 **with Bruno Snell** Snell, 1953.
161 **analysis of the problem** Meyer, 1992, 177–215.
161 *Confession* Tolstoy, 1904, 1–75.
161 **Descartes to the computer** Barrett, 1986.
161 **Leszek Kolakowski's analysis** Kolakowski, 1978.
161 **Josef Pieper's dark** Pieper, 1954.
166 **glory** *Second Collection* (a), 8.
168 **Charles Fox Burney proposed** Burney, 1925–1926.
169 **Gregory Dix defined this** Dix, 1953, 2.
172 **a third possibility?** Klauck, 1989, 67–68.

Chapter Eight
176 **An example:** Watson, 1993b.
178 **alienation** Meyer, 1990, 754–760.
178 **comprehensive understanding** Meyer, 1989, 45–49.
179 **many in the Church** Schürmann, 1982, 330–331.
180 **future."** Collins, 1992, 30, citing Koch, 1980.

180 Newman, 1960; **rationalism**": 155; **heresy,**": 327; **theology.**":
 180.
181 **(Knox).** Meyer, 1989, 119.
182 **glory** Meyer, 1988.
183 **"interpretation"**) Pieper, 1979, 29.
183 **(de Lubac)** de Lubac, 1948.
183 **Anton Vögtle** Vögtle, 1976.
183 **Peter Fiedler** Fiedler, 1974.
184 **illuminating answer** Pesch, 1979.
185 **apocrypha** Meier, 1991, 114-123.
185 **his hypothesis** Crossan, 1988.
185 **primitive Christianity** Meier, 1991, 118.
186 **Arthur Darby Nock** Nock, 1972, 958.
186 **Eric Voegelin** Voegelin, 1971.
186 **(Jacques Dupont among others** Dupont, 1958.
187 *Stichwort*-**passages** Wrege, 1968.
187 **respectively** Jeremias, 1966b.
190 **occurs.** *Second Collection* (h), 243.
190 **metaphysics.**" *Third Collection* (b), 87.
190 **Dr. Joyce Brothers has** Brothers, 1978.
191 *(Geisteswissenschaften) Second Collection* (f), 104-105.
192 **in fact is so.** *Collection* (d), 259. (CW: 238-239.)
192 **of man.** ibid., 262. (CW: 241.)
193 **new beginning** *Second Collection* (c), 55.
193 **solutions.**" *Collection* (d), 266-267. (CW: 245.)
194 **"period trash"** Farrer, 1943, ix.
194 **openness to philosophy** Armstrong, 1980, 75-77.
194 **prominent in Peter Brown's** Brown, 1967, 356-375.
195 **hellinization of the gospel** Harnack, 1908, 24-65, 266-278.
195 *Dogmatik* Jeremias, 1930, 7.
195 **and wise"** Lash, 1979, 92.

Bibliography

I: Works of Bernard J. F. Lonergan (cited by short title):

Insight: Insight: A Study of Human Understanding. London: Longmans, Green, 1957; Collected Works (CW): Toronto: University of Toronto Press, 1992.

Method: Method in Theology. New York: Herder and Herder, 1972.

Collection: Collection: Papers by Bernard Lonergan. Ed. F. E. Crowe. New York: Herder and Herder, 1967; CW: Toronto: University of Toronto Press, 1988.

    (a) "Christ as Subject: A Reply." 164–197. [CW 153–184.]

    (b) "Metaphysics as Horizon." 198–220. [CW: 188–204.]

    (c) "Cognitional Structure." 221–239. [CW: 205–221.]

    (d) "Dimensions of Meaning." 252–267. [CW: 232–245.]

Second Collection: A Second Collection: Papers by Bernard J. F. Lonergan. Ed. William F. J. Ryan and Bernard J. Tyrrell. New York: Herder and Herder, 1974.

    (a) "The Transition from a Classicist World-View to Historical-Mindedness." 1–9.

    (b) "The Dehellenization of Dogma." 11–32.

    (c) "Theology in its New Context." 55–67.

    (d) "The Subject." 69–86.

    (e) "Belief: Today's Issue." 87–99.

    (f) "The Absence of God in Modern Culture." 101–116.

    (g) "The Future of Christianity." 149–163.

    (h) "The Origins of Christian Realism." 239–261.

Third Collection: A Third Collection: Papers by Bernard J.

F. Lonergan. Ed. F. E. Crowe. New York/Mahwah: Paulist; London: Chapman, 1985.

    (a) "Prolegomena to the Study of the Emerging Religious Consciousness of Our Time." 55–73.

    (b) "Christology Today." 74–99.

    (c) "Healing and Creating in History." 100–109.

    (d) "Religious Knowledge." 129–145.

Understanding: Understanding and Being. An Introduction and Companion to Insight. Lewiston, N.Y.: Mellen, 1980.

Verbum: Verbum: Word and Idea in Aquinas. Edited by David B. Burrell. London: Darton, Longman & Todd, 1967.

Nicea: The Way to Nicea. The Dialectical Development of Trinitarian Theology. Translated by Conn O'Donovan. Philadelphia: Westminster, 1976.

"Existentialism." Mimeographed edition, Thomas More Institute, Montreal, 1957.

II: Other Works (cited by name and date):

Abrams, M. H. *Doing Things with Texts: Essays in Criticism and Critical Theory.* Ed. Michael Fischer. New York: Norton, 1989.

Arendt, Hannah. *Men in Dark Times.* New York: Harcourt Brace Jovanovich, 1968.

Armstrong, A. Hilary. "The Self-Definition of Christianity in Relation to Later Platonism." In *Self-Definition in Judaism and Christianity. I: The Shaping of Christianity in the Second and Third Centuries.* Ed. E. P. Sanders. London: SCM Press, 1980.

Barrett, William. *Death of the Soul.* Oxford: Oxford University Press, 1986.

Becker, Ernest. *The Absence of Evil.* New York: Free Press, 1975.

————. *The Denial of Death.* New York: Free Press, 1973.

Bergonzi, Bernard. *Exploding English. Criticism, Theory, Culture.* Oxford: Clarendon Press, 1990.

Bertram, Georg. *Die Leidensgeschichte Jesu und der Christuskult.* Forschungen zur Religion und Literatur des Alten und Neuen Testaments 32. Göttingen: Vandenhoeck & Ruprecht, 1922.

Borg, Marcus J. *Conflict, Holiness and Politics in the Teaching of Jesus.* New York-Toronto: E. Mellen Press, 1984.

_____. *Jesus, A New Vision: Spirit, Culture, and the Life of Discipleship.* San Francisco: Harper & Row, 1987.

Brooks, Cleanth, Jr., and R. P. Warren. *Understanding Poetry: An Anthology for College Students.* New York: Henry Holt, 1958.

Brothers, Joyce. *How To Get Whatever You Want Out of Life.* New York: Simon & Schuster, 1978.

Brown, Peter. *Augustine of Hippo: A Biography.* Berkeley: University of California Press, 1967.

Brown, Raymond E. "The *Gospel of Peter* and Canonical Gospel Priority." *New Testament Studies* 33 (1987) 321-343.

Bultmann, Rudolf. "Bekenntnis- und Liedfragmenta im ersten Petrusbrief." *Conjectanea Neotestamentica* 11 (1947) 1-14.

_____. *Primitive Christianity in its Contemporary Setting.* Trans. R. H. Fuller. New York: World [Meridian], 1956.

_____. "The Problem of Hermeneutics." In *New Testament and Mythology and Other Basic Writings.* Ed. and trans. Schubert M. Ogden. Philadelphia: Fortress Press, 1984a.

_____. "Is Exegesis Without Presuppositions Possible?" In *New Testament and Mythology and Other Basic Writings.* Ed. and trans. Schubert M. Ogden. Philadelphia: Fortress Press, 1984b.

_____. *Jesus Christ and Mythology.* New York: Scribner, 1958.

_____. "The Primitive Christian Kerygma and the Historical Jesus." In *The Historical Jesus and the Kerygmatic Christ.* Ed. C. E. Braaten and R. A. Harrisville. Nashville: Abingdon, 1964. 15-42.

Burney, Charles Fox. "Christ as the *arche* of Creation." *Journal of Theological Studies* 27 (1925-1926) 160-177.

Cerfaux, Lucien. "L'hymne au Christ-Serviteur de Dieu." In *Miscellanea historica in honorem Alberti de Meyer* I: 1946; 117-130; repr. in *Recueil Lucien Cerfaux II* Bibliotheca Ephemerides theologicae Lovanienses 6-7. Gembloux: 1954; 425-437.

Chambers, Marjory B. "Was Jesus Really Obedient unto Death?" *Journal of Religion* 50 (1970) 121-138.

Collingwood, R. G. *The Idea of History.* Oxford: Clarendon Press, 1946.

Collins, John J. "Daniel, Book of." In *The Anchor Bible Dictionary.* Vol. 2. Ed. D. N. Freeman et al. New York: Doubleday, 1992. 28–37.

_____. *The Apocalyptic Vision of the Book of Daniel.* Harvard Semitic Monographs, 16. Missoula, Montana: Scholars Press, 1977.

Copleston, Frederick C. "Ortega y Gasset and Philosophical Relativism." In Copleston, *Philosophers and Philosophies.* London: Search Press, 1976. 172–184.

Coreth, Emerich. *Grundfragen der Hermeneutik. Ein philosophischer Beitrag.* Philosophie in Einzeldarstellungen, 3. Freiburg: Herder, 1969.

Crossan, John Dominic. *The Cross That Spoke: The Origins of the Passion Narrative.* San Francisco: Harper & Row, 1988.

_____. *The Historical Jesus: The Life of a Mediterranean Jewish Peasant.* San Francisco: HarperSanFrancisco, 1991.

Culler, Jonathan. *Saussure.* 2nd ed. Modern Masters. London: Fontana, 1985.

Cunningham, Valentine. "Renoving That Bible. The Absolute Text of (Post) Modernism." In *The Theory of Reading.* Ed. Frank Gloversmith. Sussex: Harvester Press, 1984.

Dalman, Gustaf. *The Words of Jesus.* Trans. P. P. Levertoff. Edinburgh: Clark, 1902. [German original 1898.]

Deichgräber, Reinhard. *Gotteshymnus und Christushymnus in der frühen Christenheit.* Studien zur Umwelt des Neuen Testaments 5. Göttingen: Vandenhoeck & Ruprecht, 1967.

de la Potterie, Ignace. " 'C'est lui qui a ouvert la voie.' La finale du prologue johannique." *Biblica* 69 (1988) 340–370.

de Lubac, Henri. "Le problème du développment du dogme." *Recherches de science religieuse* 35 (1948) 130–160.

_____. *The Drama of Atheist Humanism.* Trans. Edith M. Riley. London: Sheed & Ward, 1950.

Dix, Dom Gregory. *Jew and Greek: A Study in the Primitive Church.* Westminster: Dacre Press, 1953.

Dodd, Charles Harold. *The Parables of the Kingdom.* Rev. ed. London: Nisbet, 1935.

_____. *The Apostolic Preaching and its Developments.* London: Hodder & Staughton, 1936.

Donoghue, Denis. "Deconstructing Deconstruction." In *New York Review of Books,* June 12, 1980.

Dunn, James D. G. *Unity and Diversity in the New Testament: An Inquiry into the Character of Earliest Christianity.* 2nd ed. London: SCM Press, 1990.

Dupont, Jacques. *Les Béatitudes. I: Le problème littéraire—Les deux versions du Sermon sur la montagne et des Béatitudes.* 2nd ed. Louvain: Nauwelaerts, 1958.

Emerton, John A. "The Origin of the Son of Man Imagery," *Journal of Theological Studies* 9 (1958) 225-242.

Ezorsky, Gertrude. "Performative Theory of Truth." Ed. Paul Edwards et al. Vol. 6 of 8. New York: Macmillan and the Free Press, 1967. 88-90.

Farrer, Austin. *Finite and Infinite: A Philosophical Essay.* Westminster: Dacre Press, 1943.

Feuerbach, Ludwig. *The Essence of Christianity.* Trans. M. Evans. New York: Harper Torchbooks, 1957. [German original 1843.]

Fitzmyer, Joseph A. "The Aramaic Background of Philippians 2:6-11." *Catholic Biblical Quarterly* 50 (1988) 470-483.

Foucault, Michel. *Madness and Civilization: A History of Insanity in the Age of Reason.* Trans. Richard Howard. New York: Random House, 1965.

_____. *The Use of Pleasure.* Trans. Robert Harley. New York: Vintage, 1985.

Frei, Hans. "David Friedrich Strauss." In *Nineteenth Century Religious Thought in the West.* 3 vols. Ed. Ninian Smart et al. New York: Cambridge University Press, 1985. 215-260.

Frye, Northrop. *Fearful Symmetry: A Study of William Blake.* Princeton: Princeton University Press, 1947.

_____. *The Great Code.* New York-London: Harcourt Brace Jovanovich, 1982.

Frege, Gottlob. *Translations from the Philosophical Writings of Gottlob Frege.* Ed. Peter Geach and Max Black. Oxford: Oxford University Press, 1952.

Gadamer, Hans-Georg. *Truth and Method.* Trans. Joel Weinsheimer and D. G. Marshall. New York: Crossroad, 1989.

Georgi, Dieter. "Der vorpaulinische Hymnus Phil. 2,6-11." In

Zeit und Geschichte. [R. Bultmann Festschrift] Ed. Erich Dinkler. Tübingen: Mohr-Siebeck, 1964.

Gerhardsson, Birger. *The Gospel Tradition.* Coniectanea Biblica NT Series 15. Malmo: CWK Gleerup, 1986.

Gilson, Etienne. *Thomist Realism and the Critique of Knowledge.* Trans. Mark A. Wauck. With a foreword by Frederick D. Wilhelmsen. San Francisco: Ignatius Press, 1986.

Gould, Julius. "Oxford Days (with Christopher Hill)." *Encounter* 75 (1990) 13–15.

Gunkel, Hermann. *Zum religionsgeschichtlichen Verständnis des Neuen Testaments.* Göttingen: Vandenhoeck & Ruprecht, 1903.

Harnack, Adolf. *The Mission and Expansion of Christianity in the First Three Centuries.* Trans. and ed. James Moffatt. London: Williams and Norgate, 1908.

————. *What is Christianity?* Trans. T. B. Saunders. London: Williams & Norgate, 1901.

Hazard, Paul. *La crise de la conscience européenne (1680–1715).* Paris: Boivin, 1935. ET: *The European Mind (1680–1715).* Trans. J. L. May. London: Hollis and Carter, 1953.

Heidegger, Martin. *Vom Wesen der Wahrheit.* Frankfurt: Klostermann, 1976.

Held, Hans-Joachim. "Matthew as Interpreter of the Miracle Stories." In G. Bornkamm, O. Barth, H.-J. Held. *Tradition and Interpretation in Matthew.* London: SCM Press, 1962.

Heussi, Karl. *Die Krisis des Historismus.* Tübingen: Mohr-Siebeck, 1932. [Original text, 1943.]

Hirsch, E. D., Jr. *Validity in Interpretation.* New Haven: Yale University Press, 1967.

Hofius, Otfried. " 'Bis dass er kommt': 1 Kor xi. 26." *New Testament Studies* 14 (1968) 439–441. Repr. in Hofius, *Paulusstudien.* Tübingen: Mohr-Siebeck, 1989.

————. *Der Christushymnus Philipper 2, 6–11. Untersuchungen zu Gestalt und Aussage eines urchristlichen Psalms.* Wissenschaftliche Untersuchungen zum Neuen Testament 17. Tübingen: Mohr-Siebeck, 1976.

————. " 'Gott hat unter uns aufgerichtet das Wort von der Versöhnung' (2 Kor 5,19)." In Hofius, *Paulusstudien.* Tübingen: Mohr-Siebeck, 1989.

Horsley, Richard A. *Jesus and the Spiral of Violence: Popular*

Jewish Resistance in Roman Palestine. San Francisco: Harper & Row, 1987.

_____. *Sociology and the Jesus Movement.* New York: Crossroad, 1989.

Jeanrond, Werner G. "After Hermeneutics: The Relationship between Theology and Biblical Studies." In *The Open Text: New Directions for Biblical Studies?* London: SCM Press, 1993. 85–102.

Jeremias, Joachim. "Eine neue Schau der Zukunftsaussagen Jesu." *Theologische Blätter* 20 (1941) Col. 216–222.

_____. *Jesus als Weltvollender.* Gütersloh: Bertelsmann, 1930.

_____. *Jesus' Promise to the Nations.* Trans. S. H. Hooke. London: SCM Press, 1958.

_____. *New Testament Theology I: The Proclamation of Jesus.* Trans. John Bowden. London: SCM Press, 1971.

_____. *The Prayers of Jesus.* Trans. J. Bowden, C. Burchard, J. Reumann. Philadelphia: Fortress Press, 1967.

_____. "Zu Philipper 2,7: *heauton ekenōsen.*" In *Abba: Studien zur neutestamentlichen Theologie und Zeitgeschichte.* Göttingen: Vandenhoeck & Ruprecht, 1966a.

_____. "Zur Gedankenführung in den paulinischen Briefen." In *Studia Paulina in honorem Johannis de Zwaan septuagenarii.* Haarlem: Bohm, 1953. 146–153.

_____. "Zur Hypothese einer schriftlichen Logienquelle Q." In *Abba: Studien zur neutestamentlichen Theologie und Zeitgeschichte.* Göttingen: Vandenhoeck & Ruprecht, 1966b. 90–92.

_____ and Walther Zimmerli. *The Servant of God.* 2nd ed. Studies in Biblical Theology 20. Trans. H. Knight et al. London: SCM Press, 1965.

Johnson, Paul. *Intellectuals.* London: Weidenfeld and Nicolson, 1988. Reprint, London: Orion &Phoenixé, 1993.

Johnson, Phillip E. "Nihilism and the End of Law." *First Things* 31 (March 1993) 19–25.

Joüon, Paul. *L'Evangile de Notre-Seigneur Jésus-Christ. Traduction et Commentaire du texte original grec, compte tenu du substrat sémitique.* 3rd ed. Paris: Beauchesne, 1930.

Käsemann, Ernst. "The Canon of the New Testament and the Unity of the Church." In Käsemann, *Essays on New Testament Themes.* Trans. W. J. Montague. Studies in Biblical Theology 41. London: SCM Press, 1964. 149–168.

Kermode, Frank. *The Genesis of Secrecy: On the Interpretation of Narrative*. Cambridge, Mass.: Harvard University Press, 1979.

_____. *The Sense of an Ending: Studies in the Theory of Fiction*. Oxford: Oxford University Press, 1967. Reprint, 1981.

Kierkegaard, Søren. *Fear and Trembling and The Sickness Unto Death*. Trans. Walter Lowrie. Princeton: Princeton University Press, 1968.

_____. *Philosophical Fragments or a Fragment of Philosophy, by Johannes Climacus*. Trans. David F. Swenson and Howard V. Hong. Commentary by Niels Thulstrup. Princeton: Princeton University Press, 1967.

Klauck, Hans-Josef. "Gespaltene Gemeinde. Der Umgang mit den Sezessionisten im ersten Johannesbrief." In Klauck, *Gemeinde, Amt, Sakrament. Neutestamentliche Perspektiven*. Würzburg: Echter, 1989.

Koch, Klaus. *Das Buch Daniel*. Darmstadt: Wissenschaftliche Buchgesellschaft, 1980.

Langlois, Charles Victor, and Charles Seignobos. *Introduction to the Study of History*. Trans. G. G. Berry. London: Duckworth; New York: H. Holt, 1898.

Larkin, Philip. "The Old Fools." In Larkin, *Collected Poems*. Ed. Anthony Thwaite. London: Marvel/Faber and Faber, 1988. 196–197.

Lash, Nicholas. *Theology on Dover Beach*. London: Darton, Longman & Todd, 1979.

Lawrence, Frederick. "Method and Theology as Hermeneutical." In *Creativity and Method: Essays in Honor of Bernard Lonergan*. Ed. Matthew L. Lamb. Milwaukee: Marquette University Press, 1981a.

_____. " 'The Modern Philosophic Differentiation of Consciousness' or What is the Enlightenment?" *Lonergan Workshop II*. Ed. Fred Lawrence. Chico: Scholars Press, 1981b.

Leff, Arthur Allen. "Unspeakable Ethics, Unnatural Law." *Duke Law Journal* (December 1979) 1229–1249.

Lehman, David. *Signs of the Times: Deconstruction and the Fall of Paul de Man*. New York: Poseidon/Simon & Schuster, 1991.

Lemcio, Eugene E. "The Unifying Kerygma of the New Testament." *Journal for the Study of the New Testament* 33 (1988) 3–17.

_____. "The Unifying Kerygma of the New Testament (II)." *Journal for the Study of the New Testament* 38 (1990) 3–11.

Lewis, C. S. *The Screwtape Letters and Screwtape Proposes a Toast.* London: Bles, 1966.

Linton, Olof. *Das Problem der Urkirche in der neueren Forschung. Eine kritische Darstellung.* Uppsala: Almquist & Wiksells, 1932.

Lohmeyer, Ernst. "Kyrios Jesus. Eine Untersuchung zu Phil. 2, 5–11." *Sitzungsberichte der Heidelberger Akademie der Wissesschaften.* Philosophisch-historische Klasse. Heidelberg, 1928.

Lyotard, Jean-François. *La condition postmoderne.* Collection "Critique." Paris: Editions de Minuit, 1979. *The Post-Modern Condition. A Report on Knowledge.* Trans. Geoff Bennington and Brian Massumi. Minneapolis: University of Minnesota Press, 1982.

MacIntyre, Alisdair. *After Virtue: A Study in Moral Theory.* Notre Dame: Notre Dame University Press, 1984. Second ed. [First ed., 1981].

MacKinnon, Edward. "Linguistic Analysis and the Transcendence of God." *Proceedings of the Catholic Theological Society of America* 23 (1968).

Meier, John P. *A Marginal Jew: Rethinking the Historical Jesus. I: The Roots of the Problem and the Person.* New York: Doubleday, 1991.

Meyer, Ben F. *The Aims of Jesus.* London: SCM Press, 1979.

_____. *Christus Faber: The Master Builder and the House of God.* Princeton Theological Monograph Series 29. Allison Park, Penn.: Pickwick Publications, 1992.

_____. *Critical Realism and the New Testament.* Princeton Theological Monograph Series 17. Allison Park, Penn.: Pickwick Publications, 1989.

_____. *The Early Christians: Their World Mission and Self-Discovery.* Good News Studies 16. Wilmington, Del.: Glazier, 1986.

_____. "Election-Historical Thinking in Romans 9–11 and Ourselves." *Ex Auditu* 4 (1988) 1–7.

_____. "Introduction." In *Lonergan's Hermeneutics: Its Development and Application.* Ed. S. E. McEvenue and B. F. Meyer. Washington, D.C.: Catholic University of America Press, 1991a. 1–18.

_____. "The Challenge of Text and Reader to the Historical-Critical Method." *Concilium* 1 (1991b) 3-12.

_____. "Some Consequences of Birger Gerhardsson's Account of the Origins of the Gospel Tradition." In *Jesus and the Oral Gospel Tradition.* Ed. Henry Wansbrough. Journal for the Study of the New Testament Supplement Series 64. Sheffield: JSOT Press, 1991c.

_____. *One Loaf, One Cup: Ecumenical Studies of 1 Cor 11 and Other Eucharistic Texts.* New Gospel Studies 6. Ed. B. F. Meyer. Macon, Ga.: Mercer University Press, 1993.

_____. "The Relevance of Horizon." *Downside Review* 386 (1994) 1-14.

_____. "A Tricky Business: Ascribing New Meaning to Old Texts." *Gregorianum* 71 (1990) 743-761.

Moore, Edward. "Dante as a Religious Teacher. . . ." In Moore, *Studies in Dante.* Vol. 2. New York: Greenwood Press, 1968.

Miller, James, *The Passion of Michele Foucault.* New York: Simon & Schuster, 1993.

Newman, John Henry. *An Essay on the Development of Christian Doctrine.* 2nd ed. Garden City: Doubleday, 1960.

Nietzsche, Friedrich. *The Will to Power.* Trans. Walter Kaufmann and R. J. Hollingdale. New York: Random House, 1967.

_____. *Der Fall Wagner; Götzendämmerung; Der Antichrist; Ecce Homo; Dionysos-Dithyramben; Nietzsche contra Wagner.* Kritische Studienausgabe, 6. Ed. G. Colli and M. Montinari. Berlin: de Gruyter, 1988. (Translations of Nietzsche mainly taken from Nietzsche, 1967, and from R. J. Hollingdale, *A Nietzsche Reader.* Harmondsworth: Penguin, 1977.)

Nock, Arthur Darby. "Gnosticism." In Nock, *Essays on Religion and the Ancient World.* Ed. Z. Stewart. Oxford: Clarendon, 1971. 940-959.

Pieper, Josef. *The End of Time.* Trans. Michael Bullock. New York: Pantheon Books, 1954.

_____. *Enthusiasm and Divine Madness.* Trans. Richard and Clara Winston. New York: Harcourt, Brace & World, 1965a.

_____. *The Four Cardinal Virtues.* Trans. Richard and Clara Winston et al. Notre Dame: University of Notre Dame Press, 1966.

_____. *Hope and History*. Trans. Richard and Clara Winston. New York: Herder and Herder, 1969.

_____. *In Tune with the World*. Trans. Richard and Clara Winston. New York: Harcourt, Brace & World, 1965b.

_____. *Was heisst Interpretation?* Cologne and Opladen: Westdeutscher Verlag, 1979.

Plumb, J. H. *The Death of the Past*. London: Macmillan, 1969.

Pound, Ezra. *The ABC of Reading*. New Haven: Yale University Press, 1934.

Ricoeur, Paul. *Interpretation Theory*. Fort Worth: Texas Christian University Press, 1976.

Rilke, Rainer Maria. *Gedichte in französischer Sprache*. In *Sämtliche Werke* II. Ed. E. Zinn. Wiesbaden: Inselverlag, 1957.

Robinson, John A. T. "Rudolf Bultmann: A View from England." In *Rudolf Bultmann's Werk und Wirkung*. Darmstadt: Wissenschaftliche Buchgesellschaft, 1984. 149–154.

Rorty, Richard. *Philosophy and the Mirror of Nature*. Princeton: Princeton University Press, 1979.

Sartre, Jean-Paul. *Being and Nothingness*. Trans. Hazel Barnes. New York: Philosophical Library, 1956.

_____. *La nausée*. Paris: Gallimard, 1938. ET: *Nausea*. Trans. Lloyd Alexander. London: Hamish Hamilton, 1962.

Schlatter, Adolf. *Paulus, der Bote Jesu: eine Deutung seiner Briefe an die Korinther*. 3rd ed. Stuttgart: Calwer, 1962.

Schlier, Heinrich. "Die Stiftung des Wortes Gottes nach dem Apostel Paulus." In Schlier, *Das Ende der Zeit. Exegetische Aufsätze und Vorträge III*. 2nd ed. Freiburg: Herder, 1971.

_____. "Kerygma und Sophia. Zur neutestamentlich Grundlegung des Dogmas." *Evangelische Theologie* 10 (1948) 481–507. Reprinted in Schlier, *Die Zeit der Kirche. Exegetische Aufsätze und Vorträge*. Freiburg: Herder, 1956.

_____. *Über die Auferstehung Jesu Christi*. 4th ed. Einsiedeln: Johannesverlag, 1975.

Schnabel, Franz. *Deutsche Geschichte im neunzehnten Jahrhundert. IV: Die religiöse Kräfte*. 3rd ed. Freiburg: Herder, 1955.

Schweitzer, Albert. *The Quest of the Historical Jesus: A Critical Study of its Progress from Reimarus to Wrede*. 3rd ed. Trans. W. Montgomery. London: Black, 1954. [German original, 1906.]

Searle, John. "The Battle Over the University." *New York Review of Books* 31 (December 6, 1990).

Seeberg, Alfred. *Der Katechismus der Urchristenheit*. Leipzig: Diechert, 1903.

Simon, Yves R. *Philosophy of Democratic Government*. New ed. Notre Dame: Notre Dame University Press, 1993.

Snell, Bruno. *The Discovery of the Mind*. Cambridge: Harvard University Press, 1953. Reprinted, New York: Harper & Row [Harper Torchbook], 1960.

Steiner, George. *After Babel: Aspects of Language and Translation*. Oxford: Oxford University Press, 1975.

Stern, J. P. *Nietzsche*. Modern Masters. Glasgow: Collins, 1978.

Sternberg, Meir. *The Poetics of Biblical Narrative*. Bloomington: Indiana University Press, 1985.

Strawson, Peter. "Truth." *Analysis* 9 (1949).

Stuhlmacher, Peter. *Historical Criticism and Theological Interpretation of Scripture: Toward a Hermeneutics of Consent*. Ed. and trans. Roy A. Harrisville. Philadelphia: Fortress Press, 1977.

_____. *Vom Verstehen des Neuen Testaments*. 2nd ed. Göttingen: Vandenhoeck & Ruprecht, 1986.

Sullivan, Clayton. *Rethinking Realized Eschatology*. Macon, Ga.: Mercer University Press, 1988.

Toynbee, Arnold. *A Study of History I: Introduction. The Geneses of Civilizations*. Part One. Oxford: Oxford University Press, 1962.

Voegelin, Eric. "The Gospel and Culture." In *Jesus and Man's Hope*. Vol. 2. Ed. D. G. Miller and D. Y. Hadidian. Pittsburgh: Pittsburgh Theological Seminary, 1971. 59–101.

Watson, Francis. "Introduction: The Open Text." In *The Open Text: New Directions for Biblical Studies?* Ed. Francis Watson. London: SCM Press, 1993a.

_____. "Liberating the Reader: A Theological-Exegetical Study of the Parable of the Sheep and the Goats (Matt. 25.31-46)." In *The Open Text: New Directions for Biblical Studies?* Ed. Francis Watson. London: SCM Press, 1993b.

Weiffenbach, Wilhelm. *Die Wiederkunftsgedanke Jesu nach den Synoptikern kritisch untersucht und dargestellt*. Leipzig: Breitkopf und Härtel, 1873.

Weiss, Johannes. *Der Predigt Jesu vom Reiche Gottes.* Göttingen: Vandenhoeck & Ruprecht, 1892. ET: *Jesus' Proclamation of the Kingdom of God.* Ed. and trans. R. H. Hiers and D. L. Holland. London: SCM Press, 1971.

_____. "Beiträge zur paulinischen Rhetorik." In *Theologische Studien . . . Prof. D. Bernhard Weiss . . . dargebracht.* Göttingen: Vandenhoeck & Ruprecht, 1887. 165–247.

Whitehead, Alfred North. *Adventures of Ideas.* Harmondsworth: Penguin Books, 1942. [Original edition, 1933.]

Wilbur, Richard. "Epistemology." In *New and Collected Poems.* San Diego: Harcourt Brace Jovanovich, 1988. 3–18.

Wimsatt, William K., Jr. "The Affective Fallacy." In Wimsatt and Beardsley, *The Verbal Icon.* New York: Noonday Press, 1958a. 21–39.

_____ and Monroe C. Beardsley. "The Intentional Fallacy." In Wimsatt and Beardsley, *The Verbal Icon.* New York: Noonday Press, 1958b.

Wrege, Hans-Theo. *Die Überlieferungsgeschichte der Bergpredigt.* Wissenschaftliche Untersuchungen zum Neuen Testament 9. Tübingen: Mohr-Siebeck, 1968.

Index